Seeing Through the Spin

Also, by Jerry Bush

Release 2021 (planned)

Volume II   A Glimpse Beyond the Spin
Volume III   A View Beyond the Spin

Seeing Through the Spin

The epiphanic resolution of a forty-year battle between
the heart's knowing and the mind's indoctrination.

Jerry D. Bush

QuantumBrook Publishing

A QBP™ Book

Published by QuantumBrook™ Publishing, a part of the
QuantumBrook™ Media.

Copyright © 2020 by Jerry Bush
Cover design by Jerry Bush

QuantumBrook™, with or without the extensions "Publishing" or "Media," are
trademarks of QuantumBrook, LLC.

Seeing Through the Spin—- First Edition, 2020 Printed in the USA

Library of Congress Control Number: 2020915361

ISBN – 978-1-7353823-0-2   Hardcover
ISBN – 978-1-7353823-1-9   Paperback
ISBN – 978-1-7353823-2-6   Kindle

Dedicated to my beloved Parents
Melvin & Doris Bush

About the Cover

More than two years before publication, the author sat down to the computer to design the jacket. I didn't want simply another "pretty" cover; I wanted it to speak to my reader how it spoke to me. The moment I saw my mind-screen take form on the computer screen, it unceremoniously sprang to life pouring fuel on the flame that has burned relentlessly inside of me for more than a decade. As you might have guessed, the lad gazing into the *Spin* represents me as a child.

In the age of innocence, he looks attentively without question. He is compliant, obedient, and entirely naive. He stands awestruck by the magnitude and grandeur of the unknowable scale of the Universe, yet; he feels an inexplicable comfort in the *Infinite* and the paradox that it's *largeness fully–comprehends his comparative smallness*. In him is the seed of all that he will one day feel, and decades later, confront his deep indoctrination.

Quantum
Brook

Table of Contents

Quantum Brook

APPENDICES   214

END NOTES & BIBLIOGRAPHY   231

Quantum
Brook

Acknowledgments

First and foremost, to acknowledge Ronda, my childhood sweetheart, and wife of 45 years. This book would have never happened, if not for your encouragement, dedication, steadfast support, and forgiveness. You are the perfect wife, but you are also an accomplished businesswoman, incomparable mother to our amazing children and Grandmother to our—well, okay. Wow!

James West, my co-author for volume III and best friend for many years. Thank you for repeating the answers to my repetitious questions. If I had you as my teacher in school, I would also—have two PhDs. While there are many things on which we disagree, they are meaningless—when in the next moment I get to call you my friend. Your support is monumental and *never* taken for granted.

Ministries Today acclaimed Jeanne Mayo as America's number one youth pastor, but I knew that—fifty years ago. I was one of the original 20 in her first youth group, and now she is known to hundreds of thousands who love her (almost) as much as I do. She was a dynamo then, and—like the energizer bunny, she keeps going and going. Of the countless people I've ever known, Jeannie, you, *by far and away*, had the most positive influence. I love you, Jeanne Mayo. Myriad precious memories will live on—forever.

A big thanks to Gregg Kennard for introducing me to Bishop John Shelby Spong's work twenty years ago and, then—talking me off the ledge for the following many months.

Lynne McTaggart, we've never met, but I hope someday we will. Reading your book "The Field" was a seminal moment for me. "Everything" began to make sense. It was like someone dimming *up* the lights.

While sad about his passing in 2012, I would be remiss if I failed to mention the yet to be fully known impact that David R. Hawkins, M.D., Ph.Ds., work has had on me. David, you, Lynne, Rupert Sheldrake and other open-minded intellectuals, introduced me to a conscious universe. Because of you, I fell in love with the limitless implications *and practical applications* of quantum physics. And—the fun is *just beginning.*

Carlton Pearson, you are one of my very few heroes. People can *talk* all they want about what they believe, but you—laid *it all* on the line. Thank you for your inspiration and willingness to look beyond your paycheck and embrace a far BIGGER picture.

Neal Donald Walsh, thank you for your courage in becoming a contemporary spiritual voice and returning goosebumps to real conversations with God. Most of today's "conversation" is about how best to decorate The Box in which each doctrine's version of God is to abide.

Dr. Gardner, I wish you were alive to read this book. I know what you would say, but we could talk about it. I might not be living today if it were not for you. I miss you.

I want to acknowledge Seth Thompson's *phenomenal* research on hell that made my job comparatively easy in writing Chapter Seven. I am delighted to highly recommend Seth's website mercifultruth.com for those interested in a more in-depth study. Seth, I am grateful for this resource.

It is a big thanks to Claude Wood, a gentleman I have known since about the time I could walk, a man I have admired and respected for a lifetime. Thanks for being the first person to enthusiastically read Seeing Through the Spin cover to cover and provide me with valuable feedback. You are my dear friend.

A special shoutout to grammar sleuth, proof-reader, and friend Bryan Robinson who not only caught embarrassingly apparent mistakes but whose investigative skills rescued an unedited manuscript that somehow (pre-October 2020) made it to press.

I offer a belated request to all my former colleagues from the 80s and 90s and 2000s. If you happen to read this book for some reason: If even for a moment, you ever felt I was silently judging you. *Please— forgive me.*

And God—*thank you for letting me see what I now see*, to say something only I can tell, and prepared me to do something that you uniquely equipped *me to do*. Thank you for,

The Awakening.

A Note to My Reader

Dear Reader,

A heartfelt *Thank You* for reading my book and providing me with this chance to share my intensely personal journey with—*You*.

Depending on your background, you may at first find some of the things I've written to be uncomfortably confrontational. To tradition's thinking, it may be a bit hard to digest. For some readers, it may take weeks, even months, for the dust to settle. But with time, *it will* begin to make sense to an open mind. If I failed to choose the right words or use the right tone—if sometimes I seem a bit disrespectful, I'm human—and particularly passionate about this subject.

Important! **Please do not** skim read this book. The context required for any part of the book is all—the rest of the book. If you only have time to scan the pages, wait until you have time to read the whole thing deeply—contemplatively. Otherwise, the parts you skim may produce a visceral reaction that determines you do not return to complete the book. You will have formed, what may be, an inaccurate opinion—prematurely.

I intend to inform, not offend. As you turn the last page, whether or not we agree, you will, at least, fully understand *why* I developed this extensive, decades-long considered perspective.

Blessings,

Jerry

Preface

The way to completely miss the
obvious is to always be looking
for everything that—

isn't.

Introduction

The Premise

Light gradually appeared above the distant edge. The higher I climbed, the more I began to see, each step preparing me to take in that first view of an unfamiliar — horizon.

Looking back, I can't say with certainty when the transformation happened. It was if my eyes took decades to open. It's not unusual for highly emotional events of a single moment to burn unforgettable, time-stamped images into our memory, but I think this epiphany was *so big* it couldn't fit into a single moment; at least one I could have processed.

It was like a photographer in a developer's "darkroom" illuminated by that one red light, watching the ghostly image take years to appear on the lifeless paper at the bottom of the stirring pool, imaginings which, before, were hidden, rolled tightly inside my camera. I know what's on that roll. I took the pictures. Yet, it is as if I am now seeing them through a *very* different lens for the first time.

The exit from the funnel of indoctrination into which I was born and, for a lifetime, dwelled unaware, was eminent. It was destiny. The world I had entered from the safety of Mother's womb over a half-century ago was exceedingly naïve. The ascent from inside the funnel was steep, perplexing, and exhausting. The echoes of other voices dominated my thoughts during the climb rather than trusting *my* deep reflections. Did I summit years too late, or did I arrive—at just the right time?

"Those intolerant of confrontation and in-depth debate live in a world of self-imposed delusion and detachment from reality."—Unknown.

My best friend and mentor, James Westbrook *(a pseudonym protecting his privacy),* joins me to co-author book three of the Spin Trilogy—"A View Beyond the Spin." James has an Einstein's IQ and two Ph.D.s. The reason I lead with this snippet will become apparent later in the book, but—I'll go ahead and admit something here. I'm not a genius, but fortunately, I get to call one of the greatest minds of our time my best friend. I don't have a Ph.D., a master's, or even a bachelor's degree, robing me in credibility, inferring that I am a subject matter expert—*in anything.* But what I do have—and what I offer you here is a glimpse into a profound epiphany that led me to a *long-overdue* awakening.

My regular dialog with James helped me understand that the way I observe the world may be more unusual than I first imagined. I, too, quickly assumed everyone saw "the obvious" the way I did. I thought—it's right there, don't you see it? For almost fifty years, I pretty much *explained away* everything I silently observed—those things woven into the countless assertions of religion's *tens of thousands* of exclusive doctrinal views.

The United States Patent Trademark Office (USPTO) awarded James more than 600 national and international Patents in Physics, Luminary, Chemistry, Medical, Molecular Physics, and numerous patents in additional subcategories, including the only *molecule* ever to receive a multi-part patent. He sleeps four hours a night and is *unable to turn off his mind.* Like breaking a wild stallion, he sees a "problem," and his brain begins to work on a solution— and I might add, *without his permission.* That is the way *he's wired.* There is little that can change that reality. But once he bridles and saddles a problem, the solution becomes a patentable opportunity, and that patent becomes an enormous asset to his family and—eventually to the world.

He and I are very similar in that way. We both *easily* visualize things in 3D. My brain works analogously but with something—shall we say—less, than an Einsteinian IQ. We identify the problem, and the solution, and "watch it" on a movie screen only we alone can see. We observe the mechanism's movement. We understand the interplay of the parts, watching how one piece interacts with the other. This observation applies not only to that which is mechanical—but also to

Quantum
Brook

that which is intangible; the philosophical, religious, spiritual, and metaphysical.

Similarly, observations which years ago contemplated the things found in this book, though intangible, for me, often take on a life of their own. They persist in demanding an answer into how *"we reached this conclusion."* The way I process observations sometimes feels like both a blessing and—a constant irritant akin to James breaking the stallion. I just can't let it go. If it is this way, *why*—is it this way? Who does it serve for it to be—this way? And importantly, what are we missing? *Who is hiding some of the essential parts?* Where are these missing parts protected, *and—why?* How do the ones hiding these parts *benefit* from advancing the narrative that *includes only—the visible parts*?

W hat goes into shaping our perspective? What goes into creating an unwavering, often—dogmatic view? [1] Are we aware that people see, hear, and respond differently to that which *appears* to have only one interpretation? Why is it that some people naturally *see all things as possible* while others see the same stuff—as *impossible*? Why do some usually look for the *worst in others*, while others see *the best in everyone?* Why is the sky *always falling* for some, and *the sky is the limit for others?* Why do some people spend their lives *looking for the end of the world* and others *spend the world, living life till the end?*

When looking at anything that challenges long-cherished views, we have few options for responding. When we are emotionally, financially, or foundationally, invested, we either dig in and defend the ego or open our minds to the merits of new information that is previously unknown and—*update our beliefs*. That said, the unbending will inevitably defend the indefensible. Those open to examination, with time, release attachment to indoctrinated assumptions and commits to considering the "impossible." One of my longtime favorite stories illustrates this point perfectly: [2]

The year is 1890, and Bishop Milton Wright declares *from his pulpit*, "If God had meant man to fly, he would have given him wings." *Thirteen years later*, in the back room of their bicycle shop, his sons Orville and Wilbur, craft a handmade glider in sections to make it transportable. *Prevailing thought ridiculed the theories* on which Orville and Wilbur constructed their airplane. Since the dawn of man, everyone with a brain knows that unless you are in a craft lighter than air (a hot air balloon), it is impossible to fly. Yet, with the glider in tow, they leave Dayton, Ohio, for a long trip to Kitty Hawk, NC. After successfully flying for the first time in human history, the brothers walk four miles to The Western Union Telegraph Company in Kitty Hawk to send their father, back home, a telegram:

"Started from level with engine power alone; we flew for seventeen seconds, "notify the press" [Exhibits- Wright Brother's Telegram].

But here is a fun part of the story you may have never heard. On May 25, 1910, Orville took his 82-year-old father on his first and only flight. As Orville gained altitude, his excited Dad cried out, ***"Higher, Orville, higher!"***

There were more naysayers than just their father. Surprisingly, for ten years *after* the historic flight, physicist published numerous papers that said *the Wright brothers claim to fly* <u>*was a hoax*</u>; it was, without a doubt, *impossible to do*. [3] In 1969, just 79 years after the Bishop declared that God did not intend for man to fly. Neil Armstrong took the first step on the moon, carrying inside his spacesuit pocket, a piece of the muslin fabric from the left-wing, and a bit of wood from the propeller of the original 1903 Wright Flyer. It was little more than 300 years earlier that the sun (and the rest of the universe) revolved around the Earth. How did they know for sure? The Church said it did. The pope summoned Galileo to Rome to face the "vehement suspicion of heresy," making him recite and sign a formal abjuration of his discovery that Earth (and everything else in our solar system) revolve around the Sun [4] and, as his sentence, live out the remainder of his life under house arrest for his heresy. As late as 1893, Orlando Ferguson of South Dakota published his flat earth map (later donated to the Library of Congress) depicting a "square and stationary" Earth, based on his literal interpretation of the Bible, which references angels visiting the "four corners" of the world. [5] There are yet today (believe it or not) people *who still believe* the Earth is flat. [6] How long did it take the *vast majority* of medieval flat earth believers to become the equally *vast minority* of modern-day fruit loops? Is perception reality or, rather—a tool which relentlessly (however subtle) forms our perspective? [7]

How does some of this century's most astonishing, and, as Einstein once described, "…spooky at a distance…" scientific advances in quantum physics reshape how we define reality? This (relatively) new truth is one *Sir Isaac Newton* could have never imagined. A little more than a century ago, science viewed the universe through a *vastly different and entirely mechanical* lens. Action A produces reaction B. It was "a billiard ball universe." Today science searches for "the grand unified theory," which explains the blatant contradictions between the macro-verse and the micro-verse. Why does the subatomic world seem to operate under a completely different set of rules than those Sir Isaac Newton first envisioned?

The new reality of quantum physics potentially bridges the great divide between science and spirit, albeit you will get neither atheists nor Christian Fundamentalists to sign up for that view. Are all scientist atheists? Does science pursue unbiased truth, or is it, for some, a relentless search for evidence that supports a predetermined, mechanistic narrative? Is there any room within religion for science? Is there room in science for the spiritual? Do the religious understand that a scientific theory is not a hypothesis, but rather a previous hypothesis now supported by math and tested in the laboratory to be true? Only then does it become a theory. Does some scientist see the universe as conscious, or, is to all a lifeless machine? How are consciousness and things which are mystical, spiritual, miraculous, untestable, and (currently) immeasurable explained? How do we know? Furthermore, how do we explain these exceedingly complex concepts in a way the average layperson can understand, that literally—*everything in the universe is energy?*

"A man should look for what is, and not what he thinks should be" Albert Einstein

---

Of all the religious, political, and cultural perspectives dividing nearly eight billion people on planet Earth, what in the world of science unites us? How does belief—faith focus, move, direct and utilize unseen energy? Why do healings and other supernatural events happen with surprising regularity and—without regard to religious label? Why do these fantastic things not invite diligent scientific inquiry? Why are millions of Near-Death Experiences (NDE) around the world so similar, describing experiences as "realities that are far *more real* than this third-dimension reality." Many of them return to speak of feelings of an overwhelming, indescribable immersion in a field of Pure Love and incredible Bliss, yearning to have the vocabulary to *even partially express* what they experienced. Many "returns" profoundly and permanently changed those who once feared death, fearing death no more. So then, how do we know that the things we learned, virtually from the time we were born, are right—or not? Was Orville and Wilber's father *willing—or forced* by the new events to admit he was wrong?

Our deeply ingrained ideas and beliefs *"make deep sense"* to us. They become a part of the fabric of who we are. In the world of religion, for example, what Muslim questions "the fact" that the mortal prophet Mohammed ascended to tour the seven heavens and returned to promise not just martyrs, but each Muslim man 80,000 servants, 72 virgins, an "eternal erection that never softens", and each time they sleep with a Houri "they find her virgin." [8] Do some extremists believe it so strongly that they blow themselves up due to their interpretation of Jihad in the Koran? Yet, how appealing are the rewards they *are programmed* to *believe* they will receive in heaven if—they become martyrs. Is it true? *It is to them.* Do Muslims have their apologist? You bet they do. But, how about we Christians?

Evangelical Fundamentalists are just as passionate about the error of Islam, the fallacy of Buddhism, the mistake of Judaism, and the blunder of Hinduism as they are about the alleged, flawed Catholicism—and misdirected Latter-Day Saints reality of Joseph Smith translating the golden plates and creating the Book of Mormon. Yet, when someone outside the Christian tradition thinks it's a stretch that Jesus walked on water, they are offended at the question. And astonishingly, "we" are all easily offended when someone challenges *our doctrine*—"the only legitimate doctrine." After all, "I" am the only one who is right! For the Christian believer, such matters are not a "matter of faith," they are worshiped as—"what happened." To them, for them, it is—only reality. How do "we" know? Well—we have always known! *That is just the way it is.* Yet, the fact remains: What is common sense to some—is complete nonsense to others.

As a young adult, *I fell in love* with learning, creating, discovering, considering the bigger picture, and importantly, looking at the discovery's implications and—its practical application to humankind's betterment. I've spent thousands of hours in books, lectures, extensive recorded learning series, and debates, some of which are foundational to this book's thesis. *I fell in love*, not—with the information itself, but the view *that was forming on a Universe size screen.* I quickly learned that early conclusions that challenge tradition, like those drawn about Orville and Wilber Wright, are likely hostile to many, at least initially, even within the scientific community. I aspire here, to look at everything from a higher perspective, which includes *ALL of Humankind*, not just the self-described—*chosen few.*

Chapter 1 - From There to Here, *An Autobiography,* I share a brief glimpse of how I started *"there"* and arrived *" here."* Frankly—there are some pearls of wisdom in this retrospective. Still, I didn't become president, cure

Quantum
Brook

cancer, or walk on the moon. Later in the book, I replay astronauts Edgar Mitchel's (who did walk on the moon) *extraordinary experience* with his fundamentalist mother. Chapter 1 is a distilled view of an abnormal-normal, uber-religious upbringing. But importantly, looking back in time at the faded images, elucidates the reasons driving my thinking, and now I better understand my choices. And most importantly, I know the decisions, which ultimately determined the trajectory, of approximately, the first approximately, forty-five years of my life and—*the genesis of the three-volume Spin Trilogy.*

Chapter 2 *Perspective from a Different Perspective* presents some illuminating science as to what goes into forming our viewpoints. As a part of this examination, we take a very fresh look at our assumptions about the well-known story of David and Goliath that illustrates how we come to perceive our world.

Chapter 3 *The Lucky Chosen to be Chosen*, confronts Fundamentalism's centuries-old belief that one group or the other is somehow *more special* to God than the rest. It revisits the alleged predestined fate of *everyone outside of the faith.* This perspective will become a self-evident revelation for many and troubling enigmas for those who cherish the fundamentalist view.

Chapter 4, *The Fundamental Flaws of Fundamentalism,* **Chapter 5,** *Conundrum of Biblical Proportions*, and **Chapter 6**, *Quoting Misquotes,* all ask probing questions that examine Fundamentalism's long-held view of the Bible's inspiration, inerrancy, and—infallibility. On what have we based these claims, and—why? Challenging the myriad indoctrinated assumptions that program us to miss the essential part of the message *screaming for recognition from between the lines* will be confrontational for some and serve up ah-ha moments for others.

Chapter 7 *A Hell of an Idea* provides an in-depth analysis of the origins and surprisingly sinister misapplication of the *concept of eternal torment.* Readers with a knowledgeable foundation in scripture may find this perspective liberating. The less scholarly may find the in-depth analysis a bit dry but *will never again fear—hell.*

Chapter 8 *A Universal Loss* asks the question: Why wouldn't every believer on earth cheerlead what was once the generally accepted version of the "Good News" with everyone? This chapter also requires above-average knowledge of the Bible. For those non-theologians, this material may also be challenging to consume but well worth the read.

Chapter 9 takes yet another look at *The End of the World—Again.* The author wrapped *far too many years of life around this doctrine.* It examines "just any day now" beliefs that drove *all my decisions*, virtually paralyzing preparing for *the future*, which quickly became—*the past*. It will be a stroll down memory lane for many Fundamentalists, confrontational to many others but entertaining and revealing for most everyone with even a basic understanding of "end of the world" doctrines.

Chapter 10 *Gob Smacked* will be fascinating for most. It takes a look at a personal health crisis over a decade ago, which became pivotal in opening my eyes to the extraordinary evidence of a *conscious universe* and the shift from a selfishly narrow *"we are special"* perspective to a limitless view of an *Infinite God and unlimited possibilities*.

Chapter 11 *Conclusion & A Glimpse Beyond the Spin* introduces *extraordinary evidence* positing a conscious universe where all that appears tangible is not. *Everything* assumed to behave and function as a machine, at a subatomic level, does not; *quite the opposite*. This chapter introduces and admittedly teases a few of the kinds of things we will explore more fully in Volume II.

Volume II, ***A Glimpse Beyond the Spin***, elaborates and enumerates on little-known examples of this unbounded reality— of which *we are all a part*, not— just the chosen few.

Volume III, *A View Beyond the Spin*, introduces "The Theory of Everything." Co-Author James West PhDs reveals his new and profound hypothesis on the origins of the universe. Is it possible there could be a theory that unifies Einstein's general relativity with the invisible subatomic world of quantum mechanics?

Could there be a story in which both science and religion agree that points to one Creator? More than half the world's top Physicists embrace the evidence of a Conscious Universe. [9]

Quantum
Brook

Chapter 1

From There to Here

An Autobiography

Mother was in labor for thirty-two hours, and then, I was born—breach. "The worst kind of breach," the Doctor told her; a frank breech, flexion of both my hips, my legs straight, feet near my face, in a pike position, meaning (at that time)—"I may not ever be able to use my back as an adult." The medical team had to use forceps to extricate me from her womb—aggressively. The trauma to my head was extensive. I looked more like I had been a car wreck than in a birth canal. The injuries were so extensive that my Father, at first look, turned away. The Doctor was quite concerned as to how my appearance would affect Mother. It was three days before she would see me for the first time, and when she did, she decided to pass on purchasing the birth pictures. She was concerned about how they *may affect me* years later if I saw them. I smile about how the difficulty of my physical birth, emblematically mirrored my unlikely ascent into the perspective expressed in this book; highly unlikely indeed- given where it all began.

———————

I was born and bred in the mid-1950s in the deep South. Churches of various fundamentalist denominations sat on numerous street corners, two, sometimes three within line of sight, some with "Read-on preachers" in their pulpits. [1] Traveling "tent meeting" evangelist visiting the region would often pitch two and three pole circus-style tents on large vacant lots near the edge of town. They would preach hellfire so hot you could feel the flames burning through the wooden chairs that leaned uncomfortably on the sawdust-covered ground. Handheld cardboard fans performed double duty cooling perspiring bodies and "shooing away" the eager insects that flourished in the humid southern heat. The "cardboard on a stick" fans were not just for the outdoors, but essential

to achieve some measure of comfort in the church buildings, most of which were
without air conditioning.

My parents attended a fundamentalist "full gospel" Pentecostal
fellowship, and by default, so did I. Within days of my birth, I was in Church. To
say attending Church would become central to everything in my life is—an
understatement. It paints virtually all the broad strokes of my earliest memories.
When I say we attended Church, I don't mean now and again. I mean, we all but
lived there. Every year I was awarded a small pin that I wore proudly on the lapel
of my double-knit polyester suit, displaying the number of years of perfect
attendance. I retired the pin around age fourteen—amid a growing awareness that
advertising such things was not doing me any favors. Yet—it would still be *18
years* before I missed my first Sunday service—*ever*. If I didn't feel well, we went
to Church. If we went on vacation, the drive home was close enough to be in the
pew Sunday morning. An occasional two-day weekend, or a Sunday at the lake
was out of the question. It would be almost fifty years before weekends were two
days for me. Faithful attendance was as much a part of our culture as eating and
breathing.

We lived on Atlanta's southside in those days, just minutes from the
Church. Atlanta was small by comparison to today's massive metro with its
twelve lane freeway systems and MARTA, moving five million residents at a
snail's pace in a 24-7 rush hour. We lived within the city limits. Everything that
was a part of my world was a 10-minute drive from home. Through my eyes as a
child, the city proper seemed worlds away even though I could climb a tree in my
back yard and see the tops of the four buildings, which made up the entire 1960's
era skyline. We didn't go downtown. We didn't have a reason to. Its streets were
foreign to me. Its buildings were like objects in someone's painting.

By age six, we moved into the house Dad built, which was, maybe, a ten-
minute drive from the tiny one floor flat I went home to after my birth. It was
walking distance from Atlanta's federal prison. The new house was yet a ten-
minute drive from the first one. It sat on a gravel road that would remain unpaved
for another ten years. At most, it was a three-minute drive to both the elementary
school and the high school I would attend. For many years, there was the all too
familiar ten-minute drive to the rest of my tiny world. The distance was measured
in time, not in miles. What was true then is even more true today. Five miles can
mean thirty to forty minutes in Atlanta's soul-crushing rush hour traffic.
Every Sunday morning, Dad would crank the 1963 Impala Chevrolet and
turn the radio to WSB 750AM. It would be a bit of a stretch to call the voice in the

dashboard, a Disc Jockey; he was a host. It would be many years before I would hear the music a real DJ would play. We would listen to the news, usually followed by some impressive commentary from Paul Harvey. The radio voice would regularly announce the time, and Dad would once again set his watch.

We were never on time attending Church; we were early. Both of my parents were involved in numerous activities—*always*. Sunday school teacher, department superintendent, usher, and for many years both sang in the choir. Sundays didn't mean just going to Sunday School. As with most southern churches, morning service followed. We were a bit jealous that the Baptist "let out" at noon. We hoped our pastor would conclude by—at least 1:00, so we could make it home, grab a bite to eat, maybe catch a quick nap before returning by 7:00 pm for the 7:30 evening service. We always arrived at least a half-hour early and would depart a half-hour late, allowing time to socialize.

The Church was for many years, the center of my social and religious world. But that tradition was far more than just Church on Sunday. Year in and year out, there were *fifty-two-midweek services in addition to Sunday's hundred and four.* Then there were Bible studies, choir practices, and the three or four yearly revival meetings that assembled every weeknight, most lasting two to six weeks—in a row. I will never forget one lasting eleven weeks.

It would be one of many featuring an up-and-coming evangelist from Baton Rouge, Louisiana. I sat on the front row next to the center aisle, my young feet unable to reach the floor as I was hanging onto every word of his powerful oratory. When he warmed up, this soon to be *world-renowned televangelist* would shift into another gear. Tugging the collar of his starched shirt and the knot of his polyester tie, signaled the coat was about to come off. He would often give it to me to hold. The faithful had filled all 600 seats in the main hall, including 400 more in the overflow "wings." Not only was he a preacher, but a singer that also played the piano. After the fiery sermons, I would sometimes sit next to him at the piano while he played song after song until the "alters" emptied. As the years passed, the attendance overdose was less about choice and more the rule: "as long as you live under my roof, you will be in church," and I was—virtually every time the door was open. For all practical purposes, other than attending school, life outside the Church didn't exist. It was a lifestyle, and it was all that I knew.

My impressionable years in elementary school were awkward and, at times, painful as I tried to fit in. Among my most poignant memories was taking a note to my music teacher, letting her know that I was not to participate in square dancing lessons that day. That would become the precursor prohibiting coming of age events like a high school, Homecoming, or a Junior-Senior dance. Dancing "was against our religion," the note said. So, it was somehow better to sit alone, consumed in the awkward self-consciousness of being a complete outsider. I would become somewhat of an enigma to my peers. You see, by not participating, I was "being a witness for Jesus" and ensuring that I wouldn't go to hell if I happened to die while I was dancing. I would most surely be "left behind if the rapture took place."

As a small, skinny lad with exceptionally churchy hair, the challenge of making friends and being "normal" wasn't easy. That hair was complements of the Vaseline Hair Tonic my Dad used for the classic cross between a young Elvis Presley and "I Love Lucy's" Ricky Ricardo. I never failed to leave a big greasy spot wherever I happened to rest my head soliciting snickers and relentless bullying from my classmates. The bullying was intense. I was small, less athletic, and, of course—"turned the other cheek." I would, without provocation or warning, three times be knocked utterly (almost) unconscious by different classmates—just because—before leaving elementary school.

It wasn't long before even the nerdish among my equals began to wear a longer "dry look" influenced by a new "devil music" band that had just arrived from across the pond called—the Beatles. But "a man ought not to have long hair since he is the image and glory of God." Of course, no one defined what long was. Knee-length or, it's been a few weeks since you've had your haircut—fella. All the while, my fourth-grade classmates energetically pounded out a new rhythm on just about any surface within arm's reach. They played "Wipeout," a new single release "B side" tune on the smaller 45RPM vinyl records. The hit would spend four months on the Billboard charts in 1962 and become one of the best-remembered instrumentals of the entire period. But I wouldn't hear the song until it reappeared as an "oldie" in my adult years. Unlike the irritated schoolteachers, I loved the rhythmic beat coming from my classmate's quick hands. I barely knew who the Beetles were except to hear my few friends talk about them. I clearly remember trying to convince Mother that they were "good people." If it were not for the cigarette hanging from George Harrison's lips in a photo on a front-page of the Atlanta Journal-Constitution, I might have pulled it off. That alone made the "good people" argument impossible. If you smoked, you were going to hell; not just smell like hell. Occasionally I would overhear some rock & roll playing on my next-door neighbors' stereo. I had a tremendous love of music, one which was much more profound than realized. I wasn't permitted to listen to anything secular. Mom was sometimes a bit more diplomatic, calling it heathen, instead of devil music, but the result was the same. Even if it had been permissible, we didn't have a Stereo at the time, so playing freshly pressed 45s of new hits wasn't an option. My parents considered the heathens to be sinners and the songs they sang to be sinful. Consequently, my younger sister and I remained insulated and virtually sanitized from everything beyond the Church's walls well into our teens.

By age eight, Mom wanted me to take piano lessons. I had never heard the songs in my beginner books. They were the popular hits of the day, but if it wasn't a song we sang in Church, I didn't recognize it. The only music to which I had any exposure was songs in the Hymnal that we called The Song Book because it contained more than just Hymns. Regardless, all of them had a *dreadful* case of no-rhythm-religious-white-man's disease. I understood that taking piano lessons meant I would one day play the music that I didn't like. Lessons and practice were a burden. Early on, I resented the instrument instead of being impassioned as I would become in my adult years. To make formal training work within the responsibilities of a mature schedule, I took piano lessons at 7:00 AM on weekdays and—bought a brand-new Yamaha Conservatory Grand for my home.

The Pastors' wife of my preadolescent years was, for our crowd, an "edgy" player, a—relative term for sure. She was too upbeat for many of the faithful. The organ and piano pounded out the monotonous downbeat weekly as we clapped hands in straight time. Even to my young, unlearned ears, it was torturous—and boringly "white." I didn't know enough to know why. I just knew how it sounded and how it made me feel. The high rhythms and backbeat that made rock & roll, jazz, rhythm and blues, and, ironically Gospel, (there is a big difference between Gospel and white Christian church traditional) so magical was—deemed "worldly" and therefore absent in anything we played. If it sounded anything like 'out there,' it would never be performed 'in here.' There, however, was a surprise one day when our then, pastor's wife noticed some talent in an 11-year-old sitting on the front row. She watched as I "played the pew" between wide-spaced knees and legs that couldn't yet reach the floor. She told Mother of her discovery, so Mom bought my first kit from Ellman's department store with money she earned working a secretarial job at a local high school. It had a snare, bass, one tom, and a single cymbal. I later added a floor tom and high-hat. We dragged them in and out of the Church every Sunday, setting them up in the morning and packing them back into the car to repeat the following week. During the week, I would often dismantle, detail, and reassemble every nut and bolt. It became a new identity: "The kid who plays the drums." As I grew, the kits grew considerably, along with my skills.

Secular, Pop, and Rock were becoming more prominent as was Mother's request for promises that "I would never play them for the devil." Through the years, growth as a musician progressed at a snail's pace, but in hindsight, rather rapidly given the *enormous limitations* of the environment. We repeated the same tired patterns to the same, dull, and painfully uninteresting songs. Week in and week out, I remained sheltered in my religious cocoon, missing the emergence of dynamic talents like Elvis Pressley, Frank Sinatra, The Four Tops, Smokey Robinson, the Miracles, Aretha Franklin and the Beatles to name a very few. At the time, I had no idea that the "Negro" churches on the other side of town, who worshiped the same God I did, were making music that would *become the roots* of Rhythm and Blues, Jazz, Rock and Roll, and virtually all of other emerging genres; music "with soul" that was lively. It was exciting. It had rhythm, and it had a beat. Over the coming decades, the old and inflexible died off making way for an emerging sound that was often as good, or better, than anything you would hear in the secular arena. I would go on the play drums, bass, and sometimes "keys," in that church for 40 years.

During those days, the country deeply divided along racial lines, especially in the South. While my parents were publicly tolerant, privately they were segregationists. I don't fault them all. They were then and remain a product of their programming. They are wonderfully loving, parents who are people committed—face set like a flint to their beliefs. They were responding to—*deep indoctrination*. They were upset by Martin Luther King, Jr, a troublesome young black minister in Atlanta who had come onto the scene "stirring up the coloreds." They politically aligned with candidates like Georgia's openly racist governor Lester Maddox or Alabama's governor George Wallace, a soon to be third-party presidential candidate, committed to fighting desegregation. Their prejudice birthed from a passage in the book of Genesis 9: 20-27 [2], where Noah curses his son Ham's descendants later used to justify centuries of slavery, modern prejudice, and segregation. This curse was the 60s era fundamentalist explanation as to why black people were—black.

I went to my first "Black Church" with a group of older friends when I was about fourteen years old, and I thought Heaven had come down. The organ growled and screamed as a *fantastic player* sat commandingly at the console of the mighty Hammond B3, pinky finger stretched wide hanging long on the high notes, working cord over harmonic cord lifting the crowds (and the drummers,) energy to a fever pitch. I was aware of the room around me, but—- barely. I was entranced, mouth open, and gaze locked. The drummer played his rickety kit like a mad man. He pounded the single cymbal that was doing double duty as both his "ride cymbal" and "crash cymbal"—even though in two places it was cracked entirely through, halfway around its circumference. I wondered if it was going to fly entirely apart just any minute. He rounded the tom-toms with authority again and again, and I couldn't take my eyes off him. I marveled at his moves, and somehow—somewhere deep inside, I understood what he was doing. I heard what he was hearing. I felt what he was feeling. It sprang not from his mind, but his soul as the organist continued to wail at the console of "The Legend," with its twin rotating [3] Leslie Speakers positioned at each end of the stage. His left foot ran the Hammond's pedal base notes heal to toe so quickly that his foot was *literally* —- a blur. His right foot rocked between various "Expression Pedal" (volume pedal) positions with the perfect mix of the *253 million possible drawbar combinations.* [4]

"The Beast" growled in what would become a very familiar and lovely distortion caused by pushing its tube-driven amplifiers to the max. I was mesmerized, and that day— *I fell in love* with the Hammond B3. Over the following 50 years, the instrument would become a fixture in virtually every music genre except *classical and bluegrass.* It remains so to this day, though now in a digitally sampled form. It had a profound and everlasting effect on me, so much so that many years in the future, I would purchase a nearly mint condition 1956 B3 with a 147 Leslie for my home music room. [Exhibit- Hammond B3] [5]

The music that night was loud. The hypnotic backbeat was an-all-consuming-amount-of-wonderful. Virtually every man, woman, and child were on their feet moving to the beat, some playing tambourines as the floor flexed beneath the dynamic load. A lot of feet moving in unison created some concern to my uninformed yet intuitive mind. The church floor sat on, otherwise stable, cinderblock piers about four feet high and logic "came-a-knockin." At the time, I was unaware that my intuition was correct. It's called harmonic resonance oscillation, a driving force pushing and pulling at the supports beneath. The floor could have left its "foundation" at "what felt like" just any time. Little did I know what a perfect metaphor this push and pull at my foundation would become in the story, one which I tell until some fifty years later.

A Sin for Everything

W e had a "sin" for—everything, and everything was a sin. Pretty much anything unrelated to the Church was in some-way-shape or form, sinful. The devil was around every corner and a demon behind every tree. The Bible had been used to label everything as corrupt except, the economically advantageous—like slavery. It was said to condone slavery.[6] It was used for millennia to subjugate women, a widespread practice today accepted in some fundamentalist denominations. [7] It was a sin to dance, to play cards, roll dice, wear shorts, to go see a movie, to wear makeup, to go "mixed bathing" (swimming with the opposite sex), and to consume alcohol in any form covers a well-known *few*. It was a sin for women to wear pants, so my sister exclusively wore dresses to school. In much that same way as I greased my hair, it called attention and raised questions. It was challenging to explain to her friends why she never wore pants. To my young mind, pants made a lot of sense, especially on the playground. Modesty was supposed to be the concern, but pants were not permitted because "a woman shouldn't wear a man's clothes." When as a child, I asked why, and the answer was—"being able to see a woman's figure causes men to lust." In retrospect, I guess it could have been a lot worse. The Mennonite and Quaker sects wore (still wear) long, plain black dresses with a white apron, and a linen bonnet pulled tightly over their hair. All of which is comparatively tame to the burkas prevalent in some Islamic sects.

Even deep inside my naïve, unformed mind, I found this strange since eight-year-old girls didn't have anything over which eight-year-old boys would "lust." Boys of that age thought girls "had cooties" and wanted little to do with them. This explanation also applied to why boys and girls didn't go swimming together. It would be many years before seeing a woman wearing makeup or a female of any age in a swimsuit. Ironically, making such a big deal out of the "thou shall not" only compounded the awareness— heightened and enlivened the mystery. The Apostle Paul talks about it in Romans 7:15-20NIV [8] I wouldn't step foot into a movie theater until I was eighteen. Going to movies and virtually any other secular activity like attending a professional ball game was a "sin;" They serve beer at the ballpark.

The change was glacial, but over the next several decades, the denomination relaxed its stance on many ridiculous extremes. However, the transformation did little to alter the perspectives of many of the traditions faithful. Some would (will) never change. Some are unable to change. "Their die is cast." The programming is locked in. To them, growth is compromising, and 'reason' is an evil word.

Compressing this retrospective into a few pages makes it read worse than it was. Yes, it was irritating, confining, stifling, unnecessary and utterly ridiculous, yet—somehow it was palatable because—it was all I knew or had ever known. If you are born colorblind, there is no need for someone to describe color.

To say this is red, that is green, and those things are blue is meaningless. When there is no reference point, there is no method by which the student can understand. The blindness must heal before exploring the world of color. It just is—what it is.

Comparing my experience to old testament Levitical Law or—Islam's Sharia law pales by comparison. So, being a *glass-half-full-kind-of-guy*, I'm thankful I was not born into either of those traditions. Interestingly enough, all of the legalistic nonsense is a close cousin, a carryover of Judaism's Levitical Law— into Christianity. The average person is unaware that Judaism, Christianity, and Islam have a lot in common. They all go back to *Father Abraham.*

My parents, and many of their contemporaries, are genuine, salt of the earth, deeply loving, and well-meaning in everything they did then, and that which they do now. I am *very fortunate* to have both of them living, now in their eighties and—healthy. My sister and I were blessed to have been born into a loving home and keenly aware that every experience birthed from a place of doing what they thought was right; the only "right" they knew, and the only "right" they will ever embrace. Only narrow-minded stupidity *on my part* would fault them and immediately place me in an identical position of refusing to be open to the obvious.

F or virtually all of my early childhood, my father worked long hours driving a truck regionally for the company the supplied A&P food stores. His days and nights turned upside down, and I didn't see him a lot during the week. He was sleeping when I was up and back at work when I was asleep. Both parents were strict, but especially Dad and, as they say—*"he got it honest."* My father was one of *fifteen siblings* born in South Alabama to his sharecropper parents, thirteen of whom survived adulthood. When Dad was a child, he would often miss attending school to labor with his siblings in the cotton fields. Later he would have to work twice as hard to get a GED and complete his primary education. Visiting my grandparents as a lad, meant using a bedpan or an outhouse and drawing drinking water from a well in the back yard. That is how rural my southern roots were in the days that my parents grew up.

If you can believe it, our house's legalism was *tame* by comparison to Dad's environment. My father was unable to say the Mailman had just delivered the Mail. It had to be the Postman. Mail is a stamped envelope, but it *sounds like* Male, and too close for comfort. I'm not sure they realized the spelling was different, but Male, (or Mail in that case) was too specific to gender, and apparently, that was *talking sex baby*. Naughty huh! Dressers in most bedrooms have drawers. Saying "drawers" was too close to something you wore under your pants. Anything under your pants—was—again, too close to—sex. They instead had to call it a *dresser-draw*. *(You can't make this stuff up)* Given the environment, and the apparent otherworldliness of sex, I've often wondered how Grandfather sired so many children? Wasn't that just *way too much sex*, or perhaps because of it—Humm. *(I needed to laugh.)* And then to think of the discipline required to manage that many kids, it's no wonder he learned to be strict. Speaking of strict…

It is hard to remember why I got so many spankings but, a half-century has past so—probably deserved? Rarely a week passed that I didn't get—at least one. Corporal punishment was commonplace and based on *"Whoever spares the rod hates their children, but the one who loves their children is careful to discipline them."* [Proverbs 13:24 NIV] In this context, "rod" in Hebrew, is used for correction. Rod was also a shepherd's staff used to *steer, guide, and rescue* sheep that lost their footing on treacherous trails; the crook of the rod pulled sheep to safety—not to beat them. But, none the less, the former became a cultural emphasis. If my sister or I misbehaved in Church, Mom or Dad was quick to tell us that when we got home, we were getting *"a-whoopin."* When the time came, Dad would chew at his bottom lip, chin moving side to side as if he was working up to it while wrapping his belt tightly around his fisted hand before "wearing me out."

The ride home from Church was often more torturous than the punishment itself, just knowing what was waiting when I walked through the door. There were times Mom would spank me, and I would get a follow-up when Dad got home—just for good measure. Given my compliance and commitment to be a good boy—*maybe it's a warped memory*. Yet, there were days my sister I would go to school with sizable welts from a belt or switch. The switch was the worst. On many occasions, Mom or Dad told me to go to the woods and cut the "switch" used for my punishment. Cutting a wimpy switch just meant that I had to go back and do it again. I couldn't fudge it—but at least it would buy some time before the big sting, a sting often drawing blood. Wearing pants made it easier for me to hide the fruit of my misbehavior, but my sister wasn't as lucky. In a dress, she wore the proof of her mistakes like an add on a billboard. While the quantity and severity were overboard, *their motivation was right*. Again—they were responding to their indoctrinated lifelong programming. My sister and I needed discipline. We needed boundaries and looking back through the lens of Love and right intention as the motive, and I'm good with that. My parents learned from their parents, their teachers, and their preachers. The aims packaged as discipline were based on Proverbs 13:24.

But in retrospect, was it discipline or serial punishment? What can we learn? Perspective? Was the emphasis on what we *did right* or what we *did wrong*? Is this crucial learning or—parsing semantics to make it fit a more enlightened narrative? Was the glass half empty or half full? Was this just perception or perhaps the subconscious projection of the wrathful, Old Testament God? Was the view of my Heavenly Father an extension of my father's earthly father—or the other way around? Was there anything I could learn, change, or do to grow, evolve, or years later, would I emerge from the die in an identical form?

There is no way to measure the proper quantity of "discipline" objectively. But both my sister and I grew into well-adjusted adults. Still, my wife, Ronda, and I would make adjustments in raising our children. My wife was rarely *if ever* spanked. We added personal experience with new thought recommendations from the American Academy of Pediatrics, emphasizing discipline over punishment. My childhood experience was in stark contrast to the modern, "time out" for everything. But a little experience mixed with some new thought, adding a tablespoon of common sense and stir, goes a long way in achieving balance. Spankings for my kids were rare but, I was not above placing a few well-placed swats on a bare behind if talking and "time outs" didn't work. The occasional use of a bolo paddle on a bare backside stings sunburn red, leaving memories— without marks.

———————

I married young; *way—too young*. I was fast approaching Twenty, and my childhood sweetheart and now wife of 45 years was a few weeks from turning (*clearing my throat*) —Sixteen. While in retrospect, I robbed the both of us of the magical years of exploration and the coming of age, she became, and remains, unequivocally the perfect wife, whom I've failed, but who has never once failed me.

Lookbacks beg for the backstory, the why and— the "*what the heezy*" were you thinking?" It is a real-life retrospective into how doctrine *heavily* influenced my every decision. But the underlying premise was this: To make the rapture *(or heaven if I died)* sex had to be—"legal," and that meant— married. Of course, it could be that I was the only young man of my day with that affliction?

As always, context is critical: *We were "not going to be 'here" much longer."* Just any day now was relentless repetition from far back as I can remember, from the pastors, evangelist, teachers, and parents. A popular song in those days put it this way: *"Any day now, we will be going home. Count the years as months, count the months as weeks, count the weeks as days— any day now, we will be going home."*

If we "count the weeks as days," for every day I have heard this tiresome refrain, that makes me well over 3,100 years old.

Tens of thousands of "just any day now" later, rethinking my immature yet—rational thoughts are as clear to me now as they were then. I didn't want "the rapture to take place" and not get to marry my sweetheart and, after all—Matt 22:30 said that in Heaven, there is no marriage, and if there is no marriage—there is no sex. To have sex, you must be married. Plan for the future? There was no future! There was *"biding time" till the rapture.* Imagine processing this perceived reality in a 24/7 testosterone-fueled stupor, no doubt something to which all but the dead, *and—the buried* can relate.

When I was 18, my parents sold our house in south Atlanta and moved to Buford, Ga. where Dad bought 13 acres of land and built the house in which they still reside 46 years later. He devised a brilliant plan for the build. Driving from South Atlanta to Buford during the months required for construction would be both costly and inefficient. Selling the house gave him the capital he needed for the build but with no place to live. To solve the problem, he purchased two mobile homes and parked them side-by-side, sandwiching between them a room that would later be a prebuilt part of the new house. He had always said, "a dollar saved is a dollar earned." I've had to tweak that one bit. By the time you pay taxes, a dollar saved is *two dollars* earned. Dad worked extremely hard all of his life, and he knew how to stretch a buck. This "room in between" provided interim storage for the furniture and serve as a passageway between the two mobile homes while the house was under construction. It was a place for us to live with no interim rent to pay, wasted time or fuel traveling back and forth, or other typical encumbrances to consider. After moving into the new house, Dad sold the two mobile homes— for a profit. However, what all of this cleverness failed to provide *me* was the proximity to Ronda.

She, too, grew up in South Atlanta, a five-minute drive from our previous house. She went to our Church; we went to the same school; she excelled academically, was gorgeous, and was quite popular. In a school with over 2800 students, her class voted her onto the Homecoming court. Smitten from the first time I saw her; hair in pigtails when she was in the—eighth grade. And while I

Quantum Brook

subconsciously processed our relationship through the layers of bullied insecurities written deeply into my programming, she had the high school jock's attention, and I had unwanted competition. Like all relationships at that age, ours was on again and off again. In 20-20's retrospect, anything serious at that age is— *completely crazy.* Yet, in fairness to my younger self, the prism through which I view the world today is dramatically different from the fundamentalist equation driving my decisions back then. Still, hindsight with all the experience and learning brings a new viewpoint. When it was off again, it wasn't me "breaking up." She was receiving a lot of well-deserved attention, and the heartbreaking breakups were her decision. [Exhibit-Ronda- my "steady" girlfriend, circa 1974] Spending time with her became more challenging. When my parents moved North, her family moved South. Each Date was a 150-miles round trip, not including the miles for the Date itself, which sometimes doubled the distance before returning home.

From the time I was a kid getting a $0.50 a week allowance, making $0.50 an hour painting houses with Dad, $3.18 an hour washing and unloading trucks for UPS, and $88 a week during summer months as a draftsman for a small engineering firm, I had never spent a dime. I saved it all. Dad required that I have 1/3 of the cost of whatever car I wanted to buy, as down payment knowing I would qualify for financing and afford payments on the balance. When the day came, with Dad in tow to negotiate the deal, I bought a brand new and "decked out" 1974 Monte Carlo. In less than two years, I put 56,000 miles on the car, most of which was 150 miles listening to a full-length eight-track mixtape I made at my best friend Lindsey's house. Lindsey's dad had a stereo reel-to-reel recorder. We recorded the songs from vinyl 45s directly from the turntable, and in the sequence we wanted, then made a copy the new collection to his new eight-track tape recorder for each of us. The tape began with Barry White's "Love's Theme" fading into "You're the First, the Last, my Everything." Artists like Olivia Newton-John followed, singing, "I Honestly Love You." Gladys Knight's, "You're The Best Thing That Ever Happened to Me," The Best of Bread's "Everything I Own"; "If a Picture paints a Thousand Words" and "I Want to Make it With You"; Skylark's "Wildflower" and the Chi-Lites' "Oh Girl" to name a—very few.

On our latest' get back together" date, music tugging at heart and lamenting the distance and painful separation, out of nowhere, Ronda—popped the question! "Why don't we just get married?" Given how tentative everything had been for months and that this Date was the first "on again." I blurted out, "Great idea, when?" as my brain went to work on—the how. The remarkable timing, sequencing of events, resources required, and how effortlessly- it all seemed to fall into place, would seem, eerily—divinely ordered.

I remembered that Tony, my older cousin, who I rarely got to see, had also married young. He had to obtain written permission from his girlfriend's parents. I called him and set up a time for the four of us to meet for dinner. As I lamented our situation, I probed for information as to how he did it. Marrying that young was impossible in Georgia, but as it turns out, not in Walhalla, SC. But still—a marriage that young required notarized consent from both parents. The more Tony talked, the more the ideas began to flow. I was "of age" I didn't need my parent's permission, but Ronda's parents would have to consent in writing. There was no way. Or was there?

Ideas and angles began to roll around in my head like the "dingy- ding-dings" of a Pin Ball Wizard playing in the finals. "Exactly what did this document look like that you had to show the Justice of the Peace I asked? It was a one-page notarized statement of permission on 8.5 x 11 paper. On my mind's movie screen in 3D, I watched the page enter a typewriter waiting patiently for further instructions. How do we get a notary to stamp and sign a page without anything on it I asked? "They won't," He replied, but they will notarize a sale. I have a 22 250 Browning rifle I can 'sell you.'" Witnessing agreements between two parties is what they do at the pawnshop up the street." Ding, Ding. Eyebrows raised! I *visually* pulled the 8.5" x 11" page from the typewriter and promptly replaced it with an 8.5" x 14". The Date appeared at the *very top* of the page. Directly beneath the Date, the statement began: I Tony xxxxx, do now sell this 22 250 Browning, serial number 12345678 to Jerry Bush for Two Hundred Eighty Dollars - $280 My Signature, his signature. Then dropping to *the bottom* of the page, the text would read:

Notary Public, Date of commission
Notary Public, Signature
Seal:

We returned to Tony's house, straightaway typing up a "bill of Sale" on legal-sized paper for the Notary to witness. The pawnshop was just a few blocks away from where we presented the document as I happily paid the $15 fee for service. In less than 10 minutes, we were done and, on our way, back. A *carefully* ruled line made its way *precisely 11 inches* from the bottom of the page to meet a pair of scissors, then turning the legal-size page into a notarized, blank

8.5 x 11. Again, into the typewriter, and the top of the newly created page would read:

Date

To whom it may concern: We the parents of Ronda xxxx, born, xxxx in Atlanta, residing at xxxx do with this give our consent to marry Jerry Bush, also a Georgia resident, currently residing at, xxxx

Mothers, Signature
Fathers, Signature
Notary Public, Date of commission
Notary Public Signature
Seal:

The courthouse in the Walhalla required that *we both* be present to register —24 hours—in advance—of the wedding. The 7:30 PM appointment with the Justice of the Peace, the following day was a separate appearance. Serendipitously, during the time we were testing the viability of various strategies, my sister was getting married in a traditional afternoon formal church wedding where Ronda was a bridesmaid, and I was a groomsman. As usual, rehearsal typically falls on the day before the wedding. After the practice, we planned to immediately drive from the Church in south Atlanta to Walhalla, register and make a speedy return back to Peachtree City, where I would drop her off knowing that the following day, she would be my wife. The cover story was the traditional "chase and pester" the newlyweds following the wedding. Ronda was to stay with our best friends Lawrence and Susan Jeffords' apartment. I, too, was to stay with Lawrence and Susan at their residence, though—both of us failed to inform our parents that it would be— at the same time. After my sister's brief post-wedding reception, Ronda, Lawrence, Susan, and I piled into my Monte Carlo, radar detector readied for the averaged 95-105 MPH drive up I-85 to North Carolina. The speed just entered the comfort range for the 350cube engine that I had "souped-up for performance." Ms. Monte looked like a good girl on the outside, but she was a bad girl under the hood. Maintaining that speed enabled us to make the 7:30 appointment in Walhalla with— five whole minutes to spare.

As we entered the JOP's office, we were immediately bemused by the "art" hanging on his wall. One picture was a dusty country road bordered by a split rail fence. On each fence post sat *badly* out of proportioned birds, apparently cut from a book or catalog without consideration for context and scale. The four of us listened as the Judge began to tell us about "man and woo-man." Eccentric, partially but inadequately describes this interesting man. After responding to all of the standard "I do" vows *in the midst of which we barely had a clue,* what we were saying we left—married—"legally"—-with the hope that by now we've reached the statute of limitations. *I do not look good in Orange.*

Lawrence and Susan took the front bucket seats, separated by a console, while I called dibs on the back seat for the return home. I insisted that Lawrence make the return as fast as possible. A siren's whoop-whoop and flashing blue lights appeared in the rearview little more than 20 minutes into the trip and maybe 15 MPH over the limit. Really? 95-105 up, and now we get pulled over! From the back seat, I explained to the officer, best I could, and ask, "how much is the fine?" "Thirty-Five dollars," He said. My wallet was out before he could finish the sentence explaining that I didn't need a receipt.

When I had to take Ronda "home," the day after we were married, we knew that was no longer her home and—it was challenging to say goodbye. On the drive back to Buford, trying to look for the positive, I remember thinking, well, at least I got to marry her and—I got to make love to her. One day we can get a place of our own. I paused and added a little prayer: *"Dear Lord, please wait a while before you return. I'm in no hurry, and I'm not sure how heavenly Heaven will be without sex anyway. So, take all the time you need. Thanks."*

The plan was to keep the marriage a secret until Ronda finished school. But that didn't last long. Two days later, I fessed up to Dad and then the same day to her parents, which went better than imagined. Her Mom and Dad had always liked me, but both *immediately and unequivocally* embraced me as their son-in-law. For more than two years, Mother wanted nothing to do with us and slipped out the back when we came to visit in what would become the *first of many* perspectives to clash over the coming years.

I went to work for a new division of Exxon Oil Corporation selling fax machines (yeah, I didn't make the connection between oil and fax.) It wasn't what I wanted to do, but it was work experience, exposure, and an income. Besides—I was biding time. "Just any day now, we'll be going home," So, in the scheme of things, it was not about planning, preparing for the future or living dreams. I had to keep everything in perspective. I was a kid, salaried with commissions with an expense account making calls on Atlanta area businesses demonstrating how they could send a document from one office to another. As ubiquitous as faxing became over the coming decades, it was somewhat of a mysterious concept in the '70s. "You put a document in the machine at location A and six minutes later a copy appears at location B. Yes—it took 6 minutes to send a single page in those days. In the wake of email, faxing all but died. In seconds, high-resolution images, including scans of existing documents, go to virtually anywhere on planet Earth, eliminating the need. We look back now and think, why would you ever need to explain faxing to anyone? Our perspective has changed. Our frame of reference is different. It's something we now take for granted.

WHEN COMPARED TO WHAT?

Well, compared to what the Bible says, of course. "If the Bible says to do it, we do it." It is now apparent, the denomination I grew up in was as generous with sin and "do not" labels, as the noonday is bounteous with sunshine. As I aged beyond my 20s and began to travel beyond the metaphorical village's borders, I quickly learned that there was an astonishing array of gray in doctrinal differences on virtually everything, all of which depended on who was applying the copious interpretations. My exposure to "scholarship" had not been scholarship at all. It was doctrine packaged by Fundamentalist Bible schools for Fundamentalist consumption.

I tend to conceptualize things such as those I described above, abstractly, be it concepts, philosophy, or especially views driving doctrinal claims. It's like a weighbridge or—a dial that incrementally measures. It increases or decreases by degree. Movement one way or the other tilts the scales. A blindfolded Lady Justice lets the weight of the evidence tell the tale. She is without bias. She wants objectivity in defining truth. Attorneys purposely biased, make their arguments for either side. They are paid handsomely to present things from a fully biased and— polar opposite perspective. They will take all they have learned and pass it through their filters and *spin* an argument that presents the most compelling view of the facts in evidence, possible.

Conditional salvation in my world, with all the fear and insecurity that came with the package, was a crucial doctrine in my denomination. The underlying message supposed to have been 2 Corinthians 5:19. [10] Becoming a born-again Christian meant that you were no longer guilty of Adam's "original sin." The "good news" was— (*supposed to have been)* that Jesus' became sin on the cross and paid the debt. That didn't mean you were *innocent*. That said, you were found- *not guilty*. Innocent means—you didn't do it. Being found not guilty means you are legally acquitted of something for which *you may be guilty*. Your attorney was just—that good. But in a guilty verdict, the Judge (God) who would otherwise pass sentence instead, *became the crime,* [11] Adam's Sin that "you committed"—when you were born. But Instead, the Judge hides evidence of the crime. He bleaches the metaphorical bloodstains, [12] eliminating the evidence from its ability to incriminate you. He expunges the record and throws the proof of the murder of your unborn soul "into the sea of forgetfulness never more to be remembered." [13] He finds you not-guilty because there is no evidence to convict you. The Apostle Paul goes to great length to explain all of this in his writings. Suffice it to say; *it depends on the reader and who taught the student how to understand what is written.*

All of the things Paul writes are constructed around "sin entering the world through one man. Adam." Before he became Paul after seeing the vison on the road to Damascus, Saul was a Jews Jew and steeped in the Pentateuch, all of which begins with the story of Adam. But that is all about original sin. What about the future "sins" to follow birth? Well, the rebirth experience was supposed to cover that too.

For many years the women in my youthful world, as mentioned, didn't wear makeup. My father-in-law, "Pop," one of the most beautiful people I've ever known (rest in peace Pop, I genuinely miss you) used to on occasion, call Ronda, Jezzie, short for Jezebel. Ronda wore enough makeup to look put together, but— natural. Yet to Pop, she was (in jest) Jezebel of 2 Kings, 9, a despicable woman, responsible for many atrocities. An exciting or bewildering perspective? The thing most noted in this example was not the atrocities she committed but rather that "…she painted her face…" (vs. 30.) Wearing makeup was part and parcel of being a bad woman as being rich was part of being a bad person, [Chapter 7, A Hell of an Idea] and, therefore, one of many items on legalisms lengthy list. Choosing to "fix-up" a bit turned a woman into a whore, attracting men. What a distressing concept! No sleeveless dresses, no hemlines above the knee, and the hair teased into beehives. The more homely in appearance, the Godlier she became. What made the "acceptable" dress of the day—- acceptable? Why did my denomination not require black, floor-length dresses with white doily collars and white bonnets? The Amish does. Who made the rules for either? Which laws are the right rules? How do you know? Is it possible that all such things entirely miss—- *the point?*

"Pop" had a few thou shalt not "pets." But his list was shorter than my parent's list. *Considerably.* For instance, he didn't have to be in Church every time the doors opened. On occasion, he served as an usher, but the Church wasn't the center of his universe. He wouldn't have been considered a committed Christian by many of the self-righteous yardsticks. Yet, Pops list of "thou shalt not" included all the biggies, but add: no makeup, no going to movies, no rolling dice, no playing cards, no saying gosh or golly both, which were allegedly Christian versions of swearing and too close to the real thing. The requisite "Oh my" was the acceptable replacement for expressing exasperation. And—if you slipped up, he would call you out. Like the many things that made such a profound impression on me as a child, I began to ponder *the rules*. I couldn't escape the enormous inconsistencies, that advertised measurements using the same scale, but with—exceedingly confusing results.

Who decided what too much makeup was? None, a little, or clownish? Who decided when a man's hair was too long? Who decided sleeve length and which hemlines were too short? Precisely at what point did the scales tilt from it being "right" to it being wrong—- an eighth inch, quarter-inch, half an inch? Who sanctioned what was sinful and what was acceptable? Who nodded their approval or snorted their derision? Who was the authorization committee, who assembled it, and who empowered either? These are but a very few examples of the sanctimony *that way too late*, started my blood boil. For some, doctrine becomes so all-consuming that, at some point, it fails to be doctrine. It becomes the God which the theory envisions, fashions, creates. It becomes—the reality to which *everyone* must conform. Some can remain devoted to their views while coexisting with those who see things differently and—*without judgment*. In my experience, such things are, however— **rare**. The sanctimonious see coexistence as compromise and compromise as a bad thing. Allowing others to "row their own boat" instead of making the biggest waves possible, is—a flag of surrender. There is no better example than demonstrated in this exemplary story.

———————

Both of my children's weddings were exquisite, but the Receptions- elaborate. My daughter's wedding Reception included a full-service sit-down dinner for 150 guests. Enchanted, flowered "trees," five to six feet high appeared to grow from the center of some of the tables, creating a fairytale wonderland inside a venue in Peachtree City explicitly designed and equipped to host such events. A large parquet dance floor centered the room, and a full bar served all the guests. My son's Reception was held at the historic, columned, colonial style Taylor-Grady House in Athens, Ga, where he and his bride and my daughter earned their undergraduate degrees at the University of Georgia. The event spilled into the back yard where a large tent sheltered the dance floor, sound system, and open bar. My parents, however, refused to attend either Reception. I chose to respectfully prepare them that both of my children wanted to serve alcohol at their receptions. It was a party; they wanted to dance and celebrate. I encouraged Mom and Dad to participate without partaking in anything with which they were uncomfortable. Persistent appeals for reasonableness fell on deaf ears. Both events were *unacceptable.*

More than a decade earlier, I purposed to throw an extraordinary celebration for my 25th wedding anniversary. Previously I disclosed that my wife and I eloped at a very young age. It's every girl's dream to one day have a storybook wedding; to walk the aisle with all eyes on her. The only regret Ronda had ever expressed was not having a wedding, so I purposed to make our 25th very special indeed, and, to the extent possible, provide her with some of the experience she had missed.

For well over a year, I secretly planned a surprise, Black-tie event announced by ribbon wrapped, engraved invitations along with a plea for discretion in keeping the surprise a secret. We designed the party for the Grand Ballroom at Atlanta's blue-domed, Hyatt Regency hotel. Black drapes framed an enormous rear projection screen positioned front and center of the room. The curtains right of the screen concealed a cart, which on cue, would roll an oversized vase with 26 perfectly arranged long-stemmed red roses onto the oversized dance floor. A single ribbon marked the 26th rose for easy retrieval. Popular Atlanta Radio DJ Mark McCain would serve as master of ceremonies and "hit spinner" for the night, providing a continuous mix of music from the 1970s and contemporary hits of the day. Beautiful ice sculpted Swan sits centered and elevated to prominence, on white skirted, arched tables that serpentine for fifty feet in the middle of the room. Tall silver wire vases showcase mixed flower bouquets that seem to stand guard on each side like centurions reaching skyward. To the right of center, a three-tier wedding cake awaits cutting while on the left, a requisite punch in a large bowl is ready to be consumed. A variety of classic cheeses and exotic hors d 'oeuvres occupy the rest of the table. Pastries prepared by the Hyatt's top chefs, one of which many years later will become family; the grandfather to my two beautiful Italian granddaughters— and, who also becomes a dear friend.

For months I had gathered old photos, home movie footage, and other memory milestones chronicling our years together. I worked for weeks, carefully spreadsheeting all the elements I envisioned packing 25 years into a thirty-minutes. Some parts of the editing required converting analog videotape to digital files, considerably more labor-intensive than the all-digital tools we enjoy today. Using a script, I developed, we painstaking sequenced each picture and movie clips to coincide with transitions, timed with messages in the music that had become so much a part our history, most of which were favorites from our 70's mixtape. I hired Bryan, a professional videographer and editor, to shoot some new footage as if he were a roving reporter around town, asking friends and family what they knew about Ronda.

The day before the big event, I drove to Alpharetta and joined Bryan in the edit suite. Dennis owned the studio and gifted us with the time for its use. He and his wife would be in the Ballroom the following evening watching the fruit of our labor. Bryan and I worked all night and late into the next morning to create something I would be proud to show our guests the following evening. I headed home from the studio, bone-tired attempting to catch a few hours' sleep before going to the Hyatt. Nervous energy competed with the time crunch and stress-induced, sleep deprivation making rest impossible. Bryan had work yet to do but promised to finish up and come straight to the party with the master tape. I was nervous about testing the projection system with a stand-in. Murphy's law had foiled many presentations in my career, and I didn't want this to be one of them.

At 7:00 PM, on a Saturday evening. Ronda, family, church friends, and business colleagues began to arrive. The first hour was a "cocktail reception" 110 guest glad-handing and catching up. Music backdropped an already lively mingle. Groups began to form, taking seats around the 20 draped tables. The bartender served a variety of beer, wine, and Champagne, punch, and soft drinks, for the many teetotalers attending.

Promptly at 8:00, as the lights begin to dim, McCain asks everyone to take their seats. Ronda and I are sitting at a table up front, next to the dance floor. Music precedes the fade from black to the picture taken the day we were married, [Exhibit—-Wedding Picture], and for the next 30 minutes, the memories roll. The last scene scrolls a lengthy poem I had written to Ronda. My recorded voice-over recites the poem, cues Bryan to enter the back of the room camera rolling, and slowly makes his way through the tables to the front of the room. A Hyatt staffer rolls the 26 roses to the dance floor, as I stand, pull number 26, and get down on one knee and present it to Ronda. I extend my hand, inviting her to dance as Mark plays Lionel Richie's megahit "Truly." Servers make their rounds placing and filling Champagne flutes for each of our guests, offering the real thing or sparkling grape juice. After the dance, I propose a toast to Ronda and—- another 25 years. The lights come up, with "Who Let the Dogs Out?" the dance floor fills, and quickly after that, my friend of many years, Mark Thompson leads an impressive array of participants in the Electric Slide, after which McCain seamlessly crossfades into the O'Jays' 1972 hit "Love Train." Ronda's no makeup mother and the rest of the fearless crowd jumps to be a part of the train that soon encircles the grand ballroom. Around and around we go as Pop remains at the table, chatting it up with my parents.

As the evening began to wrap, and for days to follow, I received numerous phone calls heaping praise and many "thank you." Most every man in attendance gushed a stream of almost embarrassing compliments telling me I had created problems for them; I "set the bar" —- and future expectations to a troublesome, unachievable level. All sentiments were *pure praise*—save— those of my parents, who made their condemnation known with palpable energy to which, at the time, I was quite susceptible. *"It was too worldly."* A verbal denunciation was a higher priority than a halfhearted attempt to find *a trace* of good. *An audacious, mind-bending allegiance to tradition*, one with which, for some, Love will never compete.

That momentous moment planted the seed that grew into a book.

"When you change the way you look at things, the things you look at change." Max Plank -Nobel Prize Winner, Physics

---

Chapter 2

Perspective from a Different Perspective

Perspective is fascinating and fascinatingly personal. One of the few things we all have in common is that *we all* see things from different perspectives. Our vantage point greatly influences our assessment, and our assessment develops into what often becomes *an inflexible perspective.*

The Origins of our Perspective

As children, we see what—IS. Our minds are uncluttered, our opinions unformed. We know the world around us—unfiltered; our reactions are uncensored. In short—real. If you ever want to know how it really is, then—"out of the mouth of babes." *"You have something on your face." "I don't like those shorts with all the pockets, Papa."* My nine-year-old, and oldest of my four granddaughters, recently informed me that what I was trying to explain to her was boring. The things I would like for her to be interested in, are for now, irrelevant to her interest. *"It's boring, Papa."* The very young have not yet learned to spin their answers to fit their audience. There are no filters. They call it the way they see it, not necessarily like it is, but certainly like it is for them. But then, what determines what really—IS?

Photographers with high-end cameras purchase lens filters to create a specific look artificially. Some are designed to gaussian the edges and sharpen the middle. Some "soft focus" the entire image. Some polarize. Polarization distorts the light. It saturates specific wavelengths and keeps others out altogether. Desirably, it alters what the camera "sees," creating a fanciful interpretation of reality and provides a perfect metaphor for this thesis. New technology for sunglasses *polarizes* the light. (it bends some of the wavelengths, it blocks some wavelengths entirely, and enhances other wavelengths) regardless, it distorts the reality of what is there.

Similarly, photographs and contemporary movies are "Photoshopped" to create remarkable special effects or correct significant imperfections. Hundreds of processes saturate or bend hues, or completely change color to enable filmmakers and marketers to cultivate realities unimagined just a decade ago. Fine restaurants dimly light their tables in warm incandescent, avoiding the harsh blueish wavelength of fluorescent lights under which "attractive" is only possible for the young and the beautiful. Filters do not just shape what we see but—also what we hear.

In the late 1970s, cassette tapes were the new thing bringing portability to albums of music. A problem inherent in this new technology was an annoying hiss that backdropped the recording. Ray Dolby developed a circuit (a filter) to eliminate the unwanted noise. Flip a small switch, and the hiss went away, but-"the fix" also compromised desirable high-frequency elements of the recording. What you got was less noise—and less of the beautiful crisp high-end. So much so that this listener often chose to deal with the hiss; the switch remained off.

Contemporary records, in some genres, autotune vocal tracks, creating an illusion that the artist can sing. If the vocalist goes sharp or flat, Autotune pulls the note back in the pitch. It *misrepresents* what the artist can do. These are just a few examples of the *desirable deceptions we tacitly give our permission.*

But what about the things of which we are entirely unaware? Something that will have a profound, perhaps lifelong impact on creating and reinforcing perceptions; *perceptions* unbeknownst to our conscious mind are sculpting our *perspectives*, creating our beliefs, impacting our future choices, and forming our worldview? Allow that question to sink in a minute.

As infants, our brains produce very slow *theta and delta* waves and remain in that range until approximately age seven. Only then do children begin to think more 'like adults,' producing the faster *alpha and beta* brain waves [1]. In the much quicker *beta wave,* the brain is open for business; it's on high alert for critical thinking and problem-solving. When deeply relaxed, the much slower *Alpha waves* occur as in the early stages of meditation. *Theta waves* are even slower than alpha *in frequency* (the number of oscillations per second) *and yet greater in amplitude* (how high and low the waves extend) [2], *which occur in sleep and deep meditation, much like entering a hypnotic trance.* When a person enters stage three of the four stages of sleep, the brain begins to produce slow, deep *delta waves* where a person is far less responsive and increasingly unaware of their external environment. They enter the twilight stage between lighter sleep and deep sleep, sometimes called "the land between asleep and awake."

So, you may be wondering why this (potentially dull to some) information matters at all. This brief explanation is not to study brain waves. It is instead to inform the reader who may be unfamiliar with this science. It is essential to understanding *why our brains indiscriminately record everything, from birth to about age seven, and the profound effect* it potentially has on the way we process our world— *for the rest of our lives.* Soon after that, it will begin to, more and more, critically judge what it perceives. It will accept or reject the information based almost entirely *on the operating system program installed in the formative years*. In later years, the Conscious will appear, at times, to accept new information as if it wishes to do so. The acceptance will depend almost entirely on the latest information's *congruence with the subconscious' gatekeeper*. If— the subconscious judges the information to be incongruent with its programming, acceptance is temporary. The subconscious rejects the conscious mind's request to permanently assimilate the data as a new part of the operating system. It is much like a virus detection program on a computer "guarding the gate." It perceives the incongruent information as a threat and places it into quarantine to delete later.

Quantum
Brook

In the article "How to transform the subconscious trance," Bruce H. Lipton, Ph.D. explains it this way: *"The predominant delta and theta activity expressed by children younger than age six signifies that their brains are operating at levels— below consciousness."* [3] In later chapters, but more intensely in Volume II, we will explore Dr. Lipton's breakthrough discoveries and expertise in cell biology, revealing how (fortunately) we can reprogram the subconscious. Dr. Lipton explains how a child's newly minted brain is a magnificently, sophisticated recording device. It absorbs everything that it sees and hears; without filters. The filters are unformed. Everything the little eyes and ears perceive in their environment becomes, figuratively, lines of code. Technically they are becoming new synaptic connections in the brain. They are unobtrusively but systematically forming the brain's operating system (the OS.) The human body's "OS" sends **11 million bits per second** to the brain for processing, yet the **conscious mind can process only 50 bits per second.** [4] The conscious mind *thinks it is in control*. The reality is, the *subconscious mind* is *mostly in control*.

For my reader unfamiliar with operating systems, it's all the smarts behind the "desktop" you see when you first boot up your computer. It simultaneously runs countless operations in the background. My MacBook Pro's OS enables me to retrieve Microsoft Word from the application folder. At my request, it then opens the "file cabinet" to extract the folder containing all the files I created to write the book *and* places it on my desktop so that I can work on it. The OS is the *coded intelligence* that recognizes which letter on the keyboard I type. It translates that letter to appear as a group of black dots, packed tightly together to form the shape of the *Text Font* (the style of each letter) I've chosen for the book. It faithfully recreates the cosmetic look of the Text Font precisely as the person who artfully designed the font to look. When I want to print a Draft, the OS notifies the printer over the wireless network. It then disassembles the entire document into a language the printer understands. It reinterprets my command for not only the words I've chosen but also in the order I've chosen them. It also builds the style, which for now, exists only in my mind's eye.
Every waking second, a child's brain is writing the program for its operating system. The subconscious world from which it will, (*without aggressive intervention),* operate the rest of its life. As we mature, we slowly allow the OS to fashion the lens and filters that will shape our version of reality. The subconscious program, growing more and more robust every day becomes the gatekeeper, and self-appointed "virus" detector. It will decide what gets in and what stays out. It will *preprocess* all that we see and hear, displaying surprising control over how we respond to future input. I learned of these marvels more than fifty years after I was born. *It shed a lot of light* on what went into my half-century-long perspective.

If you are an American, visiting England, and the band begins to play the song, God Save The Queen, you hear the words: *"My country tis of thee sweet land of liberty, of thee I sing."* Your British host understands: *God save the Queen, God save our gracious Queen, God save our noble Queen.* It is, of course, the same melody but different lyrics. The country in which you grew up, determines which words you connect to that melody now embedded into your memory. But what if that experience was much more profound. What if there was a very positive, or, likewise, a traumatic, deeply emotional event that happened while hearing that music? Not only would the words involuntarily appear when hearing the melody, but a panoply of emotions would surface, much in the same way we connect emotionally to certain popular songs during the days when we first fell in love. They become a part of our history; they become momentous threads in the fabric of who we are.

If you were *a child* born in America to parents who survived the great depression, they likely taught you to hang on to every penny you earn as if it were your last. They probably conditioned you to see everything from a perspective of lack, and you will view new opportunities as high risk—all destined to fail. Your worldview is disproportionately small; your experiences and education may "cause" you to pass on the chance of a lifetime. Likewise, *a child born into affluence,* complete with an Ivy League education, will be taught to view money as a tool that creates great wealth. Their teachers and caregivers *condition them* to see opportunity from a *perspective* of absolute success, which accepts occasional loss as just another lesson and a normal part of living life. Both live in the same country. Both are afforded equal opportunity, albeit on very different roads leading to the same destination. Yet, as adults, both will see opportunity through a radically different lens giving the appearance that both will choose the success in front of them. But that choice will emanate from the operating systems programmed from birth.

If you were born in the Northeast in the late 1800s or early 1900's you are likely the child of Italian, Irish, or otherwise European immigrant parents. They entered the USA in the shadow of the Statue of Liberty and documented at Ellis Island. If you were born in the South during the same period, you might have been, like my Father, one of many children in *a vast* family who worked in a sharecropper's cotton field. These experiences not only shape our perspective, but they also become *deeply* ingrained into the subconscious. They become the person we see in the mirror. We will, by and large, be—*wired that way.* "How we envision Truth depends on whether we observe the object of Truth or its shadow? What is the source of illumination? Do we see what is true or—Truth?

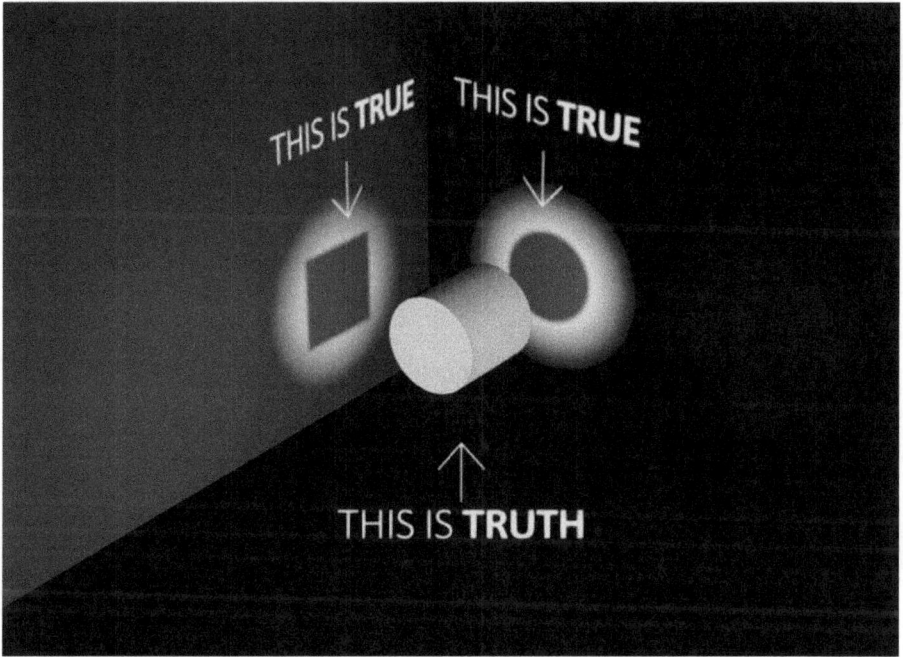

Backwards Bike

While researching examples that help illustrate this mystery, I stumbled across something unique and—- uniquely capable of demonstrating how we sometimes unwittingly wire our brain to think about things in a specific way. What we think about and practice long enough becomes a part of who we are. What we practice becomes integrated as a habit, "muscle memory." We are no longer driven by our conscious mind, but rather by our unconscious mind. We don't think about what to do or how to do it. We—do it.

Fundamental to my thesis is the difficulty, but not the impossibility, of rewiring how we view and—participate in our world. But research in Neuroplasticity, also reveals that we can reshape our brain. We can retrain that which we once thought to be permanently hardwired and inflexible.

It's just like riding a bike, huh! An engineer by education posted a must-see video on YouTube. "The Backwards Brain Bicycle" [5] Barney, a friend at the welding shop where Destin Sandlin works in Huntsville, AL, challenged him to ride a bike to which his friend had made one, "small" change. Turning the handlebars left, turned the front wheel to the right. Likewise, turning the handlebars to the right turned the wheel to the left. Everything Destin, you or I learned about riding a bicycle was now backward. But, no big deal—right? Just tell yourself *"when on this bike— left means right and right means left. While I am on this bike, I have to think in reverse."* Easy- peasy? Wrong. Very wrong. Destin devoted five minutes every day for eight months before something finally "clicked," rewiring the connection in his brain, enabling him to ride the bike— which then created another problem. He was unable to return to riding a regular bicycle. Destin never rode a "normal" bicycle during the eight months, which created yet another problem. He was now unable to ride a regular bike. Destin challenged people in various lectures he gave around the world, offering $200 to anyone who could ride the bicycle a mere 10 feet across the stage. No one succeeded. Our conscious mind is not the captain determining which way we steer our ship. Our subconscious or the unconscious mind is in control. Reprogramming, the way we think, see, hear, and process our world requires relentless determination and employing recent discoveries to assist in the effort.[6]

Ships Unseen

You can see what is right in front of you. Right? Not always. There are baffling stories of ships visible to the physical eye, but invisible to the mind of native observers. These stories in various forms are a now frequently mentioned phenomenon, documented, in the journals and ship's logs of early European explorers to the new world, notably Christopher Columbus (1492), Ferdinand Magellan (1520) and James Cook (1770). Each explorer describes natives being unable to perceive, to 'see' the large ships. The ships were beyond their understanding. They were outside the scope of their experience and, therefore, outside of their ability to perceive. Their brain could not assimilate what their eye was seeing. Joseph Banks, a botanist aboard Cook's ship describes the frequently mentioned phenomenon this way: [7] *"The ship passed within a quarter of a mile of them and yet they scarce lifted their eyes from their employment; I was almost inclined to think that attentive to their business and deafened by the noise of the surf they neither saw nor heard her go past them. Not one was once observed to stop and look towards the ship; they pursued their way in all appearance entirely unmoved by the neighborhood of so remarkable an object as a ship must necessarily be to people who have never seen one."*

Medical science long ago discovered that what we see, hits the eye's retina—upside down. Our brain inverts the image, turning it right-side-up. It takes raw information and *converts it into something useful.*[8] Amazingly, the image that hits our retinas are flat, 2D projections. Our brain then overlays the separate images to form a single, seamless, 3D image providing astonishing accuracy and depth perception. It enables us to catch a ball, shoot baskets, hit distant targets, judge oncoming traffic, draw a level bead by the line of site, etc. Our brain fills in the blanks where visual data is missing entirely. What is more astonishing is *the hole* in our vision, where the optic nerve connects to the back of the eye. There are no visual receptors there, yet the brain creates visual data that, in reality, is not there and fills in the hole to create a seamless image. ***The mind assimilates the incomplete data and uses assumptions based on our previous experience.*** Scientists call this "unconscious inference." It draws on our past experiences. It is not something with which we are born. We *learn it. Just because the eyes see the image, it is useless until the brain 'makes sense' out of what the eye is consuming. And how the brain makes sense out of what it sees depends on how the subconscious labels the information. Again, our perceptions create our perspective.*

Kittens n' Stripes

Many years ago, Harvard Medical School, and later MIT, performed experiments where they took a group of kittens and raised them in a room where visually everything was horizontal, even the walls were horizontal strips. Likewise, they took the second group of kittens and nurtured them in a place where, visually, everything was vertically striped. After the kittens matured, they brought them together in a more realistic room containing both vertical and horizontal visuals and furniture. They immediately observed that "the vertical group" could not see anything horizontal, including chair tops, tabletops. Likewise, the horizontal group was unable to see vertical things like chair legs and table legs, and they continually ran into them as if they were not there. Yet as cats love to do, the horizontal group naturally jumped onto the horizontal chair seats, tabletops, and countertops.

When the researchers later examined the kitten's brains, they found that *each group did not have the physical inter-neuronal connections to see the "other type of world."* The way the kittens experienced their surroundings, through their senses, *literally programmed their nervous system to serve the singular function of reinforcing their initial perceptions.* This study demonstrates how our early upbringing and belief systems, instilled at an early age, creating our views of reality and shaping how we understand our world. This system of reality becomes hardwired into our brains unless we *purposely reprogram it.* [9]

"Every man takes the limits of his own field of vision for the limits of the world." — Arthur Schopenhauer

---

"Yanny-Laurel"

Unless you were hiking the Antarctic in May 2018, you probably heard about the audible enigma, "yanny-laurel." When this mystery first hit the internet, I distinctly heard *'yanny' the first time I listened*. I could not hear 'laurel' and didn't understand *how anyone could*. The two words are not remotely close in pronunciation or intonation. A couple of days later, I listened again. This time all that I that heard was 'laurel.' I have been unable to hear 'yanny' since then. Go to *vocabulary.com*. Search for the word laurel. Turn the volume up and press the speaker shaped icon to the right of the word Laurel. What do you hear? This example is the audible sibling of the blue-black, gold-white dress enigma. It is

Quantum
Brook

both fascinating and—*perplexing*. While writing this portion of the book, I asked my wife to sit for a minute and tell me what she heard. When I pressed the speaker icon, I again heard—"Laurel" but didn't say anything.

"What did you hear?" I asked.
"Yanny," she said. "What did you hear?
"Laurel," I answered.
"How did you get Laurel from that? "She asked. "Do it again!"
I pressed the button. "What did you hear?" "Yanny," she said. I pressed the button yet again and asked. This time, wide-eyed, she responded, "Laurel— I heard Laurel" Head tilted, dropping one brow "they are playing some trick, switching it up!" She said.
"That would be quite a trick then," I said. "It wasn't 'switched up' for me, and we are both sitting here, listening to the same thing, and sometimes hearing the opposite thing." It is almost always 'Laurel' for me but a mix of 'laurel' and 'yanny' for her.

There is still a lot of mystery and speculation as to why some people hear yanny and some hear Laurel. After all, you should hear laurel. *Laurel is the word we looked up in the dictionary*! Right? Maybe some brains are tuned to higher frequencies and others to lower frequencies. If true, why do some hear both as she did, and— as I did in 2018? Regardless, the discussion here is not to solve this mystery but rather to immerse ourselves in understanding the book's central premise.

People perceive the world around them differently. They observe what they hear and see in ways, accurate to them, just as someone else's experiences are real to them. Our brain processes the things our senses perceive, and those perceptions create our perspective. It is those differences that make us unique.

"The Dress"

A phenomenon that broke the internet in late February 2015 overturned our understanding of how color vision worked. We thought we knew. No one could fathom why some people saw "the dress" as *white and gold*, yet others saw it as *blue and black*. Those colors are not subtle shades apart. They are starkly different. Most people assume that everyone understands what they see. And for those who do not, it suggests one party or the other is ignorant, advancing a specific agenda, or just plain crazy. We believe what we see with our own eyes and assume everyone sees the same thing. If, as I do, you see the dress as gold and white——the actual dress is blue and black. Though, as it turns out, most of us see white and gold, at least at first.

Research with 13,000 people, and two years later, researchers now have a much better idea of what may the reason for the varied perceptions: It seems the way we *perceive lighting* determines the color we see. If the observer (*subconsciously)* assumes the dress was photographed in a shadow, they are more likely to see a white and gold dress.

In judging color, the brain self-assuredly fills in *a significant* gap in our knowledge and makes assumptions, like the lighting conditions under which 'the dress' was photographed. It makes these assumptions based on *what each person encounters most often during their day* to day living. It's impossible to assess the real lighting conditions in 'the dress accurately,' so the brain assumes.

In the study, "Larks" (people who get up early in the morning) are naturally exposed to more daylight. The "Owls" who to go to bed later and sleep in later in the morning, experience relatively more incandescent lighting than do the Larks. The people who self-identified as a Lark were more likely to see the dress as white and gold. Conversely, Owls were more likely to assume the lighting was artificial and saw the dress as black and blue. Shadows overrepresent the blue wavelength. The brain, in turn, subtracts the bluer light from the image, making it more yellow. Natural light has a similar effect. If the observer assumed illumination by natural light, they were more likely to see the dress as white and gold. The daylight blue sky overrepresents short wavelengths, compared to the relatively longer wavelength of artificial incandescent light.

In either case, the brain's subtle subconscious program subtracts the blue wavelength, leaving more yellow, or subtracts yellow leaving a bluer hue. The study's author described himself as an "extreme Owl," Initially, he "strongly saw the dress as white and gold." But after four days of looking at the image repeatedly and learning the dress was black and blue, his perception "quite abruptly" changed to a black and blue, and he was then unable to see white and gold again. [10]

"There are things known and there are things unknown, and in between

are the doors of perception." ⎯Aldous Huxley

"It is a narrow mind which cannot look at a subject from various points of view." — George Eliot

Goliath- The Underdog

The story found in 1Samuel 17 of the Old Testament, has become an iconic story of the underdog's triumph over impossible odds. It is universally known within Judeo-Christian circles and well known by virtually everyone regardless of religious affiliation. Storytellers historically frame the famous account as a young shepherd boy volunteering for deadly face-to-face combat with Goliath. In his book David & Goliath, Malcolm Gladwell goes into much greater detail than I do here, presenting a *very* different perspective. *"...everything I thought I knew about that story turned out to be wrong."* [11]

This retelling using notes from Gladwell's lecture provides a perfect example of how storytellers shape our perceptions, especially in our formative years.

There is a beautiful area of soft sloping hills in Israel known as the Shephela (or Shfela), which lies between the mountains and coastal plain that runs along the Mediterranean. It is beautifully oak forested in areas with wheat fields and vineyards. The Shephela connects the mountain range and coastal plain with a series of valleys and ridges that run east to west. The cities of Jerusalem, Bethlehem and Hebron are in that mountain range. It was the same 3000 years ago at the time of the story of David & Goliath.

The Shephela had an essential and strategic function. It was how hostile armies on the coastal plain could make their way into the mountains to conquer those who lived there. At the time of David and Goliath, the Philistines were Israel's greatest enemy. They lived on the coastal plain. The Philistines threaten to may make their way by sea, then up through the Shephelah's valleys and into the mountain to occupy the highland area by Bethlehem, splitting the Kingdom of Israel in two. Saul, Israel's King, learns of the plot, assembles his army, and marches down the mountainside to confront the Philistines in the beautiful Valley of Elah in the Shephela. The Israelites set up camp, along the northern ridge; the Philistines set up camp opposite the Israelites along the southern ridge. Both armies remain entrenched for weeks, each staring down the other from their respective encampments. Neither side is willing to make the first move. Leaving the mountainside's safety to go through the valley and up the other front leaves the advancing army wholly exposed.

To break the deadlock, the Philistines sends their "mightiest" warrior, Goliath, down the mountainside to the valley floor to challenge the Israelites. Hand to hand combat, by a single warrior from each side, was a tradition in ancient warfare where the contest would decide the victory and spare the inevitable bloodshed of thousands in a major battle. Goliath's challenge:

"Choose a man for yourselves and let him come down to me. If he is able to fight with me and kill me, then we will be your servants. But if I prevail against him and kill him, then you shall be our servants."

A lot is riding on (believed to be) an inevitable loss by anyone who fights Goliath. Not only would the warrior lose his own life, but Israel would become slaves to the Philistines under the terms of the challenge. This war is one of creating perception, one, won, or lost in the mind. The Philistines are winning the war by framing the conflict through traditional understanding. Goliath is a visually imposing 6' 9"-inch giant. [12] All who see him are terrified and mentally defeated from the first sight. He is armored head to toe in "glittering bronze." His custom-made sword, javelin, and spear are enormous. For forty consecutive days, Goliath makes the trip into the valley, repeating his challenge. Not one of the Israelites wants to fight him. To do so is a death wish. Or is it? This story is a perfect example of the tribe's conditioning to look at something through a specific traditional lens. It is predetermined. But let's take another look:

The young shepherd boy David arrives at the Israeli encampment to deliver supplies for his brothers, who are part of Saul's army. Keep in mind they had been there for about two months; many weeks before Goliath began his daily challenge for forty days. David arrives,

"…as the army was going out to the fight and shouting for the battle. For Israel and the Philistines had drawn up in the battle array, army against army."

David, (by some estimates) at a height estimated to be five ft. three [13] approaches King Saul telling him to hold off, that he will fight Goliath. Saul observes David as just a boy and the man he will fight as someone who has been a warrior ever since he was a child. David explains that he has killed lions and bears caring for his sheep, and he will kill Goliath. David is not a part of Saul's army and not conditioned to look the challenge through the same Military lens. Saul agrees if—David will agree to wear Saul's armor. David suites up and quickly and tells Saul he cannot wear the armor; he has not "tested it," meaning he had not practiced with it; and he removes the armor.

Every warrior in Saul's army envisions being within swords reach while looking into Goliath's face. David saw Goliath through a different lens. He is thinking about the challenge unconventionally. He is not a part of Saul's army and has no reason or obligation to approach the battle through the lens of conventional warfare. Instead, David picks up five stones and puts them in his shepherd's bag and walks down the mountainside. Goliath sees a figure approaching and calls out with some trash talk to intimidate his challenger. *"Come to me that I might feed your flesh to the birds of the heavens and the beasts of the field."* As David gets closer, Goliath is insulted —*"Am I a dog that you would come to me with sticks?"* Goliath sees that he's carrying shepherd's staff instead of a weapon. David removes one of the stones from his bag and puts it in his sling, turning the sling like a propeller before letting the stone fly, hitting Goliath where he was most vulnerable, right between the eyes. He falls dead or unconscious. David runs immediately, takes Goliath's sword, and cuts off his head. The Philistine army turns and runs.

David is supposed to be the underdog. The term David & Goliath became a part of our lexicon as a metaphor for overcoming impossible odds. So, let's start with generally accepted assumptions.

David is the underdog because he is a little kid.
David is just a shepherd.
David only has a sling.
Goliath is big, strong, a giant.
Goliath is a skilled warrior all of his life.
Goliath outfit is impressive "modern" weaponry.

Saying that "All David has is a sling," is our first mistake. There were three kinds of warriors in ancient warfare. Cavalry: Men on chariots and horseback; Heavy Infantry: Armored foot soldiers with spears, swords, and shields. Artillery: Archers, and most important to this story: Slingers.

Slings were of leather construction, a pouch with two long cords, one attached to each side of the bag. Projectiles, rocks, or lead balls were put in the pouch and, holding the end of the two cords was spun rapidly like an airplane propeller, then letting go one of the ties sends the projectile towards its target like a bullet. The "sling" was not the "kids' toy" slingshots we know today. It is, instead, an incredibly devastating weapon. The centrifugal force building in the sling that David spins at six or seven revolutions per second means when the projectile is released, it travels at approximately 35 meters per second, substantially faster than a baseball thrown by baseball's greatest pitchers.

It is important to note that the stones in the Valley of Elah are not your garden variety stone. They were barium sulfate with a mass *twice that of ordinary rocks*. Calculating the ballistic stopping power of the stone that David fired from his sling approximates a bullet fired from a .45 caliber handgun. According to Gladwell, we know from corroborating historical records that experienced slingers could hit, maim, or kill targets at distances of up to 200 yards. We know from medieval tapestries that slingers were capable of hitting birds in flight. Slings were incredibly accurate. When David positioned himself to confront Goliath, he was not 200 yards away; he is quite close. David experienced many kills with Lions and Bears. When he stands before Goliath, he has complete confidence that he will hit Goliath right between his eyes. Historical records of ancient warfare record that *Slingers* were the decisive factor in winning the battles against the infantry. Goliath is heavy infantry. Goliath's assumes the warrior he will face will be heavy infantry and fight as heavy infantry. Furthermore,

When Goliath says, *"Come to me that I might feed your flesh to the birds of the heavens and the beasts of the field,"* the key phrase is, *"Come to me."* He says: Come to me because he expects to fight his challenger in traditional hand to hand combat. Saul has the same assumption when David says, "I want to fight Goliath," and it is why Saul tries to give David his armor. Saul, too, expects David to fight Infantry to Infantry. But David has absolutely no expectations. He's not going to fight Goliath that way. Why? He's a shepherd who has spent his entire career, skillfully using a sling to defend his flock against predators. That was his strength, and he played to his advantage rather than conforming to the prevailing wisdom. So here he is. A shepherd, experienced in using an agile and devastating weapon, against a lumbering, mass laden, giant that is weighed down by a hundred pounds of armor, and incredibly heavy weapons, which are effective ONLY in hand to hand combat. *Goliath is a sitting duck. He doesn't have a chance. So then,*

Why do we call David the underdog? Why do we refer to his victory as improbable? Are our expectations conditioned to frame the retelling of the story in a way that plays into our assumptions! We also profoundly misunderstand Goliath. Goliath is not at all what he seems to be. There are many hints in the Biblical text that we miss; we read right over them because we do not have a compartment for what our subconscious has declared as irrelevant information. We *re-see* the story the way it was first conveyed. It doesn't support the now

Quantum
Brook

ingrained presupposition, so, while we see it, we do not see it *for what it says*. We see it for what we were told that it says; things which are in retrospect, quite puzzling. They do not square with Goliaths image as a mighty warrior.

Firstly. The Bible says an attendant leads Goliath *onto the valley floor*. Unusual? Why is this mighty warrior challenging the Israelites to one-on-one combat being led by the hand presumably, to the point of the battle?

Secondly, the Bible calls attention to how slowly Goliath moves. A rather odd description for the mightiest warrior known to man at that point. It is also important to note how long it takes Goliath to react to seeing David coming down the mountain; clearly, he is not prepared for hand-to-hand combat. There was nothing about David that indicates to Goliath; I am ready to fight you. David is not armored; neither is he carrying a sword. Why does Goliath not immediately react to something so strange? He appears oblivious to what's going on that day. And then there is the equally peculiar comment he makes to David when he finally does speak: "Am I a dog that you should come to me with sticks?" David only has one "stick"; his shepherd's staff.

There's been a lot of speculation within the medical community in recent years, that something may have been fundamentally wrong with Goliath. In an attempt to make sense of these and other apparent anomalies, many articles have been written. The first was the 1960 Indiana Medical Journal that started a chain of speculation explaining Goliath's height. Goliath was head and shoulders above his peers in that era. When someone is that far on the fringe, it needs an explanation. The most common form of giantism is acromegaly. Acromegaly is a condition caused by a benign tumor on the pituitary gland. It creates an overproduction of HGH (human growth hormone). 8'11" Robert Wadlow, the tallest person in history was still growing when he died at age 24. He had acromegaly. The wrestler André the Giant had acromegaly. There is even speculation Abraham Lincoln also had acromegaly. Acromegaly has distinct side effects with vision. As the pituitary tumor grows, it often starts to compress the optic nerves in the brain—the result is either double vision, profound nearsightedness, or both. Goliath's words and movement classically appear as someone with *acromegaly* explaining much of what was strange about his behavior. Why does he move so slowly escorted down into the valley by an attendant? Because—he can't make his way on his own! Why until the last moment is he so strangely oblivious to David that he doesn't understand that David's not going to fight him? Because—*he can't see him!* When Goliath says, *"Come to me that I might feed your flesh to the birds of the heavens and the beasts of the field,"* "come to me" is another clue to his heavily veiled vulnerability. Come to me. *I can't see you clearly from where I stand.* What about when he says: "*Am I a dog that you should come to me with* **sticks**?" (plural) sees David's staff appears to Goliath as, at least two sticks when David only has one.

The Israelites positioned on the mountainside identify him as an extraordinarily powerful foe. What they didn't understand, the very thing *perceived* to be *the source of Goliath's strength, was his greatest weakness. In David's mind, Goliath was the underdog. David never had a moment's doubt. He would have, never in fear, approached Saul about fighting Goliath. David could see things for what they were, not what the masses, the conditioned group-think believed them to be. David had an incentive, not a reckless teenager's death wish.* "The king will enrich with great riches, the man who kills Goliath, he will also give him his daughter, and give his father's house exemption from taxes in Israel."

And yet there are other perceptions reliant, not upon the habit programmed into our subconscious, but on the label, we assign to the programming. How you process what you see, literally and figuratively, depends entirely on where you stand when judging which label you pick. For example: Running out of fuel late in the evening leaves you stranded alongside a desolate road in the middle of nowhere. Zero "ticks" render your phone useless to call for help. Your wide-eyed reaction to the unexpected flashing blue lights in your rearview mirror is delightful and pure relief. If, however, along that same road, in the same place, and at the same time you are greatly exceeding the posted speed limit, the flashing blue lights in that same rearview mirror, elicit a much different response. It is not happiness, though there may be sweat. The blue lights have not changed, but the label your perspective applied to the blue lights went from Oh Yes! to Oh No!

Conclusion

The backward bike beautifully illustrates how the ego assumes *it knows* while rejecting the subconscious' now innate bias. It insists the *conscious mind* is in control. Yet, in reality, the information previously integrated into the subconscious operating system consistently refuses challenges to its long-held beliefs. It also demonstrates the rewards of relentless perseverance with unexpected breakthroughs. "Something clicks" in "ah-ha" moments. There is an epiphany, a revelation, creating a new neural pathway to—truth. Our immediate perception is continually under the influence of our ingrained beliefs. Our fully formed perspective fails to *understand* what our eyes see, what our ears hear, and overall what our senses perceive. *We insist that we know,* while the filter in our subconscious *blocks the new information entirely* as false. How many of us fail to realize that their programmed obsession only looks for what is wrong, finding evil in virtually everything, blinding them to the excellent and beautiful happening all around them?

"Ships Unseen" suggests that seeing is more than just an image hitting our eye's retina. Our brain assimilates the visual input and constructs our visual experience. It is not how our conscious mind understands *the picture,* but how our *subconscious mind gives our conscious, our deliberate mind, permission to accept and assimilate what it is seeing or hearing into understanding.* The kittens in the Harvard Study, programmed from birth, to understand their world in a specific way, illustrates our environments influence on forming the way we perceive and respond to the world around us. "The Dress" elucidates how two or more people can reach a radically different conclusion when looking at the same thing. It posits how the simple activities of daily living may influence our biology to the extent that it significantly impacts our perception. On the day of this writing, my very young granddaughter saw blue and black; my wife and I, viewing the same image simultaneously, both saw gold and white. Yanny-Laurel provides more complicated, yet further empirical, proof of radically different interpretations of the identical thing—listening at the same time! Two people can listen to the same thing and hear something very different. The 'why' is unknown.

The fresh perspective of the story of David & Goliath illustrates how teachers frame a story to bias our interpretation. And upon considering a different perspective, we learn that everything is not always as it appears to be.

Are flashing blue lights in our rearview mirror one of relief or one of dread? If out of gas on a desolate country road, it is a relief. Twenty-five over the speed limit will bring completely different meanings—same blue lights. As with everything in life, it depends on where and why we apply the label. Our teachers thrust their perspective upon us, and sometimes we evolve, to later determine what works within our formula. Knowingly accepting the world in simplified broad strokes of black and white, whether in science or religion's Fundamentalism is a voluntary delusion to fit an individual narrative. Containing truth in so simple a package is folly. Every element in all creation demonstrates infinite shades of gray and billions of colors.

Chapter 3

The Lucky Chosen to be Chosen.

I'm a proud parent and—a grandparent. The idea of a favorite child or a favorite grandchild is something I can't grasp. It's something I don't have the framework to process. I don't have a slot that says, *"revisit this one later."* Both of my children are remarkable. Besides the apparent gender differences, they are unique. And it is the sum of their differences that synergistically makes them—- *distinctively*—who they are. They are both talented; they are both accomplished. Both are magnificent parents. One child is in no way superior to the other. As a Father—I am proud to say—he is my son. I am just as pleased to announce—she is my daughter. I am privileged to say *those are my children*. Yet, neither is my favorite. *Both* are my favorites. As of this writing, I have four granddaughters under the age of ten. All four are stunningly beautiful and scary smart. [Exhibit-Granddaughters] (yes, I had too. I am a grandparent) Yet they are profoundly different in numerous ways. On the power of their personalities alone, each of them can one day change their world. How could I possibly have a favorite? And if I were to choose, the immediate question becomes, on what grounds would I make that choice? Is my selection an arbitrary roll of the dice, or is it based on *something I observe* that makes one more special than the others?

Of the thousands of parents, I've known, I don't know any who would admit one of their children is their favorite, let alone write it down for future generations to unravel. But, being human implies being available to fail. Perhaps one of the children has been more challenging to raise than another. Possibly one has chosen to remain closer than another after leaving home. Conceivably, one has accomplished great things while the other has nearly broken our Spirit in what feels like a botched, exhausting effort to give them wings. Yet, for most of us, even in the depths of our humanity and under weighty conditions, we still love our children- unconditionally. *Our* blood flows through *their* veins. The evidence of *our* DNA is prominent in *their* features. We say he has my nose; she has my eyes. There is nothing on earth with more gravity, more meaning, and permanency than to say *that is my child*. And as imperfect as we are marinating in liquors of our humanity, these feelings, however argued, *is unconditional Love.* It is the most Godlike part of us.

Unconditional Love is the essence of our Creator. In the Christian tradition, we say God is Love. In other cultures, they say— Love is God. Love expressed through *any* filters of the human condition pales in comparison to the Love of our Creator. One of our— frankly— tragic failures is equating the *conditional* Love that *we call unconditional,* to the real, *unfailing and unconditional— Love of the Divine.* Comparing the two is as futile as comparing the Finite with the Infinite. The finite in any form is *measurable.* The Infinite is forever without form and *eternally immeasurable,*

The Spirit, which incarnates into each new fetus before its birth, is a part of the Divine. That Spirit is born of *The Infinite, The Eternal.* It contains the imprint, the spiritual "DNA" of our Creator. The Spirit enters the unborn child who soon emerges to have a temporary, human experience, *a minuscule comma* in time, yet a comma that will be unique to all other commas. The accomplishments, successes, failures, passions, loves, hates, lessons learned, those…collective experiences become—memories. Those experiences, those memories become the soul of that Spirit's experience. In some traditions, the soul departs the body at the time of death and moves into the afterlife. According to others, it reincarnates to work out its failures from previous incarnations, and when they do, they too will restfully evolve, enlightened, eternal in the afterlife. Whether the reality is incarnation once or reincarnated many, [1] it is a reality that will ultimately be familiar to all. It is not a technology or property of an elite group. It's not exclusive to the rich, poor, weak, strong, secure, or insecure. It is indiscriminate— ethnically or intellectually. It is not the stuff of a specific race, creed, or national origin. It is Divinity's gift of Life—*to all.*

———————————

From the time I was old enough to hold up "this many" fingers when asked "…how old are you?", I began learning that God had his favorites. The nation of Israel was God's chosen people. Later, Christians *(but only born-again Christians)* became his favorites too, adopted "into the promise" that God made to Abraham. Christians became the ones predestined to be THE ones who were unique, *above all others on earth.* Christians, or the ones with the right Christian label, go to Heaven. Non-Christians, or Christians with the wrong label, go to hell. How do we know these things? The Old Testament tells us about Israel, a doctrine originating in Deuteronomy, the last book of the Pentateuch.[2] But— a problem arises when you do that math. To say *one group* is chosen (by default) means the remainder *is not*. But really, they—are. They are chosen *to be the not-elite, the not so special, the unchosen*. They are, therefore, predestined to be *unchosen and selected to go to hell*. "For those God foreknew, He also predestined." God *foreknew everyone*. Much more on this subject in the next chapter.

When I was in grade school, I was small, skinny, athletically unskilled, and bullied, all of which was accompanied by the requisite humiliation. In retrospect, I didn't lack talent—I lacked instruction and the environment to cultivate the seeds that were already there. Seed not sown and watered will not grow. Over the coming years, instead, I would become the go-to guy for creative, design-build, or art [Exhibit-The Potter]. I later excelled in individual sports, but when it came to team sports, I was predestined to be the *last kid—chosen*. Another way to say it: Due to my "teammates" *foreknowledge of my lack of athletic prowess*, I was elected not to be selected *before the choosing ever began*. If, on the other hand, I had been the "star," I would have been the captain, and the one doing the choosing. *I likewise* would choose the players most likely to help me score points and emerge the victor. But those were just games; I'm human— and those who predestined me—the unchosen were also human. So, I have a broader perspective about choosing favorites and the humanness that permeates such ideas. In Christendom, many confidently claim they are the captain and get to declare who will make it on God's team. They do so by *self-proclaiming* their specialness—as their teachers have defined specialness, interpreting scripture, and *creating doctrine which they incorrectly reason to be unassailable.*

As father and grandfather, I played an undeniable role in my offspring being here, but—I didn't have the *foreknowledge* that God has, of who and what they would become. But— **if I did** have these superpowers, I would possess *timeless foreknowledge*. I would know that my Old Testament children becomes a nation that— unequivocally rejects me. Why then— would God choose them in the first place? His foreknowledge knows that he will eventually annihilate them, scattering them to the winds? [Chapter 9, The End of the World—Again.]

Is this then— a declaration meant to serve as evidence that God's Love is not at all *performance-based?* Is Israel's massive failure to live up to His wishes — the whole point? Is the announcement of being chosen as special, literal or symbolic? If it is authentic, having superior favorites provides empirical proof that all of the remaining *non-favorites are inferior*, **regardless of performance.** Once again, we have gone full circle to face the problems emanating from such irrationalities. Isn't it interesting that you can look at the same thing *from opposite perspectives* and make it fit— the narrative? So, how do you pick? Could it be

Quantum
Brook

that when looking at the big picture, one story seems SO much more plausible than the outlandish other? But as it turns out, it's the kind of thing you can see— only *if you really want to see it.* Most Evangelical Fundamentalists are conditioned not—to see it. Like the kittens raised in the room of horizontal or vertical stripes, they cannot see it. It is not from a lack of desire. It is the way their brain is wired to see the world around them.

Do we then break the inferiors (the numerous chosen not to be chosen) into *subgroups* of bêtes noire, anathemas, and abominations? If the rational and reasonable *voice is permitted to speak,* could there be a more straightforward explanation: Did God say: "I have chosen my favorites," or did *those who claim to speak for God make the claim of favorites?* Since God is said to talk through those *who write*— *"thus saith the Lord,"* who holds them accountable? When the prophets speak for God and direct his "chosen" to rape, pillage, plunder, and slaughter thousands of babies and other innocents [3], is that what God—said, *or is it perhaps the unevolved, worst in humanity—speaking on God's behalf?* Who does the audit? Is commonsense allowed to play a role in the discourse, or— have we become *so conditioned* to accept this Jekyll and Hyde juxtaposition that our programming ensures we remain complacent— *and compliant* in the *mind-numbing stupor of our indoctrination?*

Christians become apoplectic at the notion that anyone outside of the faith may also be a child of God. The neck tightens, the teeth grind. It doesn't mean anything to them that God created—- everyone. It is also meaningless that these *"other people"* were born into traditions that do not wear the Christian label. If the preverbal shoe were on the other foot, the response would be, *"How dare you tell me I am not a child of God!"* In all of our specialness, *the obvious gets swallowed up* in the assertion that the Bible is the *inspired, infallible and inerrant* authority, one untouched by humans, unsullied by *all sorts of bias* and personal agendas. AND **most importantly**, *thinking is not allowed.*

Would Evangelical Fundamentalists accept the competition's assertion that we are worthless to God, and they are the ones who are special? (I ask a lot of rhetorical questions.) The Koran said so? Yes, they, too, have their apologist. What is the chance their apologist can convince us of their story? None? How do we parse who is in and who is out? Do all of Christendom's different stories and divergent assertions align? Are all of our doctrines on the same page as to who is unique, who is exclusive, and especially *who is— right?* How do we determine which angle to emphasize and which ones we downplay? Do the efforts to talk one up and take one down serve to advance the overall message *that <u>supposed to be</u>— God so loved the world?*

Is it sadly apparent that the deeper we look, the more embarrassingly self-serving the picture becomes? Do we know that we are talking out of both sides of our mouth? Does it matter or has it gotten to the point that we have damaged our credibility— so severely that it is now beyond repair? Is it possible to put Humpty Dumpy together again? If— we can, for what singular purpose, and— who is driving that agenda? Any chance there would be religious politics at play? Will the voice of reason, *ever again,* play a role in theological discourse, or has the doctrinal waters in which we've languished, long ago come to a boil and cooked our proverbial goose?

You won't get a lot of agreement (or disagreement) in the Vedas, the Tripitaka, the Sutras, the Koran, or sacred scripture of other traditions that Jews and Christians are more special than all others. After all, who wants to advance the idea that they are the "redheaded stepchild?" Putting forth the idea that you are (at best) a second-class citizen is like learning that one of your siblings has, all along, been Mommy and Daddy's favorite. Where does that leave— *you?*

Arguments from a mind pickled in doctrine are like being underwater and explaining why your apparent wetness is an illusion.

The idea that one person or group is more special to God than any other person or group— is, from this author's well-thought-through perspective, the fruit of human imaginings. The evidence supporting such claims *comes from the Biblical authors making a claim.* Due to the antiquity of the writings and the weighty issues, we will cover Chapter 6 *Quoting Misquotes*; the claim to chosenness can neither be proven nor disproven. If, however, the voice of reason ever again becomes a part of the discussion, there is no need to seek proof that God loves *this one* more than *that one.* There is no concept in the history of humankind that is more **Un-God-Like**. The religious egos behind this wishful thinking, in no way, resemble the Divine. Yes, of course, that is just my opinion. And since this book is not written on papyrus thousands of years ago, it's unlikely to hold water for too many Fundamentalists.

Chapter 4

The Fundamental Flaws of Fundamentalism

I've gone to great lengths to treat the following material with care and respect, yet—it will quickly become apparent that I'm unable to hide my passion for this subject. Let me say unapologetically: *I earned it!* I am acutely aware that many of my fundamentalist friends and readers, may be *unwilling* too, or—in light of the material covered in Chapter 2, *unable* to grasp the point of this vital message. I am genuinely both empathetic and—sympathetic to the challenge because—I lived there. Despite my best efforts, some of my readers will ignore the scale and magnitude of this certainty. My reader may also find some of the material to be repetitive. That is by design.

"Repetition is the mother of learning, the father of action, which makes it the architect of accomplishment." Zig Ziglar

I've lost count as to the number of times I've written and rewritten this material. I've wrestled with how to frame each thought; wanting to avoid stepping on toes; to carefully choose each word without—*compromising the message*. It rests with *You* to determine if, for you, I succeeded. Sadly, for some, it will be too confrontational. But after years of introspection and prayerful meditation, what was once just a seed grew into a powerful message that I am passionate to share. I've concluded that anything less than an unveiled examination of the enormous implications of *my tradition's* self-serving assertions—would miss the point. I hope that my purpose will quickly become perspicuous, but in any event, let me be clear: I do not intend to dismantle *anyone's* faith. Neither is this work about debating doctrine. *I've wasted years in fruitless debates.* The material presented here speaks for itself. This portion of the book examines and challenges Fundamentalism's *myriad presuppositions*. It is a high-level examination that purposely avoids slogging through the very details that create debate. It is the author's perspective that incessantly arguing "the details," is responsible for the present, implausible, theological quagmire unimagined 2000 years ago.

*How murky are the views of the tens of thousands of
unbending declarations claiming to see so clearly? We
each possess an obscure vision of reality; perspectives
confidently claimed to be less mysterious than it—is.*

My beloved Father, an amazing man, often quotes "Festus," a character in the 1950s-60s era TV show, Gunsmoke, but certainly not for the same reason I do here. Festus asks the lead role, Marshall Matt Dillon: *"Matt, how do you know the feller that wrote it, writ it right?"* A question which is undoubtedly, *far more* profound than the writers for the popular TV series intended.

For decades I've asked myself what inclines so many to declare "their version" of the thousands of competing "truths" to be *the truth?* On what authority do they make these claims when each (Christian) doctrine points to the same source? If there is but one truth—why isn't there just one easy to understand, uncontested version of "the truth?" If there is genuinely but one version, where can humanity find it? Please?

Fundamentalism 101 — Day One.

"The Bible is the inspired, infallible, and—inerrant word of God:" On what authority do we make these claims? Who was the first to make this claim and—why?

Inspired

The word Inspired, comes from the Latin inspiratus (the past participle of inspirare.) Since the middle of the 16th century, it has meant *"to breathe into."* When one is inspired, they—live. When one ex-spires, they die. My face to the sun on a crisp spring day—inspires me. Inspirations present in innumerable forms like the works of Shakespeare, a Leonardo da Vinci masterpiece, Claude Monet's panoramic oil on canvas, the sculptures of Rodin, the poetry of Robert Frost, the oratory of Dr. Martin Luther King, the compositions of the Broadway legend, Andrew Lloyd Webber, David Foster's arrangements and *heavenly* chord progressions, the astonishing, awe-inspiring, goosebumps generating, eye puddling interpretations, by newcomer Croatian cellist Stjepan Hauser or—Neil Donald Walsh's world-renowned, *Conversations With God.* All of them move our emotions in numerous ways that we cannot explain intellectually; the way we connect with them is palpable yet intangible. They are *spiritual.*

Quantum Brook

Inspiration breathes charity, philanthropy, helping a neighbor, sharing a kind, encouraging word. Inspiration in-spirits, driving everything good. Yet, whether it's art in various visual, audible, and written forms, the characteristic shared is: They are *all* art, but—they are *all* different. Yet, when it comes to scripture, somehow, the more ancient the inspiration, the more ***exclusively inspired*** the work is supposed to be.

Inspiration is subjective. I am passionately *inspired* to write this book, but some will argue that *anything that challenges fundamentalism's cherished perspective cannot be divinely inspired.* Is Psalm 139 inspired? From my viewpoint—*you bet it is.* Is Isaiah 13:16NIV inspired? It doesn't inspire me. It perplexes me. It sickens me—that it is attributed to God. Oddly, the presumption is, the more antiquated', the less influenced by the human condition it is reputed to be. Instead, fundamentalism determines scripture to be perfect—or so those claiming perfection believe. They are declared to be entirely unwavering and committed to a single meaning—one, infallible, inerrant, and importantly— coherent interpretation. *But most perplexing*: If the numerous writers of the Biblical canon were inspired to write one single, doctrinal truth, for all humankind—why isn't *every reader* equally inspired to see but *one "truth"—that God intended?* But that is *nowhere close* to reality is it. So, which writers' intention or reader's interpretation is the *most* inspired? Furthermore, who decides? Who decrees? To whom are my readers willing to give that power? For the majority of my life, I signed away my rights to,

—think about these things.

In the fourth century, the "inspired" Pope decided. But then along came Martin Luther and from Luther's time till today, there are tens of thousands of *other "inspired" readers* who claim to speak for God—yet— they do not say the same things. Do they make the same claims? Quite the opposite. Do they compete? You betcha! How do we reconcile the myriad differences and declare all of the other "inspired" readers to be beneath our own? (A rhetorical question— of course.) *But this discourse is the reality*—- *within ALL of Christendom.* How about our Abrahamic cousin Judaism? Have you ever noticed how "truth" is always relative to the belief the claimant holds to be the truth and ***all with theological apologists*** of their own? How about the tenants of faith within Islam? For some of my more scholarly readers, swap out a few nouns, and see if this rings a bell?

"There is only one God; God has sent numerous Prophets, (with Muhammad being the last); God has revealed Holy Scriptures, including the Quran; God's angels exist, even if people cannot see them; there will be a Day of Judgment, when God will *determine whether individuals are sent to Heaven or hell*; **God's will and knowledge are absolute, people are subject to predestination, or fate, though they also have free will."** [1] Even Islam's last line is an oxymoron. Perhaps something is in the water?

Infallible

Numerous, competing interpretations of anything— is *textbook fallibility.* Oxford defines *In-fallible* as "*incapable* of making mistakes or being wrong." On which definition do we all agree to be— the right one? How about which is the wrong one? Of course, the wrong one is *all of the ones the individual "we" did not choose.* When countless versions are incongruent with the competing versions, all declaring themselves to be right and their competition wrong, *by default,* all are *wrong.* All are fallible until credentialed scholars authenticate a single text unanimously agreeing to infallibility. *Anyone can claim infallibility*, but when there are multiple competing claims, there is no consensus. When there is a failure to reach an agreement, *infallibility is impossible*.

Inerrant

When the object claiming inerrancy contains thousands of *documented* errors, numerous conflicts, and irreconcilable contradictions, by any reasonable standard, it cannot be infallible nor— can it be inerrant. To believe otherwise is— a statement of faith. The errors historians and forensic scholars have uncovered (in the New Testament alone) are estimated to be between 200,000 - 600,000. Still, most agree the number is closer to 400,000, or— as one world-renowned, historical scholar describes: *"...more errors than there are words in the New Testament."* These errors are even more troublesome when coupled with unintentional and—- *intentional* scribal changes to *critical* New Testament passages— evidentially changed to advance the scribes preferred theological narratives. *Much more on this subject later.*

THE IMPORTANT QUESTION IS: HOW DOES IT BENEFIT GOD FOR "HIS" CREATION TO FLOUNDER IN CONFUSION AND CONSTANT CONFLICT? WOULDN'T IT HELP BOTH GOD AND CREATION TO KNOW, NOT CLAIMS TO— A TRUTH, BUT **THE** TRUTH AND— WITHOUT ALL THE FUSS? IN WHAT WAY DOES THIS INTELLECTUAL DISHONESTY SERVE HUMANKIND?

If discussion permits logic and reason, wouldn't an error-free, uncontested, clear, and straightforward word of God best serve everyone? If the Bible is the *one and only—instruction* from our Creator presumably, God would want it to be clear and uncomplicated for the least scholarly among us. But in reality, we have thousands of the brightest academic minds on Earth unable to reach a consensus on even the most basic Biblical claims. Isn't it easy to imagine that God would want to make such an important thing chrystal clear? But God is not "a Christian." Wasn't Jesus a Jew? And more than 75% of the Earth's population, something other than Christian. Why then does Christian Fundamentalism with its countesses competing voices so quickly declare all non-Christians (and most Christians) to be second class citizens all of which are said to be on their way to hell?

Truth?

Which Version?

When on the inside looking out, "The Box(es)" in which Christianity has placed God, appears large. It seems inviting and—inclusive. And it is for all who *agree—to agree*. But precisely which Box should *we all* accept? There is not just one. There are amazingly many. On which doctrine do we base our agreement? All of the arguments that create each Box emanate from the Bible. *There are thousands*, each wrapped attractively, uniquely, invitingly. All Box's compete with others to be the most impressive, persuasive, and authentic. What, in Fundamentalism's view, should the onlooker find most appealing? The wrapper or the contents? *All Boxes purposely contain the best, the superior—the one and only "true" gift.*

I didn't construct the following description to illustrate this point, yet it is pure serendipity as a (real) pastor self-describes his eclectic version of "The Gift."

"I am a Pastor of a small Church in [location removed] [...] I am postmillennial in my eschatology, Paedo-Calvinist Covenantal in my Christianity, Reformed in my Soteriology, Presuppositional in my apologetics, Familialist in my family theology, Agrarian in my regional community social order, belief that Christianity creates culture and so Christendom in my national social order belief, Mythic-Poetic/Grammatical Historical in my Hermeneutic Pre-modern, Medieval & Feudal before enlightenment, modernity & postmodern reconstructionist, Theonomic in my Worldview. One-part paleo-conservative/one-part micro Libertarian in my politics, Systematic and Biblical theology need one another, but Systematics has pride of place."

In a Nutshell

Consider there is but *one way* to consume the following material. Seek to understand *the point*. Discern my motive. Understand that the questions expose the "question behind the question." It invites my reader to ask: what if these examples were me? *It is always an open invitation—- to think.*

"You do not define anyone with your judgment. You only define yourself as someone who needs to judge." —
Wayne Dyer

All of Christianity's Catholics, Protestants, and fundamentalist doctrine rest on one basic premise: If you are Christian, you will, importantly, avoid hell. When you die, you will go to Heaven. The problem: there is no unanimity on what makes a *Christian—Christian*. However, if you are—anything but a Christian, according to Christian teachings, *it is over for you.* You will go to hell. What makes you a Christian, *and keeps you—Christian*, has been debated ad nauseam for 500 years. Before Luther, you went to confession. If you were Christian, you were Catholic. But today traditional Catholicism privately views Protestantism, in its many post Reformation, Lutheran forms, as—Heresy [2]. Publicly, Catholicism had to (at least) appear more accepting over the past 100 years.

Meanwhile, Evangelical-Fundamentalism now views *traditional Protestants* as too liberal, and therefore non-Christian. Generally, if you are not "born again" *(if you have not formally recited the sinner's prayer.)* You are not "saved." Catholics, and virtually every traditional Protestant doctrine which fails to view the world through Fundamentalists lens, is generally—*not Christian*.

Martin Luther, responsible for the Protestant Reformation in 1517, decried the Pope as The Antichrist. Today, Mormonism suggests the Book of Mormon is another testament of Jesus that—clears up millennia of squabbling and the very finger-pointing within mainstream Christianity that we are contemplating in this book. On the other hand, traditional Christianity frames Mormonism as an illegitimate doctrine whose own Fundamentalists are also at odds with the LDS mainstream. Then there are other Christian sects like the Jehovah's Witnesses who knock on my door at least twice a year. They set up literature displays in a nearby public park hoping to convert enough souls to earn their way into the 144,000 who go to Heaven. **Entire ways of life** are built around esoteric interpretations of the scripture, creating a "Box" to which sincere, lovely people devote lifetimes. It <u>deeply saddens me.</u> I nod and smile with a hello, knowing how *sincere* and loving these people are and what a waste of time a conversation with them would be.

Fundamentalism derides the former as cults, yet anyone who challenges the basis for their interpretations is a heretic. Yet **somehow** Christianity is the self-proclaimed Crème de la crème rising to the surface as *the only way to God for all of humankind,* regardless where on the globe you reside or into what tradition you were born.

No one escapes developing biases. No one reaches for a conclusion they believe—to be the wrong conclusion.

PEOPLE. REAL—FLESH AND BLOOD PEOPLE "SEE THINGS THE WAY THEY SEE THEM, BECAUSE—THAT IS THE WAY THEY WERE TAUGHT— PROGRAMMED—INDOCTRINATED—TO SEE THEM.

Selah

(Selah is a word used poetically in the book of Psalms. In essence, it means to pause, reflect, think about what was said.) [3]

A teacher asked her 3rd-grade class to write letters to God. I will share some of these *real and really adorable* 'letters' throughout the remainder of this chapter." [4]

Dear God,
I bet it is very hard for you to love all of everybody in the whole world. There are only four people in our family, and I can never do it.
Nan

Quantum Brook

Always

All of these differences are constructed with scripture and there is *always* a scripture ready to argue an opposing view using—another scripture. It is akin to being in a shootout where, characteristically, the bullets fired are reused to—return fire. The only causalities in the fray are religious egos. There are no winners, no real losers, but everyone gets to show off their weapon while they waste time. They get to impress the opposition with their big guns, with how many bullets they have in their arsenal and—how quickly they can pull together their response. The thing is, seldom—do these arguments demonstrate or require *thinking*. Instead, they rely on memorization. It gives little recognition to anything outside of—*Their Box*. It rarely invites *genuine inquiry*. It prefers instead to defend its flag; *the flag perceived—believed, to occupy the only Truth*. The arguments emanate from the narrow, and responses flow from the shallows of indoctrination. And, when the indoctrinated speak, the opposition is unable to listen. When each position exhausts its depth, it politely *simulates* listening. The opposition regards information outside *"the ultimate authority of the scripture"* as inadmissible; unless of course—the argument happens to support the cherished view chiseled in the stone anchoring its flag. If support for the argument is there, it embraces the "insight" as *conclusive evidence* for making its case. Otherwise, it is banned from the debate and explained away with yet——*another scripture*. This circular, repetitive waste of time does little to serve. Instead, it undermines the creditability and *consume-ability* of the entire Biblical message.

———————

Doctrine wants to *package God*. But you can't put God in a box, any box! A Box, by definition, *contains*. It defines, confines, restricts and limits the contents to the boundaries of— its meaning. Boxes, by design, separate its content from everything which is *outside the Box*. It makes portable that which it contains. But here is the thing: *All attempts* to quantify God to doctrine—fail! Efforts to doctrin-ize God creates an idol, a—mini, measurable, diminished version of that which is *immeasurable. Infinite* cannot be measured. Doctrine create a two-dimensional God with borders; a God compelled to the limits of the words on a page. It creates an image, and it remains *just an image*. No matter how inspired the conception, it is penned from each author's conditioned perspective——and worshiped——*as if it were God.*

God, "Himself" did not scribe the parchments, scan, and email them in an unalterable PDF that would forever remain untouched by traditions, culture, or human bias; one incapable of being miscopied, or otherwise corrupted by the recipient. Instead, it becomes "A God" that is labeled and limited— to what the label says. It will be someone's ability or (more accurately), everyone's inability to describe what is *impossible to describe.*

Yet, today, from the pulpits of far too many churches, God is explained from an anthropomorphic lexicon of humanity's worst attributes. The Created brazenly thrust the things most loathed and born of frailty's flaws upon the Creator: Anger, jealousy, vengefulness, hatred, wrath, a brutal serial killer ordering the predestined slaughter of tens of billions of innocents, and all those predestined—broken. "We" attribute this pettiness to The Infinite, to the one who is both The Macro and The Micro. The one who is not only IN the Eternal Now, but who IS the Eternal Now. The I Am. The Beginning and also the End, yet which is *mind twistingly—without Beginning or—End,* The Everything, The Eternal! The All. Yet every description, no matter how inspired it may be or— may have been, can only measure—*the attempt at an explanation.* The one thing we can endeavor to explain is "His" *love* for all of humankind. Who created all of us? Everyone reading these words is an integral part of "His" creation—(my statement of faith.)

What need can anyone fill for a God who needs nothing, or can ever possibly want for anything? There is no void to fill. You cannot add to that which is already FULL. In what way could it satisfy an ill-imagined, debased need to eternally punish that which He created, to forever punish his child which, in human form, is of relative size and intelligence to a single atom in all of the Earth's oceans.

"I would rather err on the side of the goodness and the greatness of God than on the side of his presumed pettiness and wrath. It is more important to believe what Jesus taught about God than what the churches have taught us about Jesus" — Bishop Carlton Pearson— The Gospel of Inclusion

What Can We Learn?

We no longer live in a day when messages are delivered from one medieval kingdom to another via runner, the messenger praying to escape death at the hand of an angered royal that does not like the message. Pigeons no longer deliver notes on tiny scrolls to the privileged few. The "town crier" no longer delivers the news in the public square. We no longer ride horses to exhaustion to get letters from town to town. The literate few no longer read to the ignorant many. We no longer have just one translation of the Holy Scriptures. The King James Version heralded for hundreds of years as "the authorized version," critical scholarship *long ago* exposed as a *woefully inferior translation*. Today we have as many as 450 translations—just in English. [5].

We no longer have inaccessible silos of ingrown groupthink echoing doctrine among religious elites, crafting and redefining scriptural strategies that fend off the thousands of traditional and—new thought competitors. Today, information is accessible with the tap of a few keys and the click of a "mouse." A mere thirty years ago, writing this three-volume series with its many layers and interconnected topics, would necessitate vocational level exposure to information mostly inaccessible to those outside the vaulted halls of secular and religious academia. Access to all these things would have required *years in a library*, flagging pages, compiling lists of handwritten notes, and manually cross-referencing voluminous texts. Even still, the author measures this effort in decades.

Today *ignorance is a choice*, not a destiny. Millions of books on virtually any topic are available with just—one click of a "mouse." Digital editions are immediately downloadable and instantly portable on smartphones and laptop computers—that new material—highlightable, searchable, the notes sequenced, and exportable. If preferred, there is still the good-ole paper version. And yes—it too appears on your doorstep *the following day*— with one click. As for the Bible, there are at least two notable "search engines" like BibleHub.com with topical, Greek and Hebrew study tools, concordances, commentaries, and— BibleGateway.com with 200 keyword searchable translations in 70 languages. Knowledge is no longer for the privileged few who package, disseminate, and control biased narratives for a career. It is available to anyone who *genuinely seeks to expand their views beyond the echoes of their programming*. So, the primary and most important question ever asked remains: *How can anyone, anywhere at any time, for any conceivable reason, reconcile a doctrine that promotes a God who creates eight billion people, in this generation alone, to send the vast majority of them to hell?*

Conundrum's Carousel

W hat is virtually unknown, or perhaps ignored in Evangelical Fundamentalist circles and, by learned clergy of all evangelical denominations, is that: none—zero, of the Autographs *(the original manuscripts)* of the 66 canonized books of the Bible—exist. All of the resulting translations and iterations are a product of translating copies—that were themselves copies of copies of copies of copies of a *yet-to-be-determined (and some suggest will be forever unknown)* number of generations of copies. All copies compounded the errors contained in the previous generation copy. Furthermore, *we do not know in what order the copies were written*—making it all but impossible to ever determine the origin of the error—or determine what the original text would— *most likely say.* As previously mentioned, the errors uncovered are, on average, estimated to be 400,000. Most of these errors are misspellings and relatively minor, but some are significant. [6] These (minor) errors are most troublesome when coupled with unintentional ***and intentional scribal changes to critical*** New Testament passages—apparently to advance the scribes *preferred theological narrative* [7] Yet, Christianity as a whole rest its most weighty doctrine, the doctrine of "original sin" and eternal torment for billions of people on an "inspired, infallible, and inerrant" collection of manuscripts. Much more to follow on this subject.

A t a very early age, I was taught that I became special to God when, around the age of eight, I became a "born-again" Christian. I prayed the sinner's prayer, based on [Romans 10:9] *"if you confess with your mouth, "Jesus is Lord," and believe in your heart that God raised him from the dead, you are "saved." For it is with your heart that you believe and are justified, and it is with your mouth that you confess and are saved."* Quite importantly, I was also foreknown and predestined to be a Son of God. [Romans 8:29-30 NIV] *For those God foreknew, he also predestined to be conformed to the likeness of his Son, that he might be the firstborn among many brothers. And those he predestined, he also called; those he called, he also justified; those he justified, he also glorified."* This passage is more Presbyterian (Calvinist) in its doctrine than the predominantly Pentecostal (Arminian) version advanced in my denomination, but one which is none the less, central to this thesis.

So, in God's foreknowledge, he knew me—and he knew that I would be born into—circumstances that would teach me, not only to allow me but prepare and assure that I would take steps to become a born-again Christian. As I shared in Chapter 1, my world as a child was *tiny*. As are all children, I was naive, but for the first 18 years of my life, I was completely ignorant of most everything outside the boundaries of my metaphorical "village." Was this destiny?

I grew up in the Assemblies of God. My status as a born-again Christian assumed that I didn't sin right before the time of death, or before "the rapture," [Chapter 8 - The End of the World—Again] If I did, I would go to hell. The first of several problems was, there were very few things that were not a sin. Or another way to put it: It seemed that virtually everything considered by most people to be normal and enjoyable was in some way—sin with many of nose in the air faithful saying "…well I never…" like somehow it is *always* about *their experience and their experience determines the high watermark*. No "going to a movie, dancing, having a beer with a friend, or a glass of wine with dinner. If there was a life outside the church, the odds did not favor being ready to die or make the rapture. You see, the reward was not living *an abundant life here*, but making sure to *make eternal life there*, and all of that was up to me. Ultimately, it was about endurance and survival here to reap the eternal rewards in Heaven; to be crowned, to rule and to reign.

Every day, the End of the World was "at hand" while ubiquitous demons and an equally pervasive devil *(though there is supposed to be just— one devil)* to tempt and torment eight billion people. Meanwhile, the fundamentalist Baptist, a close cousin to my 'full gospel' denomination, believed that to be saved, following the sermon you go to the front of the church, shake the preacher's hand, and answer a few questions resembling the sinner's prayer thereby making a public profession of faith, and you are newly minted into the family of God. The difference, and a big one: From that point forward, you would always be a Child of God. You were "eternally secure" [John 10:29NIV] *"My Father, who has given them to me, is greater than all; no one can snatch them out of my Father's hand."* This doctrine seemed to have the most scriptural support and always made the most sense in my decades of study. Yet, while the pulpit in our church condemned the Baptist Church across the road for *preaching false doctrine*, the pulpit in *their church* condemned the "demon-possessed tongue talkers" on our side of the street.

Out of the tens of thousands of competing denominations in existence, [8] there are numerous—close doctrinal cousins, all with a different *Spin* on the same scriptures about "salvation." Each new doctrine creates another claim of being 'the thing' to believe. For example, the Church of God (COG) substantially aligns with the Assemblies of God (AG) but notably added sanctification as "a separate work." The Church of Christ (COC) doesn't permit musical instruments in its services and believes you are not saved until baptized by immersion. The Catholic sacrament of baptism by sprinkling—just won't work for Protestants. It must be by immersion. For the COC, it was not the prayer of faith— but the immersion itself that ushers you into the faith. The AG, COG and other Pentecostal variations encourage baptism by immersion, but, if you died, or the rapture happened before you were baptized, you would still go to heaven even though you had not yet been baptized. The Pentecostal Holiness held to the same belief as to the AG with minute differences, at least for one sect, a noteworthy extreme like snake handling in the Appalachian Mountains (truth is stranger than fiction). All other denominations will argue the value and permissibility of reason and common sense *here*. Interestingly, this form of worship was based on Mark 16:18—one of twelve verses which, at some point for some reason, someone decided *to add* into the later manuscripts; *none of which appeared in the most ancient, (the more reliable) manuscripts.* Death is the high price of ignorance when attached to the business end of an angry rattlesnake.

Then, there are the numerous Protestant and Catholic mainstream denominations. The Methodist, Presbyterian, Episcopal, Lutheran, Anabaptist, Orthodox, Seventh Day Adventist, Anglican Communion, and Roman Catholic, which, as previously stated, Fundamentalism judges to be so liberal in their theology that they were generally labeled as barely Christian— if Christian at all. A perplexing conclusion considering the legalistic, high holiness history of Methodism as an example. In any event, all who do not formally recite the sinner's prayer are not 'born again'; they are not 'saved.' Then, add fringe sects like the Latter-Day Saints, Jehovah's Witness, Quakers, Mennonites, and Amish, to name a better known few.

"We must look at the lens through which we see the world, as well as the world we see, and that the lens itself shapes how we interpret the world." — Stephen R. Covey

When a pet doctrine becomes the topic of conversation, the voice of reason is asked to leave the discourse.

TRUE | FALSE

Have you ever considered what truth is *to You*? What is good to you? What is bad to you? What degree of difference makes your right "their" wrong and your wrong their right? What is unacceptable or objectional to *You?* Why? What makes *you* saved? What keeps *you* protected? Is everything black and white, absolute for you— or are their shades of gray? All judgements point to the same source. How did you determine yours?

Quantum Brook

Chapter 5

A Conundrum—

of Biblical Proportions

UNIVERSE

From Latin: unus versus, vertere
"to turn, turn back, be turned; convert, transform, translate; be changed.
——-one, unique verse——

If there is a God—

"He" is certainly not the diminutive, anthropomorphic creation of human imagination. He is *Infinite*. He is pure consciousness. He is the All. He is the unified Multi-Verse of many layers, realms, and dimensions. He is a boundless Orchestra of perfect players, each moving with infinitesimal precision, eternally performing an inexplicably intricate symphony. Each player follows the wand of the ultimate Impresario—the *One Composer*. He is but one conductor, He is also the innumerable players yet, just—one player. He is the melody. He is illimitable harmonies. He is the rhythm, the timber. He is every incomprehensible vibration— pianissimo to fortissimo. He is reverberation of the highest highs in fathomless synchronicity with the lowest lows. He is eternal Resonance in Perfection.

He is, I Am.

The day I was conceived, my parent's DNA became a permanent part of me. Their blood began to flow through my veins as my body formed in real-time. I grew in Mother's womb, to emerge nine months later as— me. I may have survived a complicated physical birth, but according to the "The Doctrine of Original Sin," I was born spiritually dead. The doctrine asserts that a fellow named Adam blew it *for everyone*— with one bite of "the forbidden fruit." Over the ensuing, thousands of years, one mistake that is said to have caused you— me— and all births after Adam to be born *spiritually dead*. The doctrine of Original Sin was a relatively new idea that emerged in the *late fourth century*. [1] [2] It was wide-reaching, gaining credibility when advanced by St. Augustine 354-410. Yet it is a doctrine which had little recognition before then. "Tragically, Augustine's misreading and misinterpretation of sin based on looking at Scripture through a *prism of dualism* is the accepted dogma by most contemporary Christian theologians. The doctrine owes more to Augustine's desire to emulate the philosophers of his day than—Scripture. [3] It was doctrine with *profound implications for **all of humankind***, regardless of religious label. It derives a portion of its philosophy from the book of Genesis, the first book of Pentateuch *(the first five books of the Old Testament.)*

Fundamentalism has long held to the belief that Moses wrote the Pentateuch, known to the Hebrews as the Tora. Yet, Biblical Historian and world-renown authority in Bible history and textural criticism, Professor Bart Ehrman, M.Div., Ph.D., a former evangelical fundamentalist educated at Moody Bible Institute; Wheaton College and Princeton Theological Seminary—- put it this way: *"The Pentateuch, was not written in whole, or even in part by Moses, or— by any one person — certainly by no one living as early as the 13th century B.C.E. The Pentateuch, as we now have it, is composed of a variety of written sources woven together, all of which are themselves based on earlier oral traditions that had been in circulation for a long period of time— as storytellers told and retold the stories about much earlier times. Today scholars are virtually unanimous in rejecting Mosaic authorship."* [4a] [...] *led the majority of scholars to conclude that they are the product of many hands and many centuries* [4b] *"It has long been recognized that the traditional view —not stated in the Pentateuch itself, but already assumed elsewhere in the Old Testament— that Moses was not the author of the Pentateuch."* [4c]."The Making of the Pentateuch: A Methodological Study" is often cited as evidence of Mosaic authorship [5], although Whybray's findings regard the Pentateuch as fiction. [6] John Van Seters, a Yale-educated, Canadian *scholar of the Hebrew Bible and the Ancient Near East,* proposes *the Pentateuch should be understood as ideological fiction rather than history.*[7] Additionally, out of the Genesis story, we also have several very similar stores of a great flood, *all of which have heroes other than Noah;* the sources of these stories are *many centuries before the J and P sources (the ancient manuscripts) of the story of Noah* found in Genesis. Find two of the stories in [Appendix- The Great Flood].

We know Moses was not the author of Genesis. We know the Earth is not six thousand years old [8]; instead, it is ~4.543 billion years old. [9] There are clearly major problems with Genesis. Yet, *the proposed fate of all humankind* rests on a single line in a story that begins in Genesis, which is, at best, a "reality" impossible to verify and, empirical scientific evidence does not support. It is instead— a statement of faith, a faith that unbendingly and enthusiastically sets the stage for the *fiery demise of most of humanity.*

But it is not the Genesis account of Adam's sin per se: It is the Apostle Paul's reference to the Genesis story. The thing which long ago became a great fascination for me is— *why*— Evangelical Fundamentalism has chosen to— *literally*— fixate their **eisegesis** *(the interpretation of a text by reading into it, one's ideas (Webster))* on everything in the following verse except that which *would seem to be* most welcomed and—-the most essential thing in the Christian faith.
—in Christ ALL—?

"Therefore, just as sin entered the world through one man [Adam], and death through sin, and in this way, death came to all people, because all sinned." [Roman 5:12] "For as in Adam all die so—in Christ—**all will be made alive"** [1 Corinthians 15:22]

May I invite serious consideration for a broader view of the doctrine that alleges to send most of God's creation to hell? In light of all we learned about the origins of the Pentateuch: *Even if* there was empirical proof that God emailed the book of Genesis to its authors, yesterday—and tens of thousands witnessed the event, just maybe the fate of billions *born into other traditions* might still be open for discussion?

Regardless of pervasive wishful thinking, God *did not*—dictate Genesis or any of the books of the Bible. So, maybe in light of what we've examined so far, we confront the hubris of the doctrine of original sin to understand the consequences this doctrine promotes—fully:

In the 'mid-50s, the spiritual "DNA" in the real me, the eternal me, incarnated into the fetus forming in my Mother's womb. The singular purpose was to have a temporary, physical experience in a flesh and blood body. The body was a— tiny comma on an eternal timeline. According to the doctrine of original sin, I required the God in whom I have always existed to intervene and save me from eternal damnation, ...and ironically *for something I didn't do.* According to the Genesis story, the single act Adam commits in the inferior physical dimension was—somehow—able to corrupt *all* of the yet unborn beings in— the *superior,* spiritual dimension, the minute their mothers give birth. So, it seems a *mother's flesh corrupts*—-the *incorruptible spirit* me. Adam, the creation - reportedly damaged *All of God's future creation.*

How does the lower, weaker, finite *created*—- somehow sneak up behind—- and overpower the higher-stronger, all-powerful— *Infinite Creator? But Fundamentalism does not allow "the math" to enter the equation. I invite you dear reader to Do The-Math!*

Selah

After this happened, it is said that I would be one of *the few* lucky ones, **predestined to be God's chosen.** The people "He foreknew-and- *predestined"* to be born and indoctrinated into Christianity—but most importantly, into the *right brand of Christianity.* But as we have already asked, which brand would that be and—how do you know? Note: There is (believe it or not) a school of thought that suggests God purposefully flawed the Bible to intentionally confuse and blind many to the truth *so that only a few* will see the spiritual meaning beneath the words, read in between the lines as it were, and *"be saved."* No matter how messed up (from my perspective) that thinking is, it demonstrates this book's essential underlying premise. If this happens to be accurate, I hope my readers are a part of the brand that emerges victorious, (whichever one that happens to be.) All births and deaths between the time of Adam and Jesus are said to have been "in the bosom of Abraham," This statement of faith was included in the Apostles Creed, but one most Protestants reject. Jesus "...descended into hell," is another mistranslation we explore in detail in Chapter 7, "A Hell of an Idea." The only thing clear about the meaning of hell is— the ambiguity, but all will become clear by Chapter 8.

There are other creative doctrinal imaginings not accepted within Fundamentalism: Purgatory for intermediate cleansing, or Paradise, which fundamentalist often interpret as Heaven because Jesus, tells the thief dying next to him on the cross, "today you will be with me in Paradise" There is no need for *an in-between* for Jesus; but, none the less is it straight to heaven or a—pause *before heaven*? Do the millions of amazingly similar Near-Death-Experience accounts of meeting loved ones, reflect "in limbo" interpretations? Either way, there is an array of colorful **eisegesis** *(the interpretation of a text by reading into it one's ideas)* doctrinal threads citing Latin, Greek, Hebrew, Aramaic, and one inadequate translation, or another: "It could have been, or it might have been, maybe it was—that *settles* nothing. And there lies the eternal rub.

Free Will

"Free will" is an additional argument. It points to Adam's *free will* as an example of our own. It suggests that it was not just Adam's Sin but- the array of sins we commit of our own free will when we come of age. The doctrine suggests God *loves us so much* that he w*ill not violate our free will*, in order to save us and—he loved Adam so much that he allowed Adam's "free will" to seal the fate of all humankind. It is the one thing (doctrine claims) that God "self-limits" his ability to do. It's amusing *(to me)* that doctrine determined God's boundless Love for—not violating our free will—and a love so great that it supersedes a Supreme Love that would ultimately fail to rescue all of humankind (not just born-again Christians) from their fiery demise.

God has zero limitations yet—"He" fully understands the many limitations *under which all of humankind lives.* However, it's Christianity's avowed certainty that everyone who is not a Christian *chooses—-**not to hear God**. If they did, after all, **they would hear what they are supposed to hear.** Pause for a moment to think about that. Would Christians become Christian if *they did not—want to hear from God; to please God*? But how is it that Christians seem to understand things—very differently? If there is but one message, why is God not saying the same thing whenever he speaks? According to those who disagree with what God said to someone else, the accused are allegedly *seeking the wrong answer.* How about non-Christian faiths who have the heart to know God. Are they *insincere* when they *hear something different* than the Christian message? If so, what would be the purpose of *insincerely* seeking God be? That, too, is entirely nonsensical. Sadly, too often, Fundamentalism's go-to answer is: "*they are listening to the voice of demons and devils.*" If you are not hearing what the accuser hears, then it is something demonic. Could a "religious spirit" be pointing the judgmental finger, or has it all reached absurdities of epic proportions?

Quantum
Brook

I recently read about a Coast Guard helicopter that flew to a capsized boat on a search and rescue mission. By the time they arrived, it had looked as if the only survivor was the mother. It was soon apparent that her husband, son, and daughter had perished in the accident. The diver lowered from the helicopter, desperately tried to rescue the mom, who was hysterically shedding her life vest. Grieving the loss of her loved ones, she didn't want to be the only one who lived and was wildly trying to end her life. She kicked and screamed, giving the diver an enormous black eye as she cursed and yelled for her rescuer to let her die. But the swimmer refused. "I am bringing you in, I don't care what you do to me." And she did. The mother was unaware that one of her children had survived, having drifted some distance from the capsized vessel. She later apologized and thanked her rescuer for *saving her—against her will.*

Most of my readers would agree the rescuer did the right thing. That is what *true Love is, and for someone the rescuer did not know.* That is what those who genuinely care, do. In the real world, the vast majority of "unregenerate" non-Christians would do the same thing. They would behave like the rescue diver. They would view the situation through Love, context and understanding valuing the life they were rescuing. Yet, doctrine paints a picture of a stubborn, pouting deity who will abandon the billions he created who are drowning, simply because they do not want his help, and "he" *cannot* violate their free will. Yet, *ironically…*

The majority of the New Testament attributes the writings of a man who's *free will* life's mission was to persecute and kill Christians. That was his *passion.* Before Saul became Paul, he was a "Pharisee's Pharisee." The ultimate Jew. Did Saul change his mind because some stranger bumped into him on an evening's stroll and told him about Jesus? Can my evangelical reader envision having a similar conversation with a Muslim, Jew, Buddhist, or Hindu trying to convert them? How about *them* trying to *convert you?* Really? How productive would a standard "come to Jesus" conversation have been for Saul on his trip to Damascus? Acts 9:3-9 tells us that Saul was thrown from his horse and blinded for three days by a vision where Jesus asks (then Saul) "Why are you persecuting me?" Did this *violate Saul's free will?* Was Saul seeking Jesus? I think not. Was Saul sincere in what he was doing? Perhaps. Muslim Jihadists are sincere too. Yet, how many people on planet earth would refuse such an in-your-face personal appeal from the one he was persecuting? I think it is fair to say; it wouldn't be many. Is everyone that God created who have legitimate doubts not equally deserving of such a convincing personalized experience *in this age of tens of thousands of versions of The Truth? But which truth would they hear?* You can argue several things, but for our religious purposes here: God either predestined Paul to be one of the chosen few *despite his previous passion for killing,* and— to become more special to God than virtually ALL of humanity, or the rest of humanity is predestined *unworthy of a similar, convincing appeal. But, no need for such clarity now. The scriptures are inarguable. They are inspired, inerrant, and infallible.*

As it stands, 2000 years later, regardless of tradition, Christian doctrine expects *(literally)* everyone on planet Earth to without questions, rely on *Paul's personal experience* in the middle of the most doctrinally fragmented time in human history. If there is just one path to God, which version? If Jesus appeared to Paul, why is he not *equally eager* and able to perform TO ALL, not through the voice of an enormously indoctrinated few, and—- *clear up some things? It is not the choir who needs convincing.* Or, will it be as Fundamentalism teaches today, only the predestined elect receive God's grace?

With that in mind, regarding the doctrine of free will, I invite my reader to immerse yourself in this illustrative imagining. Vividly experience the story *as a Parent.* Parents will do anything for their children. Yet, as easy as it is to comprehend that kind of Love, it is nevertheless a love that exists entirely in the realm of human frailty. In Fundamentalism's words: "Storge" *(Greek for a parental love)* in contrast with "Agape" *(Greek for God's Love).* One is vastly inferior to the other. Venture to guess which? Speaking from a parent's point of view, who would say with confidence say God will not violate free will…

You are getting a promotion for a few pages that follow. You are the *Infinite God!* You must think and feel with a Godlike parental, Love. You've created *billions of children.* Each child is unique. Each of their spirits timelessly exists in—- You. In their current physical manifestation, you create them of a lower, slower energy; *A MUCH* lower frequency than your Infiniteness. This relatively temporary, flesh, and blood biology will host each eternal Spirit and provide your offspring the experience of something outside of the *Infinite— You.* You will incarnate each Spirit, into time. Time does not exist in the infinite. Time is Finite, measurable, and *inferior* to everything *Infinite.* Spiritual incarnation into an "earth suit," is not about the biological conception; it is about the eternal Spirit's incarnation into a temporary host. But You create these organic beings to replace themselves, through their prodigy, providing yet another host for their future, spiritual siblings to inhabit temporarily. The saints, mystics, and sages have taught us for thousands of years that you (Infinite God) are **Omniscient** *(all-knowing).* You are **Omnipotent** *(Supreme, The Ultimate. The I Am, the All),* you are **Omnipresent** *(universal, present everywhere at the same time).* Quantum physics (viewed through a spiritual lens) also suggests the universe *is all of these things.* It is pure consciousness.

Omnipotent: The *Infinite* unified Multi-Verse has always existed. Thirteen billion, seven hundred million years ago, just as Mother dilates to give birth, The Infinite-Conscious-Multi-Verse, dilated and gave birth to the lower, slower, Finite energy—TIME. In quantum mechanics, *time is energy.* Time-Relative is a primary constant in every mathematical equation describing the Universe. TIME *does not exist* **in the Infinite.** It exists only in the Finite.

Omniscient: *Everything* in the Universe is interconnected. Information is energy and—energy is information. To get information *here*—does not require going *there*— to get it. *There* is simultaneously—here. At the quantum level, everything is—HERE-NOW. There is no Future. There is no Past. The future is already, **here-now.** The Past is still present. It too, is, Here-Now. In the INFINITE Multi-Verse HERE-NOW is NOW HERE and *EVERYWHERE*— NOW. It's vibrating somewhere in—Time." Remember—You are God. You are all-powerful. You are INFINITE. You have always existed. You are present everywhere and—in You, *there is no past or future.* **It is all—in the NOW.** You do not want anything. You do not need anything except—to show how much you love your creation. They ARE YOU, vibrating at Finite, yet incalculable frequencies within this realm, within this dimension, Within Time. Their frequency is less than You—slower than You—the INFINITE. (We will explore many of these things far more deeply, and in a practical context in Volume II: "A Glimpse Beyond the Spin" and Volume III: "A View from Beyond the Spin."

Omnipresent: Quantum physics tells us that there is no "stuff"—here or—stuff—there. There is *no* **matter** (material stuff) as such. There is only energy. The Universe is 99.9999999% empty-space, and the atoms which appear to create any *there-stuff* is in reality 99.999999999999% nothingness. They are instead Waves of Energy which, *in the presence of an intelligent observer*, collapse into particles, which for a brief moment in TIME, are just lower forms (frequencies) of energy, all of which exist in an INFINITE SEA OF POTENTIAL.

POTENTIAL IS REALLY ——THE ONLY THERE——THERE!

So, God, in your foreknowledge, did You create countless billions of children that would be born spiritually dead and or *that you already knew would make bad choices for innumerable reasons?* Of the approximate 108 billion people that have walked the earth, [10] in your foreknowledge, did you already know that human frailty makes countless mistakes, sometimes egregious and appalling mistakes? Did you remember that many of them would possibly result from early life experiences, impoverished conditions, negative influences, or just lessons they must learn for numerous reasons arising from the human condition? In your infinite foreknowledge, did you know by the destiny of birth, ¾ or 80 billion of them are born into non-Christian cultures? In your all-knowingness, did all of this escape you? Under Fundamentalism's model, "free will" sends them to hell. *If you already know how the sundry "free will" outcomes will play out with your countless offspring, how about— just not creating them in the first place?* What does *it do for you* **already knowing they will fail** and send them to hell— assuming it is their failure and not Adam's failing?

Your child stands beside you on a sidewalk. In your foreknowledge, you know that the animated, conversational distractions cause them to stumble in front of a truck—barreling down the road at sixty miles per hour. Would you let them? Would you have created them—anyway, *so that you could then watch them die— and go to hell?* Or—if we can stop thinking like paid theologians with too much time on their hands and think and feel *more like—God:* Is it more reasonable to believe that you would do something much *less human* and MUCH *more Divine*? But, more about that truck. What if the threat was not *an enormous truck* but the microscopic world of germs?

Jesus, *the great healer,* walked the Earth 2000 years ago, and scripture makes it clear that healing was a big part of his three-year ministry. But surely, *God who becomes flesh* would be acutely aware of the lethal danger of microorganisms— (germs, virus', bacteria). The fate of all humankind allegedly hinges on Adam eating the fruit from *one tree: the tree of the knowledge of good and evil.* Why then did eating from the tree of *knowledge* kill humankind spiritually and— yet fail to offer helpful information— like *knowledge about the world of Microorganisms?* Fast forward from Adam to Jesus. Of all the comparatively esoteric things Jesus, had to say *in all his teachings,* wouldn't a paragraph or two, even a single verse about the hidden dangers of microscopic organisms, have **healed billions through prevention** as compared to the relatively few he healed during his ministry? *Selah.* Yet curiously, the Bible is silent on the subject. It instead represents Jesus, saying *quite the opposite* about a practice now heavily stressed in preventing the spread of the deadly COVID virus.

"The Pharisees and some of the teachers of the law who had come from Jerusalem gathered around Jesus and saw some of his disciples eating food with **hands that were defiled, that is, unwashed.** (The Pharisees and all the Jews do not eat unless they give their hands a ceremonial washing, holding to the tradition of the elders. When they come from the marketplace, they do not eat unless they wash. And they observe many other traditions, such as the washing of cups, pitchers and kettles.) So, the Pharisees and teachers of the law asked Jesus, "Why don't your disciples live according to the tradition of the elders instead of eating their food with defiled (unwashed) hands?" Jesus responds in verse 15, **"Nothing outside a person can defile them by going into them. Rather, it is what comes out of a person that defiles them."** [Mark 7:1-5,15 NIV]

The Pharisees *(as always)* were coming from a legalistic, religious, ceremonial perspective and Jesus is making a spiritual point, but—wouldn't this (or any time) have been *the perfect opportunity* to teach his disciples, *and everyone over the coming 2000 years*, about the dangers of the invisible world of microorganisms? And maybe even to have *sided with the Pharisees on this point?*

How much do we know today about the importance of proper hygiene and isolating sewage from drinking water? Washing our hands is potentially critical to survival. Of all the things the Bible would teach, wouldn't this certainly rank near the top of the list? With all Fundamentalism's emphasis on sins *of the flesh*, there is not a word about what germs will *do to the flesh and the penalty of death under the various conditions we've—belabored.* With all of the Apostle Paul's insight, there is nothing—from him—either.

From the 1700s to the 1900s, an average life span s*lowly* went from aged 29 to 33 years. Before that time, Doctors went from performing autopsies to delivering babies—without washing their hands. Excrement piled high in cities with runoff into the rivers forming thick disease-bearing sludge. The brown water was often drawn to drink and—to wash cloths. Later, a mostly Christian England still ignorantly fails to isolate sewage from drinking water. During the related cholera epidemic, *the local clergy determines it is "God's punishment."* The first recorded case of influenza dates back 6000 years. Medical text dating from 2700BC describes Malaria and Smallpox emerging over 3000 years ago. These diseases (and others) killed *hundreds of millions of people.* Highly contagious Typhoid spreading through contaminated water destroyed 1/3 of the population of Athens, Greece. In the sixth century AD, the Bubonic Plague takes *25 million lives* over 200 years, followed by another outbreak in 1348 that kills 25 to 50 percent of Europe's population in just three years. In the 19th century, Tuberculosis slew 25% of Europe's adults. In the early to mid-1800s Cholera kills tens of thousands. As late as 1854, 616 people died in Soho, London, where Cholera had made its way from a cesspool into the drinking water. Fortunately for all of us living today, in 1861, Louis Pasture published his theory that microscopic organisms caused disease, and Surgeon Joseph Lister presented his argument, and recommendations for sterilization. Meanwhile, Robert Koch announced a proof that a specific bacterium causes Anthrax. *Slowly* the battle against disease-causing microorganisms gathered steam with the development of vaccines and antibiotics, approximately **2000 years— *after Jesus walked on Earth.*** The average lifespan in the last ~300 years went from 29 years to 33 years and in the past 100 years, from 33 years to 72 years. Why did it take 1900 years since Jesus's day to significantly increase life expectancy? [11] Do kudos go to science or religion here? Jesus said: *"The thief comes only to steal and kill and destroy; I have come that they may have life and have it to the full."* [John 10:10NIV] *What am I missing?*

In God's foreknowledge, ***was this by design?*** Of all the things Jesus could have taught us, why was this unimportant? Did Jesus know but purposely withheld the information? Was all this part of a grander plan where these billions of people over thousands of years were disposables predestined for eternal punishment? ***What role could free will possibly have played in these and similar scenarios?*** What is the possible *eisegesis* artful enough to provide a satisfactory explanation?

For what conceivable purpose, in the most ingeniously imagined and exquisitely crafted way possible, does a doctrine that dooms people to hell, at all: serve-promote-value-exalt-extol-appreciate-esteem-uplift or -amplify God?

Yeah, But What About?

Ever since the Protestant Reformation, "yeah but" and "what about" have been the impetus for reweaving doctrinal sweaters fraying around the edges, to get around pesky problems, conflicts, and contradictions. "It could have been..." or "It was likely that..." are explanations or better yet, *eisegeses* I was taught, for the newborn,—seems to pave the way for a slightly more loving Godlike God, one which, gets around St. Augustine's and St. Anselm's big-ole theological problem—"original sin":

The workaround posits that a child is protected until they reach the abstruse "age of accountability." But what determines that age? And isn't that honestly—

Quantum Brook

more civilized than sending babies to hell? If the age of accountability does exist—where? *Hint: The only place you will find it is in Fundamentalism's dance hall. (I thought dancing was a sin)* But—if it did exist, why is it necessary? ***If the baby is already predestined to be lucky—or unlucky? Why would it matter?***

St. Augustine's Original Sin is a doctrine on which virtually all Catholics and Protestants build the need for a redemption narrative. As we've discussed, it is Adams Sin, not just an individual sin that sends babies, children, and adults to eternal torment. If you choose Augustine's model, you doom innocents to hell. *If the child is foreknown,* apparently (and reasonably) the child is already *"known"* to God, to be *either in Heaven—or hell.* That dear reader is the meaning of *foreknowledge.* Catholics have the artful Purgatory as an in-between, a place Protestants claim does not exist. For fundamentalist evangelicals, it is hell—or Heaven. But, as a matter of pure inquiry, **why would we need an "in-between" if the result is** *foreknown, predestined, the conclusion—forgone?"*

To further illustrate the dramatic difference in interpretation: Just for grins and giggles—go and Google the phrase "bible verse purgatory." Click and read about the first seven or eight search results—- just on the first page. You will be *astonished* at the intricate arguments—"for and against." These arguments are a real-time, portrayal of the tragic, yet comedic stalemate, *none of which seems to matter to the multitude of oblivious players.* One site I stumbled upon was: **allaboutgod.com**. I laughed out loud. This site was going to teach me *ALL* about God with the GIVE HERE button prominently displayed on the homepage.

But what about adults around the world born into something other than Christianity, or shall we say, into the yet-to-be-determined, correct version of Christianity? Evidentially they too were predestined to go to hell ultimately, as soon as there is consensus on the "correct version." So, if there is a Purgatory pause for the adults, why take time for the hiatus? Again—*What is the purpose?* Is it a form of delicious, hand rubbing, pre-torment, dangling visions of what could have been, should have been, would have been if—Adam had not eaten the forbidden fruit? Or perhaps if they had been just a little bit luckier and been predestined to be *the right kind of Christian?* Will they be offered an opportunity to confess Adam's sin in Purgatory? If they will, then ***aren't they already foreknown and predestined* to "be saved?"** Yes? Then why did they need to go to Purgatory in the first place?

The "Reverend" J. Furniss, C.S.S.R. (1823-1865)

"The fifth dungeon is the red-hot oven. The little child is in the
red-hot oven. Hear how it screams to come out; see how it turns
and twists itself about in the fire. It beats its head against the
roof of the oven. It stamps its little feet on the floor."

*From the Sight of Hell — Quoted from Christ Triumphant
by Thomas Allin.*

Back to Augustine and Anselm's problem: Fundamentalism does not
believe in Catholicism's Purgatory, and, maybe, for a good reason. As we've
learned, it depends who's asking and—who's answering. Could it be that a more
Godlike-God turns a blind eye to "the crime" of Adam's sin—for which the baby
is punished eternally, but— did not commit? That would certainly make more
sense, wouldn't it? Is it okay that I'm rational? Those who are Catholic and survive
birth are, sprinkled, (baptized) to wash away their sin. Those not yet sprinkled or,
who are Protestant and have not prayed the sinner's prayer, well—that is a
problem. *They are babies who have not learned to speak or comprehend. How
could they?* And when they can, do they speak from their mind or, from the mind
of their programmer? What if destiny's programming is Buddhism, Judaism,
Islam, Hindu, Jainism, etc., or— competing Christian brand X, Y, or Z? What
exactly determines which programming it receives? But then wouldn't [Romans
9:14-16 NIV] address this issue? "What then shall we say? Is God unjust? Not at
all! For he says to Moses, "*I will have mercy on whom I have mercy, and I will
have compassion on whom I have compassion.*" *It does not, therefore, depend on
human desire or effort, but God's mercy.*" ***So, does this exacerbate the problem
or— solve the problem?*** How do you misinterpret this? It is clear-cut, until—
you read a competing scripture that applies *another SPIN*.

**DOES THIS ADVANCE PREDESTINATION'S DOCTRINE THAT SOME ARE IN
AND SOME ARE OUT? OR DOES IT SUGGEST THAT EVERYONE IS IN?**

Dear God,
why is Sunday School on Sunday? I thought it was supposed to be our day of
rest.
Tom L.

Quantum
Brook

God, Is That You?

If we allowed God to be Godlike again, couldn't he show compassion, and have mercy without the need for human desire or effort? I mean, that IS what that verse said, right? For those indoctrinated into a "wrong" belief; into "false" doctrine, a "false" religion…or perhaps they were just fallibly human? But again —which one is false? It could be any of them. And wouldn't that be in sharp contrast to God's Old Testament persona where, *(I want to be clear)* **in the words of His prophets**, He orders widespread infanticide, genocide, and—even rape? Let's take a look:

In the book of [2 Kings 8:12 NIV] the Prophet Elisha speaks for God, as prophets tend to do, **"…You will […] dash their little ones to pieces and rip open their pregnant women."** And from the Prophet [Isaiah 13:16 NIV] **"Their infants will be dashed to pieces before their eyes; their houses will be looted, and their wives violated [raped]."** Or in [Hosea 13:16 NIV] **"…They will fall by the sword; their little ones will be dashed to the ground, their *pregnant women ripped open.*"** Or, in [Nahum 3:10 NIV] **"…Her infants were dashed to pieces at every street corner."** In [Genesis 19 NIV], the story of Sodom and Gomorrah: Abraham goes to great lengths to negotiate with God down to ten. [32] "…What if only ten can be found there? He answered, For the sake of ten, I will not destroy it." Anyone familiar with the story knows God destroys Sodom and Gomorrah. **The evil included all the babies and the children? Not to be counted even as ten worth saving. What did they do? Adam's Sin?** There are numerous examples, but to continue belabors the point. Perhaps St. Augustine and Saint Anselm were right. These innocents, paradoxically, were guilty from birth and—they were neither Catholic nor Protestants, but—they could not have been any brand of Christian, could they? There was no Jesus then. What possible reprieve did they have? They were neither Jewish nor Christian. They were just nameless, faceless, apparently unimportant people, born into their place on Earth, their culture, at their appointed time, into their traditions, and into their cultures religious practice, and—for their crime, according to all we've learned—*they are in hell.*

Unlike the horrors we just witnessed, generally speaking, the civilized world places a very high value on the sanctity of life. Even in a time of war, we seek to protect civilian mothers and their infants. We abide by the rules of the Geneva Convention for prisoners of war. We abhor torture.

Back home, we spend millions keeping "preemies" alive in our hospital's NICU until the fetus is viable and, months later, take that long-awaited ride home with joyous parents. Many decades later, that once premature child may spend millions to keep the very parent alive, that gave them life, long after "*the real them*" departed their body through the cruel, dark portal of advanced dementia or a chronic illness.

Christians will march on Washington, passionately—participating in Right to Life protest devoting time, energy, and financial resources to putting conservative judges on the Supreme Court to fight for the relatively temporary injustice to the physical body of the unborn. They rightfully describe abortion as a barbaric, murderous act. At the same time, most are *oblivious to the fact* that they fervently champion doctrine(s), **which advance the belief of a permanent and eternal injustice of the unborn's soul and the souls of additional billions of toddlers and adults around the world. After all, they are just words on a page.**

Why is common sense so uncommon within Fundamentalism?

Was the God in the book of Exodus a different God than the one in the New Testament? Maricon, who proposed one of the earlier versions of the Biblical Canon but was later *labeled a heretic*, thought so. He concluded the God of Jesus and Paul could *not possibly* be the same God found in the Old

Quantum
Brook

Testament. [12] To even the most casual Bible reader, it's easy to see why Maricon might have reached that conclusion. Yet, even in my childlike understanding, I always understood the Ten Commandments frowned on these things that "God commanded," in II Kings, Isaiah, Hosea, Nahum. (pg. 86) Could it be that the prophets directed God's predestined, special, chosen ones to carry out these barbaric atrocities against those who were apparently, and unfortunately, defenseless in their physical death but predestined and determined to be vulnerable in their spiritual death? Keep in mind that only Israel self-proclaimed to be "the chosen ones" at this time in history." It would be a long time before Jesus enters the timeline in which "born again" Christians are also—- the chosen. In any case, the man murdered we just read about didn't have a prayer. Perhaps the tens of thousands, maybe hundreds of thousands of mothers and children were getting what they deserved. From what I read, that is a heavy toll that comes with being *predestined disposables*. Maybe we will again hear the convenient, well-worn not-an-answer-answer; "*...my thoughts are not your thoughts, neither are your ways My ways, declares the Lord*" [Isaiah 55:9 NIV]

In the real world, could it be that all of those innocents—were living their lives as would any of my friends and readers who were born, bred, and indoctrinated into their respective countries, cultures, and various belief systems?

Dear God,
Of all the people who work for you, I like Peter and John the best.
Samantha

Here is another chilling look at an 1800's era preacher's *enthusiastic rhetoric* about children in hell. I wonder if he was rubbing his hands together, with shoulders drawn when he said:

"Husbands shall see their wives. Parents shall see their children tormented before their eyes...the bodies of the damned shall be crowded together in hell like grapes in a wine-press, which press on another till they burst..." pg. 514
A Critical History of the Doctrine of a Future Life. Jeremy Taylor, D.D. 1877.

The wailing wall in Jerusalem

Given all that we've covered, I presume it was good the author was born in the *New Testament days*. And apparently, it was good that I was born into Protestant-Evangelical-Fundamentalism, where the skillfully imagined, age of accountability clause provided me and others with shelter from Saint Augustine and Saint Anselm's eternal-infanticide interpretation. What would have happened if my Mother's 32-hour labor and the extensive trauma I experienced at birth resulted not just in serious injury, but my death? If I had been Catholic in those days, I could be in hell wondering—what the hell happened? Or, would I be in purgatory?

With awareness of a large number of babies "stillborn," or those who die soon after birth, what purpose would it serve; how would it—benefit God to foreknow a baby will die, to send it to hell *and allow their parents to conceive in the first place?* Are they all such brats that they are guilty of causing their conception? Placing doctrinal bias aside to the extent possible, I ask my fundamentalist reader specifically, to ponder the following question: What if it were—*you?* Have you ever really stopped to consider the possibility?

Quantum
Brook

What if you were born to different parents, in a different country, into a different tradition, into a different belief system, one not choosing, but one chosen for you by your birth destiny?

My Granddaughter Mia's Christening

At one point in my career, I was responsible for our company's International licensees and distributors. I have friends in different cultures, ethnicities, backgrounds, and religions. I am also *very fortunate* to have Catholics as extended Family, very dear friends, and neighbors, some of the most beautiful people ever to grace planet earth. According to evangelical Fundamentalism's formula, Catholics are not real Christians; they are not "born again."

At one time, Martin Luther called the Pope "the Antichrist," as have many others over decades, including modern-day televangelists. Catholics do not say the sinner's prayer per se'; they instead confess their sins to a priest. And as previously examined, when baptized, they are sprinkled rather than immersed.

Catholics baptize infants as soon as possible after birth to rid them of "original sin," a beautiful ceremony I attended for two of my granddaughters, whose other grandparents are Catholic. For Fundamentalists, this doesn't pass muster as "being saved." In Fundamentalism's view, my Episcopal, Anglican, Methodist, Presbyterian, etc., friends are generally too liberal to be protected, and they do not ordinarily advance the Romans 10:9 salvation model. Catholics categorize sin as original sin, venial sin, and mortal sin. Fundamentalism talks about God's grace after being "born again," but most Fundamentalist denominations' underlying focus has been and always will be——*the law.* James 2:9-10 NIV says: *"But if you show favoritism, you sin and are convicted by the law as lawbreakers. For whoever keeps the whole law and yet stumbles at just one point is guilty of breaking all of it. "* It's a good thing my fundamentalist friends have been able to grow beyond the frailty of showing favoritism, or it won't turn out well for them. But what about everyone else around the world? What about my friend in the United Arab Emirates, an exceptionally accomplished gentleman, or his children? He, and of course his children are Muslim. I have many Muslim friends. According to Muslims, Islam is the only genuine religion. All non-Muslims are going to hell.

Quantum
Brook

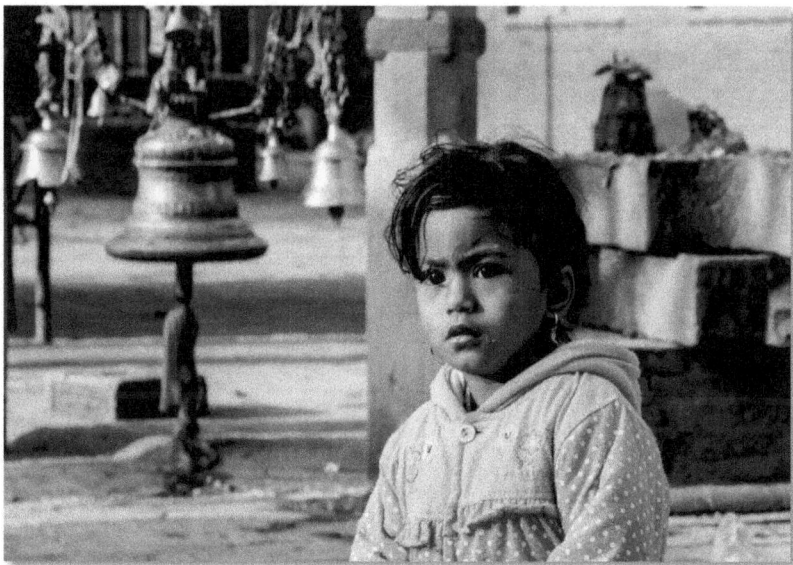

Then there is a friend of many years in Kochi, Kerala India. India is a mix of Hindus, Buddhists, Muslims, and Christians. I have Buddhist friends in Malaysia. I have friends in China. What about them?

Dawn Breaks

The *tiresome* doctrinal fog began to ever so slowly lift for me in the '90s when a dear friend on a parallel path introduced me to Bishop, John Shelby Spong's eye-opening work, Rescuing the Bible from Fundamentalism and A New Christianity for a New World. I was familiarized with the depth of Spong's scholarship when he appeared on a debate format, television talk show circa 1989. His performance against a *woefully ill-equipped* fundamentalist opponent made a huge impression on me. Spong scholarship emerged as a thorn in the flesh of numerous famous televangelists over the coming decades. Spong and other theologians' in-depth learning base their informed conclusions, in part, on the applied science of textual criticism. Historical discovery began to get in the way of centuries of unchallenged assertions. Spong was deep, and Fundamentalism most often operates from the shallows. It was quickly apparent that the lens through which I viewed everything about the Bible from the time I was old enough to read, was a remarkably different reality. Not so much because of the problems with Scripture, but to paraphrase Dr. Ehrman, it was because of the contentious, complicated, 2000-year-old history *behind the scriptures*, one in which only career historians, through the forensic sciences would ever uncover. This knowledge is either hidden from or ignored by the average evangelical.

I first became aware of this competing reality in the mid-1990s when I was the sales lead on a very competitive two-year-long evaluation at a Children's Hospital in Atlanta. Every seven years, hospitals typically replaced their aging "Hospital Information System. "HIS" is the centralized computer systems housed in a glassed-in, raised floor, heavily air-conditioned, halon protected rooms running numerous, fully integrated mission-critical application programs that serve as the information backbone of all the hospital's financial and clinical operations. Our corporate headquarters office was based in Atlanta, so no airplane hassles preventing frequent meetings with the Chief Information Officer who became a good friend. We met once, sometimes twice a week for lunch. In one memorable conversation, he informed me that he was going to Emory University to get his Master of Divinity. Months later, just a few weeks into his first semester, he said that he figuratively ran out of there like his hair was on fire. What he was learning was way too much to assimilate into his more fundamentalist conditioned paradigm. Hundreds of Fundamentalists, denominations sponsor Bible Schools that teach theological views packaged for Fundamentalism's consumption. They make for a much better education on which to build a career in Ministry. But Fundamentalism *views seminaries as cemeteries.* Seminary advances scholarship, which deep dives into the biblical history, manuscript origins, and the complicated and contentious history of the codified 66 books of the Bible. This relatively new scholarship of textural criticism has uncovered evidence virtually unknown in traditional fundamentalist circles. All of which challenge established perspectives and—cherished beliefs, most importantly, that of Biblical inerrancy and religious superiority. To the fundamentalist, this scholarship is heresy, *an idle word indicating disagreement with—presumed orthodoxy.*

> *"You could say the road to heresy is paved with Scholarship"*
> —Bishop, Carlton Pearson

In 2006, I read a book by Carlton Pearson, a man who just a decade earlier had influenced a lot of the music we were doing in our church. He was a fourth-generation fundamentalist and an emerging superstar on our denomination's stage. He had a national television show, and every Sunday, five thousand plus members packed his church in Tulsa, Oklahoma. But, after reading his book, I no longer felt alone in a barren wasteland with my thoughts. It seemed that some 25 years earlier, Carlton had a similar epiphany, an awakening like mine but one with far more at stake professionally. He was the senior pastor of a megachurch, which, in all its many facets, was the source of his livelihood, one which he worked decades to build. My income didn't depend on towing our denominations doctrinal line. If someone called me a heretic, it didn't affect my paycheck. But as Carlton said in his book, The Gospel of Inclusion, "I lost it all to find everything, especially me." It was a no holds barred, scorched Earth look at my minds muttering, challenging the reality I had lived my whole life. It *resonated deeply.* It was if he was nervously reading my mind and writing down my thoughts. Anyone, anywhere, at any time wishing to advance a narrative that benefits them personally, may have my ear, but it will come with a healthy dose of skepticism. Anyone, anywhere, at any time, promoting a narrative birthed from their being's depths, *which cost them everything—is instantly credible.* They have my sincere admiration, my respect, along with my undivided attention to learn— *why.*

Who is Driving the Narrative & Why?

Writing as a person who has spent the lion's share of my career convincing people to spend hundreds of millions of dollars in exchange for advanced technological solutions, I know what it means to be responsible for creating spin. My presentations in many a board room purposed to frame our proposal in the most favorable light. My job was to analyze my client's challenges and illuminate how our solutions could save them money, save time, and save lives— better than our competition. When my clients connected with the fact that I genuinely cared about their challenges, their day to day frustrations, their fears of dropping the ball, resulting in potentially career-ending mistakes, it was a pleasure to present a "total, end to end solution." It was rewarding to know that my customers would realize a value returned, many times over the $millions, it would cost them. But *all of these advanced— my company's narrative.* What if I walked in one day, my client's team and my team were sitting attentively around the table, and I began to share a superior discovery that reframes and challenges the standard with which I had become very comfortable? My next meeting would be an exit interview with my boss. What could I have possibly discovered that would cause me to remove myself from a comfort zone that took a lifetime to build? What would be of such importance for me to commit career— suicide?

So, when I say Carlton Pearson (and now many others) lost it all, I mean he lost everything he worked his entire life to build. But Carlton found a superior story. Carlton Pearson is my hero. His church dwindled to nothing, and the phone stopped ringing. How much do you think he believed in this great Epiphany; how can you better measure the influence of such an awakening? Why—was it so real to him and such an anathema to others in the faith? Would not this kind of commitment get *anyone's* attention? Should it not cause those paying his salary to sit up and take notice, do the math, and at least—try to argue the merit in his new perspective? Carlton is just one of a growing number of examples I repeatedly refer to because of the enormous impact it had on me. On a related note, and one with which I have a direct connection.

Christlike?

Years ago, a lovely couple I have known for decades had to make a difficult decision: Stand by their son or stand by the doctrine they espoused from their pulpit for forty years. This couple pastored an extensive Assembly of God church. Their son, himself the senior pastor of an interdenominational megachurch, had lived a lie for a lifetime. He made a *bold decision* to tell his congregation and his parents that he was gay. His church collapsed. His **ultra-conservative** evangelical parents made the difficult decision to put their Love for their son *ahead of their interpretation of the scriptures and stood by him and supported his decision.* Rumors running rampant surfaced from the denomination's headquarter offices that the consequence would be—the couple losing the pension they had earned over decades in ministry.

Which action demonstrates the greater Love here? The Love of doctrine or the Love for their son? Who has my attention, respect, admiration, and yes—Love? What is more, "Christlike"? Who are the Pharisees, and who are the Christ characters in these narratives? How does this contemporary example encapsulate the thesis of this entire book?

> *"I like your Christ; I do not like your Christians. Your Christians are so unlike your Christ."*—Mahatma Gandhi

The Crux of the Matter

Allow me a brief side-bar to share the crème de la crème example of the kind of "special interest" that too frequently triumphs over the greater good. I have referred a few times to my dear genius friend, James West. Roughly six years ago, he invented the first and only molecule ever to receive a patent; actually, multi-part patent. He spent more than five million dollars of his own money and years of exhaustive wheel spinning effort to get "Moxy" into the marketplace. So, why would you care? James depleted his finances and—- his body in an attempt to introduce *a revolutionary breakthrough* in virus and bacteria warfare. Moxy wages an effortless, unseen war, 24/7/365 on the ubiquitous, dangerous, hidden enemies in the microorganism world.

Amid the COVID-19 crisis, killing millions worldwide, threatening economic collapse, and destroying our way of life, no amount of pleading from me would renew James' drive to give it another go. He was done. For more than a week, ten hours a day, I reached out, in writing and via phone to numerous federal and state government officials, and many members of the national media as our nation sat paralyzed, afraid, hoping for the best. I felt it was essential to *get someone's attention.* I wrote that it was a matter of life and death "to hear from them today," but— I too failed.

Carefully read [Appendix COVID-19] to understand why "established interest" *wants nothing to do with this technology.* We could have avoided—the Pandemic—*entirely*—and the emergence of COVID-20 *next generation* to follow. There would have been no loss of life, no loss of income, or the many freedoms we all have willingly relinquished. COVID-19 would have been Dead-On-Arrival, never reaching our shores. Moxy's side effects? Higher oxygen levels saturating our homes, airplanes, businesses, restaurants, stadiums, malls, cruise ships, places of worship, and—hospitals making it necessary to calibrate or dial back an "always-on" to an "occasionally on," condition, otherwise, everyone would feel as if they were hyperventilating (high on oxygen.)

When does the interest of the few override the health and livelihoods of the masses? The answer is crystal clear. But it is also clear that it—***always gets down to economics.*** Protect the goose laying that golden egg— at all costs. When something of Moxy's magnitude or—the significance of this thesis enters the discourse, it threatens for some the VERY profitable, status quo. And when that threat appears, so do sharp tongues.

When lifetimes are invested in things working a certain way, including protecting doctrine that operates according to a specific formula, abrupt change is financially cataclysmic. Harmful levels of protectionism begin to encircle the status quo. In Volume II, "A Glimpse Beyond the Spin," I'll share another stunning example of established interest preventing yet another of James' patented technologies from seeing the light of day. It is sure to make your blood boil.

Is there reason to concede the presence of, at least, some level of self-serving hypocrisy? How can it be a surprise as to why there are so many agnostics? Why are there so many atheists? Which is better? Blind faith or—to remain woefully blind to scholarship?

Carlton Pearson's story argues that God's Love includes everyone, everywhere, of every religion. He argues that God is a God of love, not eternal punishment. *This viewpoint is not new.* Instead, it is a doctrine which has been around for millennia, one which once competed to be the accepted orthodoxy but, *specialness, and choosiness* won. **The literate few of the day *made the rules.*** We will take a fresh look at this old perspective in Chapter 8, "A Universal Loss."

Quantum
Brook

Conclusion

With thousands of interpretations of the Bible inspired in many places, and as we've observed, shocking in others; If our statement of faith is the redemption story, why would we not want to believe in all of humankind's redemption *instead of just those our indoctrination chose for us?* Which is the more magnificent love story?

For some of my readers, there are no perfect words- written in any sequence, any combination, or prose, that will change minds for reasons that may not serve their interest. But my purpose here (again} is not to convince. I get paid either way. Instead, it is to offer a reason to think; to inform; to, if allowed, help construct a new framework that considers *All*.

Bishop John Shelby Spong put it this way: [13]

"It is time, I am convinced, to move Christianity beyond that historically inaccurate and psychologically damaged definition of humanity that has resulted in a constant denigration of human life as helpless, depraved, sinful, and in need of divine rescue. The suggestion made by so much of the Christian theology of the past that every baby is born with the stain of original sin distorting his or her goodness is abhorrent to me. I admit only that babies are born with a loudspeaker on one end and no sense of responsibility on the other. But I regard both of those traits as morally neutral." [...] "To spend my energy concentrating on the presumed lostness, the moral depravity, of the hopelessness of human beings, so easily called sinners by traditional Christianity, is to fail to appreciate the most incredible product of the whole created order— namely, the human mind." –

John Shelby Spong

Chapter 6

Quoting Misquotes

As we examined in previous chapters, the cornerstone of Christian evangelical Fundamentalism is the belief that the Bible is *inspired, infallible, and inerrant*— and is the only legitimate word of God. I once fully embraced this statement of faith until I awakened to the irreconcilable paradox of a loving God and the God of eternal torment portrayed in my early years. My mind is unable to (even partially) accept what my heart unequivocally rejects: The *eternal sadistic torment* of 80 billion babies, children, and adults who *are not born-again Christians.*

Over a decade ago, John Shelby Spong's book Rescuing the Bible from Fundamentalism introduced me to perspectives I had never considered: The bigger picture. I had never confronted the *implausibility of all I had believed,* which set me on this quest...in earnest. While doing some preliminary research for Seeing Through the Spin, I read a few reviews of the books "Misquoting Jesus" and "Jesus Interrupted" by an author who, at that time, was an unknown— to me. His scholarship is—to say the least, troublesome within fundamentalist circles. The thing arresting my attention and bestowing immediate credibility to Dr. Bart Ehrman's work was *his journey* "From There to Here," Like my own journey, he arrived *at a destination he had early in his life, purposed <u>not</u> to travel.* That resonated with me in—*an enormous way.*

Bart Ehrman is a James A. Gray Distinguished Professor of Religious Studies at UNC, Chapel Hill, NC. Ehrman wrote and edited thirty books, including six New York Times bestsellers and three college textbooks. I learned that Ehrman was an American New Testament scholar focused on textual criticism of the New Testament, the historical Jesus, and the origins and development of early Christianity. I'll never forget the elation I felt reading his book reviews. I was thinking: "...now, this is some serious Scholarship!" His credentials would get anyone's attention, ***but it was his <u>background</u> that got mine.***

Quantum Brook

In the Introduction portion of his books Misquoting Jesus and Jesus Interrupted, Ehrman writes that he too was a teen in the 1970s; (there are very few months difference in our age.) He also grew up in a suburban home to loving parents. He went to an Episcopal church in Kansas where, unlike the Assembly of God church I attended, he said, *"They didn't overly emphasize the Bible."* What a contrast, I thought. The Episcopal faith emphasizes liturgy, tradition, and community over an immersion into studying the Bible. Ehrman didn't elaborate when he said that he *"had a born again' experience in a setting other than his church"* when he was a sophomore in high school. But he expressed the sentiments espoused in my denomination when he said *that he and his peers who had born-again experiences considered themselves to be 'real' Christians unlike those who just socially showed up to church going through the motions.*

One of Ehrman's much-admired mentors who could quote vast passages of scripture by memory convinced him to consider becoming a *"serious Christian"* and devote himself entirely to the faith. This urging prompted him to consider in-depth Bible study at Moody Bible Institute, where Ehrman would major in Theology. Moody had a sparkling reputation within our denomination as well. It was a *highly conservative boot camp* for budding ministers. In his book, *Misquoting Jesus*, he wrote that all the students and professors at Moody were required to sign this statement: *"The Bible is the inerrant word of God. It does not contain mistakes. It is inspired complete and its very words—"verbal, plenary* inspiration."* Ehrman goes on to write about the big leap from *"the milquetoast view of the Bible"* he had as a self-described, *"Socializing Episcopalian"* when he was a teen. Comparatively, *"This was hard-core Christianity, for the fully committed." Ehrman said.*

Surprisingly, one of the first things he learned in the new curriculum at Moody was that we don't have *any, zero, zilch,* of the original writings (the Autographs) of the New Testament. What we do have are copies of copies of copies—of copies—of copies—of copies— We don't know how many generations of copies existed before *the versions used in translating the Greek manuscripts into English.* Ehrman explained that the Gospels were stories handed down through oral tradition *before they were first recorded.* And then: <u>none</u> of the copies are accurate. The scribes producing them inadvertently and—all too often intentionally—*changed* them in many places. <u>*All the scribes did this*</u>— and as mentioned in previous chapters, each succeeding generation copy *compounded the previous errors* introduced into each previous generation copy. Ehrman said that we would likely never know how many earlier copies folded in—and compounded their errors into the following generation's text.

Ehrman writes that his classmates were somehow able to shrug off what he found *"most troublesome."* Again, *I deeply resonated.* When interpreting the text to allege the eternal torment for 3/4 of planet Earth, I, too, find anyone's ability to "shrug it off" most troublesome over thousands of years. One of Ehrman's courses at Moody was an introduction to Textural Criticism—a science that attempts to restore the "original" words of the text. The word criticism can be misunderstood by those unfamiliar with the science. Textural Criticism looks forensically at the available text and applies mathematic probability using computers and other modern tools to restore the text's most likely original version.

Text restoration would later become Ehrman's passionate life pursuit, but first, he explained that he had to learn the Bible's original languages, Greek, Hebrew, Latin, and even French and German. Learning these languages enabled him to study the historians in their *native tongue.* After three years at Moody, Ehrman describes that **"he purposed to become an evangelical voice in secular circles."** He contemplated that getting his degree would equip him to teach in secular settings. He chose Wheaton College in a Chicago suburb, and I found it most interesting that his friends at Moody *warned him* that he might have trouble finding "real Christians" at Wheaton.

The warning speaks volumes about Moody's conservatism. You see, Wheaton is Billy Graham's (the poster boy for Fundamentalism) alma mater. Ehrman admits that he did find it to be **"a bit liberal for his taste."** But as he studied the Greek text and the highly nuanced meanings of the "original" Greek words in translation, he pondered that most people didn't have the time or— the skill to study the text in their original form. Instead, all they could do was what he describes as **"reading the more or less clumsy renderings in English, which too often had nothing to do with the original words."** But the more significant difficulty—which much belied the problem with the translations from the original languages, was the manuscripts themselves. What Ehrman found most troublesome was the primary question burning within him: He kept asking: "*how can we say the Bible is the inerrant word of God if we don't have the [original] words that God is said to have inerrantly inspired?* Instead, **we only have the words the scribes copied.** Sometimes they copied them correctly, but many times they copied them incorrectly and often intentionally changed them. How can we say the Autographs (the originals) were inspired if—we don't have the originals? Instead, we have "*error-ridden copies, virtually **all of which are centuries removed from the originals and differ in thousands of ways.**"

After Ehrman earned his degree at Wheaton, he obligated himself to studying the New Testament through the lens of a historian—and through the science of textual criticism. At the Princeton Theological Seminary, Ehrman would learn from the world's leading expert and scholar, Professor Dr. Bruce M. Metzger. Ehrman's evangelical friends, this time at Wheaton, warned him, "*it would be tough to find real Christians at Princeton.*" Like Dr. Ehrman, I was taught that Presbyterians were not real born-again Christians. So how could they teach authentic Christianity in a Presbyterian Seminary? While immersed in his studies at Princeton and— at a granularity, most of us can't even begin to comprehend; he said, "*I resisted any temptation to change my [evangelical fundamentalist] views [...], But my studies started catching up with me.*"

One of the examples Ehrman sites was assignments studying the book of Mark that would become a turning point. The "interpretive crux" of a specific passage was the subject of a final term paper. He chose a passage in Mark 2, where the Pharisees confront Jesus about his disciples eating grain while walking through a wheat field on the Sabbath. Jesus responds that the "*Sabbath is made for humans, not humans for the Sabbath.*" Jesus reminds them that when King David and his men were hungry, they went into the temple and ate the showbread when **Abiathar** was the high priest. The problem is: **Ahimelech** was the high priest, *not Abiathar.*

Ehrman describes developing a long, nuanced, complicated, (and he admits), a convoluted but intelligent, argument the kind which *(my emphasis)* has become the mainstay among today's evangelical doctrine builders). Ehrman describes being confident that his, much revered and pious professor would appreciate his argument. "*... a good Christian scholar who obviously (like [himself]), would never think there could ever be a genuine error in the Bible.*" He said that Professor Cullen Story wrote <u>one line</u> at the bottom of his paper: "Maye Mark just made a mistake."

Ehrman mused about all the effort he went through doing some very fancy exegetical footwork to get around the problem. Again, something that resonated with me was something I had lived with the first forty-plus years of my life. Ehrman also explained that his solution "was, in fact, "quite a stretch." He concluded: "Maybe Mark *did make a mistake.* But— he also concluded that if there was one little "picayune mistake" in Mark 2, there could be others.

Intelligent, well-meaning people artfully dance between the 66 books, threading solutions to conflicts and creating doctrine which—creates other conflicts for their opposition to then do their fancy exegetical footwork, all— wishing to get around blatant contradictions with the new explanations. It is unacceptable that "*maybe Mark just made a mistake*" **because it has always been**

the assertion that the scriptures are inerrant. Yet, the more convoluted the creative explanations, the more diminished the overall credibility.

I too remember as a young boy, almost as if it were yesterday, thinking about where in Mark 4 Jesus talks about *"the smallest of all seeds on earth"* is the mustard seed, wondering if Jesus had ever seen Bermuda seed; they are so small that they are almost like dust. My father purchased a bag to overseed our lawn. I remember thrusting my hand into the bag and feeling the seed escape my grasp, running through my fingers like fine sand. But in the scheme of things, something like that is entirely irrelevant to Jesus' overall message.

But what about where the book of Mark says Jesus was crucified the ***day after*** eating the Passover meal (Mark 14:12; 15:25), and then the book of John says Jesus died the ***day before*** eating the meal. That is potentially a substantive issue. Getting your days straight during this time period is essential to critical theological assertions. How about Luke's account of Jesus' birth where Joseph and Mary ***returned to Nazareth*** a little more than a month after they came to Bethlehem—after performing the rites of purification required by Jewish law (Luke 2:39) But—in Matthew's account, ***they fled to Egypt*** (Matt 2:19-22). So, did they return to Nazareth or—flee to Egypt? Or when Paul says he ***did not go to Jerusalem after he converted*** (Galatians 1:16-17), but in the book of Acts, he says ***it is the first thing he did after leaving Damascus*** (Acts 9:26). Or how about something which may be *significantly* more critical: The genealogy of Jesus. Both Matthew 1 and Luke 3 present his genealogy. This is something where most readers will yawn, rub their tired, crossed eyes, and skip to something that is— readable. Complicating readability, Matthew and Luke are formatted *very differently*; it is almost as if they purposely wanted to confuse the reader. Matthew formats, *"Abraham **the father of** Isaac"* and <u>begins the genealogy with Abraham</u>. (I know this is boring. Hang in there with me.) Luke, however, formats his genealogy: *"Isaac **the son of** Abraham"* and to make readability worse—<u>Inverts (flips upside down) Matthews format</u> and begins with Joseph going back to Adam.

To help unscramble the brain, I created [**Exhibit—Jesus' Genealogy**] to make it—*readable*. Matthew's format is now consistent with Luke's, and both are **for the first time, side by side**. Matthew and Luke both <u>begin</u> **with Joseph** and go back to Abraham. So, here is the key question:

Who is Joseph's Father?

In Matthew 1, it is Jacob; in Luke 3, it is Heli. If Luke presents the authentic linage, in verse 24, is *Matthat the son of Heli,* or is he the *son of Jorim* as it says in verse 29? Compare the two columns carefully. I worked very hard to make it easy for my reader. Compare both columns back to Abraham. In Matthew, you will find **25 generations** to get back to King David. In Luke, there are **42 generations** to get back to King David. At least both finally get there.

Selah

As I have now stated several times, my purpose is not to argue. My objective is to leverage a lifetime of study now—within the context of my epiphanic illumination. I want to corroborate the unassailable critical scholarship of historians like Dr. Ehrman and renowned theologians like Bishop John Shelby Spong and add badly needed reasoning into the discourse. There are also realizations of former evangelicals like Baptist minister Tim Sledge, MDiv., D.Min. In his book "Four Disturbing Questions with One Simple Answer," all were thoroughly trained to explain and answer these very reasonable questions. However, they hit a wall after years of *placating explanations for the source from which creative men construct doctrine that unyieldingly judges humankind.*

Let's look at some other telling examples and understand why they exist in the first place. Do a horizontal study of the Gospels, which in many cases tell the same stories. Read the story in Matthew, then in Mark, then Luke, then John. See what each says about the account. Compare them. Where do they agree? Where do they differ? If each report presents information not found in the other stories, Fundamentalism's solution has been *to combine all of the stories and create a fifth gospel*—which doesn't exist. The problem enters when each Gospel presents conflicting accounts of the same story. Like the genealogy of Jesus. Which one is the right one? Does it matter? If for such an essential part of Fundamentalism's doctrinal thread, you wish to call the Bible *inerrant.* This is not a *mis-spelling*. It is a crucial *mis-telling.* If you can embrace it's often inspired yet profoundly human origins—its human copyists, its human translators, its social agenda, then it will read—as it is.

According to Dr. Ehrman, there is virtual consensus among scholars and historians that Mark was written around 65-70AD, Luke and Matthew were written around 75-85AD and John, around 90AD. *None of the four namesakes which were eyewitness to the events about which they write.* While these books bear the names of the authors, Ehrman explains that they *were all written* _pseudonymously (not written by the authors the book names.)_ They were written in the third person.

T hose who followed Jesus in his day were working-class, uneducated peasants, most of which spoke Aramaic. Peter and John in Acts 4:13 are said to be illiterate. The _vast majority_ of the ancient world people were uneducated, never learning to read or write. Yet, these books were written in Greek—by authors highly literate, rhetorically trained and educated in Greek composition—all of whom _were not disciples, nor did they claim to be disciples_. The stories were _circulated through oral tradition for decades_ before they were first written down. Stories were told to someone who understands someone who tells someone else and "improves," embellishes the previous telling, ultimately changing the story and even changing the changes made to the earlier telling. All of these things took place _before_ the ~4000 copyist errors, the unintentional _and intentional_ scribal changes that supported preferred narratives. Are the accounts really what the pseudonymous author heard? Is it really what the author is _said to have said_, or do the reports reflect the desires and wishes of the authentic writer more accurately? Or is the scribe who later copied the manuscript changing what was previously copied to reflect _their own bias_ for their narrative? Here are a few examples.

On what day was Jesus crucified? What time of the day did he die?

(John 19:14) John is explicit when he says it was the day **before eating** the Passover meal, (also known as _the day of preparation_.) John is straightforward because—for John perspective, Jesus _must die on the day the Passover lambs are slaughtered_. John is also unambiguous that Jesus was not even condemned to death until **the afternoon**. John says Jesus is put to death _when the lambs are being sacrificed_ for the Passover meal. _For John, it is vital to be on this day because—Jesus is the Lamb to be slain for the sins of the world._ Interestingly, John is the only gospel to make this claim. But that which was essential to John is _not_ what was important to Mark.

(Mark 14:12 15:25) Mark is precise when he says Jesus died _the_ **day after eating** the Passover meal. It was important to Mark that the _Lord's Supper_ **be the Passover Meal**. Mark said Jesus died at **9:00AM**.

Did Jesus carry his cross to Golgotha as John 19:17 described, or did Simon Cyrene carry it as Mark 21 describes it? _Or was it both as the imagined fifth gospel describes?_

Did the curtain in the temple rip in half *before* Jesus died or after he died? (Mark 15:37,38; Luke 23:45-46). In Matthew 27:51 the earth shakes, rocks split, tombs open and bodies of many "holy people" who had fallen asleep were raised and went into the city after the resurrection. This account of the biblical zombie, the walking dead, is a scene you will *only find in Matthew*. If such a fantastical event occurred—wouldn't *all the gospels* make at least an *oblique* reference to it? I would think they would have written a whole book about it!

In *Matthew 28*, after the resurrection, the three women go to the tomb. The angel instructs them to *tell the disciples that Jesus will meet them in Galilee.* In *Luke 24*, the women are instructed to *tell the disciples what Jesus told them when he was in Galilee—that he would be raised.* Then Jesus appears to the disciples and tells them *not to leave the city of Jerusalem.* They do not leave Jerusalem. In Jerusalem, Jesus tells them to *stay there* until the power comes upon you, which happens on the day of Pentecost—fifty days later. They remain in Jerusalem after Jesus has ascended to heaven. *So, did they stay in Jerusalem, or did they go to Galilee?*

How about when Peter denies Jesus? Does Peter deny Jesus before the cock crows at all, or before the cock crows twice? And in the denials, Peter denies to different people in different Gospels. Fancy footwork by fundamentalist suggests Peter denied Jesus *six times*. Then why wouldn't all the Gospels say—it was six times?

On *numerous occasions* in the gospel of John, Jesus claims his divinity. **Yet strangely**—in Matthew, Mark, and Luke he—*does not*. Neither does he claim divinity in the source documents for Matthew, Mark, and Luke known as: "Mark, Q, M, L." Only in the Gospel of John, *written 65 years after Jesus' death*, does anyone say—that "Jesus said—he was God." How could that be? Isn't this the *critical central narrative* advancing every theological thread? Shouldn't this be *pervasive **throughout all the Gospels?*** In all Jesus' travels, in all of his teachings throughout his three-year ministry, how does it evade mention *even once in the other Gospels?* I would think, above all other things, that would be—*the most important thing.*

In Mark: Why is Jesus <u>utterly</u> silent from the time of his trial through his crucifixion, except for the words to Pontius Pilot, "You say so." Then, the final words before his death ("Eloi Eloi lama sabachthani?") "My God My God why have you forsaken me?" In **Luke's account**: Jesus is *not in shock*. He talks to the women beside the road, telling them not to cry for him but to be more concerned about *the fate that is to befall them*. On the cross, Jesus asks the Father to forgive the people crucifying him because they do not understand what they are doing. He has a coherent conversation with one of the thieves hanging on the cross next to him. Jesus tells him, today you will be with me in Paradise. He is not wondering why all of this is happening to him. He doesn't ask God why he has forsaken him—because he doesn't feel abandoned. Instead, he says, "Father into your hands, I commit my spirit" He then dies. Jesus is *so composed* that it troubles the scribe to the point that he *thought it necessary* that Jesus appear human, so in chapter 22:43,44, the scribe adds: "*An angel from heaven appeared to him and strengthened him. And being in anguish, he prayed more earnestly, and his sweat was like drops of blood falling to the ground.*" Nowhere else in Luke at any time during the passion does it indicate Jesus was suffering.

Jesus' demeanor in Mark, however, is very different to what we see in Luke. Here, Jesus looked much too divine, knowing his fate and not sweating anything —especially blood. The scribe however, thought it most important that he appear to be human and added vs. 34 "My God, my God, why have you forsaken me?" Fundamentalist will not only combine Mark and Luke's account of the crucifixion but also Matthew's and John, removing each authors emphasis and instead creating a *combined fifth gospel*—which again—does not exist. How about Jesus' triumphal entry into Jerusalem? It had to adhere to the prophecy— *but which one*?

In Mark 11:2-7 and Luke 19:30-35, the disciples follow Jesus' instructions and bring him *one colt*. In Matthew 21:2-6, the disciples follow Jesus' instructions and bring him *two colts*. In John 12:14, Jesus doesn't instruct the disciples. *He gets his own colt*. Mark 11:7, Luke 19:35, John 12:14, Jesus rides a *single colt* when entering Jerusalem, but in Matthew 21:7, Jesus rides *two colts* at the same time (not quite sure how that would work.)

Jesus' cleansing of the temple is sometimes considered symbolic of overturning Judaism, but the Gospels differ on essential details: In Mark 11:15-17, Jesus cleanses the temple at the *beginning of passion week*. In Matthew 21:12-13, however, Jesus cleanses the temple *during Passion Week* at the end of his ministry. In John 2:13-16, Jesus cleanses the temple near the beginning of his ministry (well *before the Passion*.) In Luke 19:45-46, Jesus cleanses the temple at the *beginning of Passion Week*.

Before entering Jerusalem, did Jesus curse a fig tree and cause it to wither *because it didn't have any fruit*? There is no similar reference in Luke or John. There is in Matthew and Mark, but the two disagree on the details: In Mark 11:20-

21, Jesus' disciples don't notice the tree has withered until—the following day. In Matthew 21:19-20 Jesus' disciples observed that the fig tree *withers immediately* after being cursed—and they are amazed.

Where was Jesus anointed with oil? Matthew and Mark agree; Luke does not. There is no mention of the anointing in John. In Mark 14:3, Matthew 26:6-13, Jesus is anointed in Bethany at Simon, the *leper's house*. In Luke 7:36-38, Jesus is anointed in Galilee at the home of an *unnamed Pharisee*. But how and on what part of the body was Jesus anointed? Mark 14:3 and Matthew 26:7 say the oil is poured on Jesus' **head**. However, Luke 7:38 and John 12:3 says the oil is poured on **his feet**.

Who anointed Jesus? Mark 14:3, Matthew 26:7, and Luke 7:37 agree that an unnamed woman anoints Jesus. However, John 12:3 says that Mary anointed Jesus. What about reactions to the anointing? The oil was expensive and not everyone was happy about the apparent waste. Matthew, Mark, and John describe different people being upset. Luke doesn't mention it at all and Mark 14:4 says "some" rebuke the unnamed woman. In Matthew 26:8 the disciples admonish the unnamed woman and Luke 7:39 says an unnamed *Pharisee* thinks it's wrong *because the woman is a sinner*. John 12:4-5 say Judas Iscariot *rebukes Mary* for anointing Jesus.

Passion Week plays an essential role in Christian doctrine. Still, the gospels don't agree on *the sequence of events*: in Mark and Matthew it is the triumphal entry, cleansing of the temple then—the anointing at Bethany. Luke chronicles the triumphal entry, cleansing the temple and daily teaching in the temple. John starts with cleansing the temple (long before Passion Week), supper with Lazarus, then the triumphal entry, and—no cleansing the temple.

The Christian tradition frames Satan as helping to lead Judas to betray Jesus, but when did that happen? In Luke 22:3-6, Satan enters Judas before the Last Supper. In John 13:27 - Satan enters Judas *during* the supper. In Matthew and Mark, there is no mention of Satan entering or otherwise affecting Judas.

What About Judas' Destiny?

We've written *a lot* about *foreknowledge and predestination*. Did Judas' betrayal send him to hell as an inevitable part of *the plan?* Did Judas have a choice? Free will? If Jesus was to be the sacrificial lamb, could he have fulfilled that role if Judas had *not betrayed him?* Then, should Judas be scorned—or praised? Matthew 19:28 says all 12 disciples will sit on thrones and judge the 12 tribes of Israel. In Paul's writing's Jesus appeared "to the 12" after his resurrection? Was Judas among the 12? The "fifth Gospel" crowd thinks not.

From where are we to receive illumination?

Judas betrays Jesus to the temple high priest, but—when did he make the arrangements? In Mark 14:10-11, Matthew 26:14-16 and Luke 22:3-6, Judas bargains with the priests **before** the last supper, but in John 13:21-30, Judas bargains with the priests **after** the last supper. But how about the deal Judas made for the thirty pieces of silver? The price of "thirty pieces of silver" is well known even in secular traditions. But minted coins were already in use during Jesus' time. The payment was no longer "weighed out." "Pieces of silver" *had not been in use for over two centuries.*

In Matthew 27:5 Judas throws down the silver and walks away from the priests. In Acts 1:18 Judas uses the silver to buy some property. In Mark, Luke and John, there is no mention of 30 pieces of silver. In Matthew 27:6-8, *the priests buy a field* that gets its name because they used Judas' "blood money," but in Acts 1:18 *Judas buys the field* which gets the name "the field of blood" because his body bursts open there. The field of blood is not mentioned in Mark, Luke, or John.

How did Judas die? Matthew 27:5 says *Judas hangs himself.* Acts 1:18 *says Judas falls to the ground, bursts open, and his guts spill out* (how and why this happened isn't explained) Mark, Luke and John does not mention Judas' suicide—by any means.

In my studies over many years, I have run into numerous inconsistencies, conflicts, and confusing contradictions. The ones I presented here represent but *a very few*. I strongly believe decades of programming, runs interference in "the background" editing what we read with thoughts like "it might have been, or—it could have been, maybe it was that…" It still happens to me today. Our "operating system" (that we covered in earlier chapters) edits what we read in real-time, performing something akin to Ehrman's fancy exegetical dance for his assignment

Quantum
Brook

in Mark's book. You either ignore it—or pretzel your mind to look for a plausible explanation.

For this author, the troubling issue is not the *relatively* minor errors, discrepancies, or even outright contradictions. Flawed human beings wrote these manuscripts regardless of illusions otherwise. That is not a belief, that is a fact. There were no computers for continuity and fact-checking before compiling the cannon. If there had been, we might have never known just how human the sources were. However, again, for me it is not so much the errors; it is the constant building of *doctrine* around the myriad **eisegesis** *(the interpretation of a text by reading into it one's ideas (Webster))* **when—**

Thousands of the world's foremost theological scholars <u>cannot agree</u> on what the text is supposed to say. They are unable to reach consensus as to how these things *affect the meaning of <u>critical portions of Biblical message</u>.* Decade after decade there is ***massive disagreement*** among scholars on matters which are ***of utmost importance***, <u>such as the doctrine of the Trinity, the full divinity of Christ, the full humanity of Christ, the atoning sacrifice of his death, favorite stories of Jesus' life</u>, all of which stem from problems with the text. After all of the manuscripts discovered, after all the technological and methodological developments, *here is where we find ourselves:*

We have amassed more than 5,000 manuscripts. Each contains a measurable portion of the Greek New Testament, but—importantly—only eight of these manuscripts *may* date as early as the 2nd century. Forty of the documents *may* date as soon as the 3rd century. The vast majority (more than 80%) are **11th to 16th centuries**. <u>The oldest copy of the complete Greek New Testament dates to the mid 4th century.</u> Most telling is that it took *hundreds of years* for church leaders to reach an agreement on *which books should be part of the New Testament Canon.* Adding the book of Revelation took almost *40 additional years* and in my humble opinion *should never* have been. Yes, I would have been one of the numerous "no" votes. The 27 books that made it into the finals *were not the only books under consideration.* Even after declaring the canon complete, disagreement continued *for decades.* Some in leadership were unrelenting in their proclamation that several unsanctioned books should <u>continue to be considered inspired and authoritative</u>. And yet—

In 2005, two scholars put together a **new updated edition** of the Greek New Testament, which *they claim was from the original Greek.* Five—years later, in 2010, another scholar *put together another, original Greek new testament— which differed from the 2005 version,*

——in over 6000 places.

Do we have identical problems knowing the original words of other historical writings which were also initially handed down through oral tradition— like Homer's Iliad and Odyssey, Plato, Aeschylus, Euripides, etc., to which we *do not have access to the original text?* Yes, and I have beautiful leather-bound versions of these literary works. But— none of them *allege to predestine those chosen to be chosen and the eternal torment of the vast majority of the human race.*

The greatest obstacle to discovery is not ignorance - it is the illusion of knowledge. Daniel J. Boorstin, Historian

---

Conclusion

"The Bible is the inerrant word of God. It does not contain mistakes. It is inspired complete and its very words—"verbal, plenary inspiration."

One error does not support a claim to *inerrancy.* If there are thousands, only a throat-clearing statement of faith remains. The story's value in the holy scriptures is–the overarching message: *God so loved the world—not just those* which **the writers and the interpreters of those writings love(d), not only those who directly benefit from self-appointment, from unique self-serving exegesis. The message is—to all—for all.**

Quantum Brook

Chapter 7

A Hell of an Idea

If you have access to the internet, pause reading for a moment and go to **worldometers.info/world-population** and prepare to be astonished. Watch, *in real-time,* the number of babies born— and the people who die, each second. Permit the gravity of what you are watching to sink in.

Selah

Pulling away from doctrinal noise requires—*a lot of discipline*. Focusing once again on the big picture requires the ability to *think clearly*. Suppose God is good *(in the weakest possible human use of the word—good)*. *Would* He under any conceivable circumstance create billions to later torture them for trillions upon trillions of years? And—in exchange for "unbelief" for a relatively few— years? *Think.* Moreover. Why would someone-anyone **choose not to believe** if there were not countless, confusing, competing claims within different cultures, including our own? Is the implication that God does not understand this human condition; this conundrum? Is it conceivable and fair that each person will (merely) be born into the "wrong" religion, or— (if Christianity is the right religion) taken by birth into the *wrong version* of Christianity—once we finally know what that version is.

Have you ever paused to consider how long a trillion years is? If you and I were to sit across the table from each other and I were to place a dollar bill in your hand every second, of every minute, of every day, of every month, of every year, (24 – 7 – 365), it would take you and me 31,709 years to make that exchange. Now exchange each one of those dollars. Each second, *for a year* in hell. That trillion years is—just an opening act for—eternity. *Think.*

Assuming my reader is human rather than alien (meaning that you are subject to human emotions of love, and with provocation, immense anger), can you imagine a time that *you* could torture another human for even an hour? There *is general agreement* that people who could torture *anyone*, regardless of their evil deeds, are among the lowest life-forms in existence. Are we saying that God has a sadistic, serial killer side that *must be satisfied*, and "He" is even worse? Is the message: God is gazillions of times worse than the most malicious and evil Nazi, Dictator, or Warlord the world has ever seen? For those who *do believe* God is evil suggests the need for an in-depth psychiatric evaluation.

As I have stated on several occasions: my mind cannot possibly accept *what the rational, commonsense of my heart* outright rejects. (Much more about the hearts astonishing intelligence in Volume II) New science suggests that the heart is more intelligent than the mind can ever be.

Fundamentalism squirms uncomfortably in another interpretive dance suggesting that God is *not evil. Instead—he is "just."* These words do not pretend to answer the question or explain but instead seek to soothe the conscious of those who may dare to begin—*Thinking*. For at this scale— **"Just"** is a rather an intellectually dishonest, **unjust semantical argument**. "Justice" means, among other things, devising a punishment that—fits the crime. God has already done that. In the Christian culture is called sowing and reaping. In other cultures, it's called Karma. Either way, sow bad things and (it's a law of physics) acquire—commensurate bad things, not eternal torture. Ironically, under the Levitical Law, it was an eye for an eye and a tooth for a tooth. A comparative fare exchange in a relatively uncivilized society. Indeed, if we allow God is more Godlike and less human-like in "His" thinking: An incommensurate quadrillions of years of torture in exchange for, say, 100 years of unbelief or 50 years of the most heinous "mortal sins"? I have no option but to do something I hate to do and drill down—just a bit.

As reviewed in previous chapters, *according to the doctrine of Original Sin*, ¾ of the babies born every second, whether they die soon after birth or live a long life, are predestined to go to "hell." As of this book's publication date, the world's population is quickly approaching *Eight Billion*. All of these people collectively speak more than 6,500 languages and practice 4,300 religions. 1,213,000,000 of them speak the language most spoken in the world: Mandarin. Also, there are fifty-six ethnic groups spread over Mainland China, Taiwan, Hong Kong, and Tibet, which speak one or more of 297 living languages. On the second most populous continent of India, there are 60 mother tongues, 720 dialects, and 22 major languages, including Hindi, Punjabi, Malayalam, and Sanskrit. There are also 1,216,000,000 people speaking ~2000 different African Languages, primarily practicing versions of Christianity and Islam blended with their native beliefs. What role does geography, language and tradition play in religious "choice?"

The Basic Tenants

The *basic* tenants of Christianity say that Jesus loves you. It also teaches that his love is *conditional* on you returning that love. If you do not love him, regardless of the reason, God will make sure you burn in hell—forever. There is *nothing* Jesus can do about those *who do not embrace a faith that is foreign to them*. Yet, curiously the average Fundamentalists, who are most likely born into *"a version"* of Christianity, somehow fail to consider the enormous odds against themselves ever converting to Buddhism, Hinduism, Judaism, Islam, ad infinitum; why? *(a rhetorical question—of course.)*

Fundamentalism chooses to ignore the fact that if fundamentalist believers were born somewhere on the opposite side of the earth, into another tradition—indoctrinated into that tradition's faith, the odds strongly favor remaining in that tradition, practicing and defending that faith—*for a lifetime.* I urge you to take a moment and *read yourself into* the brief Bios of some noteworthy examples in the **Appendix**. Put yourself in their shoes from the moment of your birth. After reading these stories, would anyone care to estimate *the odds that* The Dali Lama would become a Muslim? How about him becoming a Hindu—or a Catholic or a Protestant? What are the chances Pope John Paul II would become a Buddhist, a Muslim, a Methodist, Presbyterian, or a fundamentalist? How about Gandhi, exposed to many faiths, including Christianity, but, in the end, the most influential would be his mother's faith. How likely would John Calvin be a Methodist or that John Wesley would be a Presbyterian? What are the odds that John Paul would be anything but Catholic? What are the odds that this author would be a Catholic? Catholicism in the mid-1950s in the deep South? The answer is self-evident. These are uncomplicated, indisputable facts of geography and human nature. You don't need a degree in social anthropology to understand. Yet apparently, they are realities Fundamentalism choses to so *easily* ignore.

Do people convert to Christianity from faith x y or z? Yes, it happens all the time. It is the exception, not the rule, just as some become disillusioned with Christianity and leave for other faiths or agnosticism. Again— the exception, not the rule. Yet, somehow, decades of indoctrination into another religion is *supposed to magically disappear when Christian doctrine enters the discourse.* Years of programming have most assuredly formed the lens and filters, creating this grand illusion.

Fundamentalism *says* Jesus is the savior of the world, but it also means Jesus *will—not save— the vast majority of the people on planet earth.* It teaches God has condemned billions— *already.* Even with verses like: *"For God did not send his Son into the world to condemn the world, but to save the world through him."* (John 3:17) Fundamentalists prefer instead to advocate for <u>the very next</u> <u>verse</u> in that passage: *"Whoever believes in him is not condemned, but whoever does not believe <u>stands condemned already</u> because they have not believed in the name of God's one and only Son."*(John 3:17) Fundamentalism preaches that these ancient, *"inspired, inerrant, infallible,"* [1] words on a page means *eternal torment for billions*, depending on whether or not they believe, yet, they wouldn't in a million years, believe something similarly written in the Koran, the Bhagavad Gita, Talmud, the Vedas, the Upanishads, et al.

Fundamentalism teaches that Jesus is a Strong-Victorious-King. Yet, the majority of Christianity's various doctrines preach that Jesus *is not* strong enough—*cannot* overcome *any resistance* to his will to save humankind.

Quantum
Brook

Fundamentalism says Jesus teaches you to love your enemies. It also shows Jesus will eternally torture his enemies; enemies defined as those who do not believe. The reason is irrelevant. What if they happen to be the unfortunate recipient of indoctrination into *a different faith*, or *"the wrong version" of Christianity?* What if my reader is one of the unfortunate?

Incongruously, for many in Christianity, eternal torment is not only a cherished belief but one championed by numerous voices within the faith, one trumpeted with **surprising passion**. They count themselves among the lucky (and relatively few) predestined to be a unique child of God—instead of those allegedly *predestined for hell*. What does this irrational thinking do to advance the "Good News?"

If you were one of those on the outside looking in, you would hope to assume that Christ's Love would cause believers to eagerly, even desperately find a scriptural narrative whereby God provides a path of salvation for the—*whole world*—not just the predestined elect. Sadly, I've found *the opposite to be true.* Craning necks continue to pluck at insignificant competitive theological threads and—*at all cost—defend a hell of eternal torment for most of humankind.*

As I've now stated many times, the purpose of this work is not to argue scripture with scripture. *"That dog won't hunt. It's dead."* Over the past fifty years, there has been a sea of books written to argue support for *any doctrine you choose.* It is truly a smorgasbord of doctrinal delights—using not just the same translation but also the same scriptures to craft creative new tradition or creatively argue the current versions.

It's as if these books were written in an enormous house with *thousands of rooms*; all the walls are two-way mirrors. Those who venture into the halls can see into the rooms, but those resting comfortably in their chosen room cannot see beyond their walls. There are only *reflections supporting the doctrine each room defends as truth.* The acoustics are lively; the echoes a muddled morass.

The following will be an *unavoidable descent into the weeds.* I hope to shed new light on Fundamentalism's pervasive advance of a God who mimics other historical andromorphic, Zeus like imaginings. There was Huitzilopochtli god of the Aztecs or Huiracocha god of the Incans, or the Canaanite god Moloch. Moloch was a bronze statue heated with fire into which the Israelites would throw their children in sacrifice. [2] But sadly, the following quote *is **not** 5,000 years old.* These are the words of the **"Reverend" J.** Furniss, in the late 1800s.

"The fifth dungeon is the red-hot oven. The little child is in the red-hot oven. Hear how it screams to come out; see how it turns and twists itself about in the fire. It beats its head against the roof of the oven. It stamps its little feet on the floor."
(The Sight of Hell - Quoted from Christ Triumphant by Thomas Allin)

Selah

The idea of eternal torment comes with an array of horrifying images. As we've previously learned, most of them emanate from Augustinianism's unbaptized babies descending by the billions into perpetual incineration. Add Dante's psychotic dreamscapes of twisted, mutilated, broiling souls and images of St. Francis Xavier advising his crying Japanese converts that their deceased parents must suffer eternal agony in hell. *Could* fundamentalists welcome news that unbiased scholarship advocate that the basis for this weird doctrine was completely garbled in transmission and- *totally lost in translation?* Sadly, most would not. And for me, the saddest truth of all is that far more will continue *to cherish—and champion* this unfathomable horror than find it unfathomably—abhorrent.

I am genuinely empathetic. I firmly believe that indoctrination often makes it *impossible* for many to see what is *right—there.* It is not by choice. It is programming. The documented facts today are this*: No truly accomplished New Testament scholar believes that scripture presents God's eternal torture chamber.* Furthermore, most fail to realize or intentionally ignore the fact that **Paul never mentions it**. The only eschatological fire he ever references brings salvation, *not eternal punishment* (1 Corinthians 3:15). It is neither found in the other New Testament epistles nor any surviving documents (like the Didache) from the earliest post-apostolic period. There are a few terrible, surreal, symbolic images of judgment in the Book of Revelation, but nothing which yields an explicit doctrine of eternal torment when *properly read.* [3] As mentioned earlier, it is not well known that the book of Revelation was "squeezed" into the canon in the fourth century. It took many years after the Council of Nicaea (325AD) for John's apocalypse to *barely make it* into the 27-book canon. Over the centuries, it continued to draw the wrath of critics, from theologian Martin Luther to authors like D.H. Lawrence. When reading from the original Greek, even the frightening language Jesus used in the Gospels fails to deliver the fiery dogma Fundamentalism applauds.

Quantum
Brook

It Came From Somewhere

Bible Historian Bart Ehrman says it this way in his book "Heaven and Hell: A history of the Afterlife: *"One of the surprising theses of this book is that these views do not go back to the earliest stages of Christianity. You cannot find them in the Old Testament, and they are not what Jesus himself taught. Then where do they come from?"*

What happens after death, for the good and evil, has morphed in numerous forms over the past three thousand years. The oldest sources of The Hebrew Bible do not speak about life after death. For all people, whether righteous or wicked, for the Hebrews, they're dead in the grave—or, in a mysterious entity called Sheol. Nearing the very end of the Old Testament period, *Resurrections were not that of individuals but that of nations*, specifically Israel. [4] Later, the evolved thought still determined that the people of the Old Testament who sided with God would return to their bodies to live forever *on Earth*. The origins seem more the musings of the great philosophers some 350 to 450 years before the time of Jesus.

Socrates and Plato in Plato's dialog *The Phaedo (Plato, speaks for Socrates)* Socrates asserts that, should he be put to death, his soul would live on forever. It was immortal and imperishable. There were various views among philosophers about different states of existence after death, including that of non-existence. The annihilated soul is lead into a dreamless sleep from which it would never awaken. Three centuries before Plato, Homer's the Iliad, and the Odyssey had various contemplations on death, but there was a constant for Homer: Death is final, and there is no coming back. According to Homer, when the *psyche*, the life-breath, and the soul leave the body, it goes to the underworld where it exists as a mere image or "shade" of the person. There is no pleasure or pain. It remains there forever.

In Virgil's twelve-book epic, the *Aeneid,* Aeneas, a fugitive from the Trojan War, is anxious to visit the Sibyl, an ancient semi-divine prophetess. Sibyl could predict the future when inspired by the god Apollo. Aeneas convinces her to lead him into the earth. On the journey, Aeneas and the Sibyl come to a fork in the road. The path to the right leads to Elysium, *the place of **eternal happiness***, but "the path to the left is ***torment for the wicked***. It leads down to Tartarus, the path to doom." Here, in this story, there are numerous elaborate accounts of the journey into Hades, crossing the river Styx and—Tartarus, a burning moat designed to keep the souls from escaping. In Virgil's report, the Souls in Hades *are **either punished for their sins or—rewarded for their upright lives.*** All the while, above, *one of the three divine "Fates"* keeps guard. (Aeneid (Book Six))

If you read the Iliad and the Odyssey and the Aeneid as Greek Mythology, as the literature that it is, rather than as a part of the Biblical canon, have you ever wondered where the idea of hell originates? If you are an evangelical fundamentalist, the answer might be, "in the Bible." You might easily assume that when you read the word *hell* in scripture, its source is a single place from which all Biblical authors describe what "they see"—and then confidently record their vision to advance, with the **"Reverend"** J. Furniss' enthusiasm, the doctrine of eternal torment. Surely it is THE single source *where all of the Biblical writers get their word and ideas* for "hell"—correct? No. The visions of a fiery hell came from Greek mythology. The word hell (hel) came from ***Teutonic-Germanic paganism's—Norse mythology***, [5] Neither the word nor the descriptions came from a single "God-inspired" source and a unique word describing God's plans and place to eternally torment 3/4 of his creation. But, as for the numerous Hebrew and Greek words translated "hell?" They are many. Where did they come from?

Most Christians have no idea that there are significant differences between English Bible translations. The late Gary Amirault [6] famously said: "I have thirty New Testaments and whole Bibles which do not contain the words "hell" or "everlasting punishment"—even once! What's going on? It is essential to understand that the Reformation period's scholarship was just *a few steps removed from the Dark Ages."* Most Christians are completely unaware that many translations do not at all contain the concept of a hell—of eternal punishment. [7] While these are certainly not popular in hellfire and brimstone circles, they are nonetheless available in most Christian bookstores. But what is most troublesome is—*why they are not more popular.*

Numerous poorly translated versions of both the Old and New Testaments liberally used the word hell (hel), especially in the King James version, first published in 1611. More accurate translations like the New International Version (NIV) *(the version I favor),* in the Old Testament, more correctly substitutes the previous use of hell with the word's **"depths"** twice **"grave"** 61 times, and **"death"** four times. In the New Testament **"depths"** appears twice, **"hades"** five times, **"grave"** three times, and **"hell"** once *with a footnote that "the Greek is*

Hades." The other word most translated as hell in the New Testament is
Gehenna—translated, hell 12 times. The term "**tartaroo**" is translated as hell
once. The **Concordant Literal Version** (CLT) of the Bible more accurately
translates (virtually all of these instances as "**unseen**." Unseen is used 75 times (or
every time but once) previously translated- hell, and there, "death" was used once.
Let's look at the real meanings of the words in the original text that was
mistranslated—hell:

Depths: also translated Hades and Unseen,

Hades: A mythological *place* and *a god* that Homer frequently described as a
king living in a royal palace and possessing orchards, fields, and herds of cattle.
The dead pass through the pylai haidou or "gates of Hades" to enter his realm.
Hades, the god the Greeks also called Pluto, is *the brother of Zeus and Poseidon*
who rule the skies and the seas. He rules with his wife Persephone in the realm
called Hades, the region under the earth, full of mineral wealth, fertility, and the
home to dead souls.

Death: the spirit departs the body

Grave: a place to lay a deceased body

Tartaroo: (ταρταρόω, "throw to Tartarus") (ˈtɑːrtərəs; Ancient Greek:
Τάρταρος, Tártaros) the deep abyss used as a dungeon imprisoning the Titans and
a place of torment and suffering for the wicked. Tartarus is where, according to
Plato's Gorgias (c. 400 BC), souls are judged after death and where the wicked
receive divine punishment. Tartarus is also considered a primordial force or deity
alongside entities such as the Earth, Night, and Time. It appears once in scripture
in 2Peter 2:4.

Gehenna: the ecclesiastical Latin gehenna from ancient Greek γέεννα from
Hebrew יֵיהָגֹּום "valley of Hinnom" which the Hebrews otherwise called Tophet
was a location in Jerusalem in the Gehinnom where worshipers influenced by the
ancient Canaanite religion engaged in child sacrifice to the gods Moloch and Baal
by burning their children alive.[8] A place appointed to torment reprobates in
Jeremiah 7:30-34. Yet, Jeremiah goes on to say: *"The time is coming, says the
Lord, when all Jerusalem will be rebuilt for me, from the Tower of Hananel to the
Corner Gate. A measuring line will be stretched out over the hill of Gareb and
across to Goah. And the entire area—**including the graveyard and ash dump in
the valley** (that is Gehenna), and all the fields out to the Kidron Valley on the east
as far as the Horse Gate—will be holy to the Lord."* (Jeremiah 31:38-40). In the

light of everything we've presented in this book so far, is it too much to believe that if Gehenna is used to symbolizes "hell" in the New Testament and "Gehenna will be holy to the Lord" *is it not also inherently **fundamentalist*** to believe that "hell" (Gehenna) too will be "holy to the Lord?" Will a lifetime of indoctrination block the ability to think beyond a bloodthirsty, tyrannical God?

Present-day valley of Gehenna, Jerusalem

Lazarus and the Rich Man.

The story fundamentalist *eagerly* turns to for quintessential *proof* of the fiery hell of eternal torture is the parable of Lazarus and the Rich Man. In Chapter 2, David and Goliath's story gets a fresh look as a prime example of how we are programmed to see things from a specific perspective *to advance a preadapted narrative.* This story, *more than any other,* demands a fresh look-see. Most believers view this account, *not as a parable*, but a story Jesus details about the sinner's punishment in hell.

Standard Fundamentalism Indoctrination 101

But a reexamination suggests traditional interpretations are *badly misleading.*[9] The following provides an, *in context*, verse by verse investigation into what Jesus was teaching. Yet, lack of scriptural context is one of the numerous things plaguing Christianity and diluting the central message. Does this story describe the condition of the lost soul burning in hell or, as Jesus ***explicitly said his parables intended to do,*** *hide its meaning from specific listeners?* Let's take a look, beginning with some important Keys.

1) When Jesus tells this story, he *never accuses, or even implies the rich man has sinned*—or is "a sinner." If the story were about sin—he most assuredly would make that point *crystal clear*. He portrays him as wealthy. He describes him as a man who lived a life of luxury and riches. We naturally *assume* those who are wealthy are bad. The assumption, ingrained in our culture, demonizes the rich and glorifies the poor. It has become our default assumption. **2)** Likewise, Jesus didn't describe Lazarus as being righteous but rather—a man who is unfortunate and unable to care for himself. If we are to take this story literally, the *reasonable* implication is the rich are evil and *predestined to*—burn in hell. If you are homeless, destitute, and needy, you—*are predestined to be saved.* I don't know how anyone can *believe either to be true.* **3)** If hell (as traditionally taught) is an abyss of fire and brimstone tormenting sinners forever, what (thinking) person believes "a drop of water" would even momentarily relieve anyone's anguish in such flames?

By some calculations, from the time man has walked the earth, there would already be *eighty billion people* in hell. How does the observer in Heaven pick out the one they wish to observe? If there were *only a billion,* it would be akin to looking at every person on the continent of China all at the same time and picking *your person* from the crowd. Realistically wouldn't Lazarus or anyone delivering the drop of water suffer the same burns? Are the souls in Heaven different in substance to the souls in hell? How do you cross such a vast gulf between the two? (Luke 16:26) Isn't the gulf's stated purpose to *separate hell from Heaven and prevent such crossings?* Does the observer use binoculars or, perhaps, a telescope to see "their person" in flames? A gulf *(at least implies)* separation by—a great distance. What is necessary to relay the request for the drop of water? Do you engage in a conversation regarding the request? Is it a communication device or a telepathic connection? If telepathic, have you wondered *how, and more importantly, why,* the rich man *zeroed in on Lazarus?* If it is a communication device, where does the rich man get Lazarus' number or one of the 80 billion unique frequencies to contact Lazarus? There is no indication of a familial relationship or other connection. Was Lazarus the only one in Heaven able to take that call?

What is "the rich man's" connection to Lazarus?

If hell exists as portrayed in this story, then *all* of "the saved" in heaven can view "the lost" burning in hell. Does it suggest that our friends, family, and loved ones, and—also random strangers tortured in flames can contact anyone in heaven at any time? With eighty billion frequently making that call from hell, who could enjoy an *eternal existence in Heaven watching* and listening to lost friends, family, and acquaintances *in eternal torment that never burn up*—forever begging for a drop of water?

These are *a but a few* of the various difficulties encountered when literalizing this account. Instead, best to understand what **the parable** is communicating **and why. Embracing** the story as literal-factual means, we then have to view *all of Jesus' parables as literal.* It is common among most Christians to believe that he spoke in parables to make the meaning *clearer* for the illiterate, the uneducated people he was teaching. Yet here, at least in this instance, Jesus explains—**the opposite to be true:**

Matthew 13:1-15

"On the same day, Jesus went out of the house and sat by the sea. And great multitudes were gathered together to Him so that He got into a boat and sat, and the whole multitude stood on the shore. Then He spoke about many things to them in parables. And the disciples came and said to Him, *"Why do You speak to them in parables?"* He answered,

"Because **it has been given to you to know the mysteries of the kingdom of heaven, but to them, it has not been given.** *For whoever has, to him, more will be given, and he will have abundance; but whoever does not have, even what he has will be taken away from him. Therefore, I speak to them in parables, because seeing they do not see, and hearing they do not hear, nor do they understand. And in them, the prophecy of Isaiah is fulfilled, which says: 'Hearing you will hear and shall not understand and seeing you will see and not perceive; for the hearts of this people have grown dull.* **Their ears are hard of hearing, and their eyes have closed, lest they should see with their eyes and hear with their ears, lest they should understand with their hearts and turn so that I should heal them.'"* (NKJV)

This passage and the corresponding scripture in Mark 4 make it clear that Jesus spoke to the people in **parables** *to hide the spiritual meaning of what he was saying.* He intended *only his disciples* to understand. He meant for the parable to *conceal from specific bystanders, the purpose.* An essential backdrop to the situation in which Jesus will tell this parable.

All the tax collectors and sinners came to hear what Jesus had to say (Luke 15:1)—making the Pharisees and scribes increasingly jealous. They complained, vehemently criticizing Jesus for receiving sinners and eating with them (Luke 15:2). They were most surely envious of Jesus's growing fame, afraid his popularity would increasingly diminish their authority and prestige. So, to those gathered around him, Jesus first spoke *a three-part parable* (the lost sheep, the lost coin, and the prodigal son). This parable showed the tax collectors and sinners (as well as the Pharisees) that God was concerned for them. It said that He would seek out the lost and welcome them into His family.

The always—self-righteous, accusing scribes and Pharisees, who Jesus recognized as the legitimate religious teachers of the Jews (Matthew 23:1-3), *should have been* the ones spreading the message that God loved them; however, their faith was in *their righteousness*. Their contempt for these tax collectors and sinners *didn't measure up to their sanctimonious standards*, so the Pharisees and scribes excluded them and—considered them accursed (John 7:49). Afterward, he speaks primarily to his disciples, but the Pharisees are still listening. Jesus related the parable of the unjust steward (Luke 16:1-13). The "lovers of money" Pharisees (Luke 16:14) realized that *Jesus was referring to them in this parable and took offense.* They scoffed at Jesus. The final part of Jesus's response to the scribes and Pharisee's contempt—was the *parable* of Lazarus and the rich man. Let's unpack it and take a look:

———————

"There was a rich man who was dressed in purple and fine linen and lived in luxury every day." Luke 16:19

The way Jesus describes the rich man is—significant. The man is clothed in *purple and fine linen*, clothing which was quite ordinary for those of considerable wealth during Jesus' day. However, this apparel has an additional symbolic meaning. *"...the wearing of purple was associated particularly with royalty ..."* [10] Moreover, the use of linen was prescribed for Priests (Exodus 28:39). "The coat, turban, and girdle must be of fine linen."[11] The rich man's garments were *symbolic of royalty and—the priesthood.* Just before giving the

Israelites the Law on Mount Sinai, God told Moses, *"you will be for me a kingdom of priests and a holy nation. "These are the words you are to speak to the Israelites."* (Exodus 19:6) The rich man's clothing **identifies him symbolically with the people of Israel** who rarely measured up to the high calling as God's "chosen" people, sending them into captivity for refusing to honor the covenant ratified at Mount Sinai.

The rich man in this parable represents the Jews of Jesus' day, exemplified by the religious teachers, the Pharisees, and scribes.

Verse 19 says the rich man *"lived in luxury every day."* Figuratively, this represents the spiritual feast available only to the Jews, the sole remainder of God's people—Israel. In the first century A.D., they are portrayed to be the only people on earth who had *the true religion*. The Apostle Paul recounts:

"For I could wish that I myself were cursed and cut off from Christ for the sake of my people, those of my own race, the people of Israel. Theirs is the adoption to sonship; theirs the divine glory, the covenants, the receiving of the law, the temple worship and the promises. Theirs are the patriarchs, and from them is traced the human ancestry of the Messiah, who is God over all, forever praised Amen." (Romans 9:3-5).

The gift of great wealth provided fertile ground for the Jew's indulgent self-righteousness. They gloried in the gifts and increasingly less in the Giver. Instead of being a "royal priesthood" and blessing all nations, they despised the surrounding Gentile people. As Paul later wrote, *"May their table become a snare and a trap, a stumbling block and a retribution for them"* (Romans 11:9).

"At his gate was laid a beggar named Lazarus, covered with sores, so 21 and longing to eat what fell from the rich man's table. Even the dogs came and licked his sores." Luke 16:20

The first thing noteworthy about Lazarus is his depiction as a beggar, an appropriate way to describe the Gentiles who "laid at the gate" of Judah. Paul describes the Gentiles' predicament before receiving Jesus. "Remember that at that time you were separate from Christ, excluded from citizenship in Israel and foreigners to the covenants of the promise, without hope and without God in the world." (Ephesians 2:12) This passage fittingly represents the Gentile nations' position before Jesus's crucifixion. They were *"excluded from the commonwealth of Israel," "strangers to the covenants of promise,"; "without hope and without God in the world."* The Gentiles were beggars. They located outside Judah. They longed for the "spiritual crumbs" from the Jew's divinely blessed table. We read that the dogs came to console Lazarus in his misery, licking his *unclean sores*. The Jews considered Gentiles to be unclean *"dogs."*; unclean most often referred to leprosy. When speaking with the Greek Syrophoenician woman while in the region of Tyre, even Jesus used this unflattering comparison (Mark 7:24-30).

Crucial to the story is the—name: Lazarus is Greek, and is a form of the Hebrew Eleazer. It—literally means *"he whom God helps."* Using this name is of particular significance to the parable's message. The Gentiles would *become "those whom God helped"* through Jesus' sacrifice. The next events are Lazarus', then the rich man's death.

"The time came when the beggar died, and the angels carried him to Abraham's side. The rich man also died and was buried." Luke 16:22

The parable has been figurative up to this point; no reason to assume it now becomes literal. First—substantial proof the language is symbolic. Jesus said: Lazarus dies and taken to the bosom of Abraham. Importantly, there is no mention of his burial. Later the rich man dies, and he is buried in Hades (vs. 23). If the story is literal, we face a Biblical contradiction, (although we have learned more than a few). Here, Lazarus immediately receives the promise of eternal life. Yet the book of Hebrews says that Abraham—and all the other Old Testament saints, have not yet received the promises God gave to them. (Hebrews 11:13, 39-40). All these (Abraham, Noah, Abel, etc.) died in faith, without receiving the promises, but having seen them and having welcomed them from a distance, and having confessed that they were strangers and exiles on the Earth—and all these (including Abraham), having gained approval through their faith, did not receive what was promised, because God had provided something better for us, so that apart from us they would not be made perfect.

Hebrews 11 explains that **the great men and women of faith have not yet been made perfect and given eternal life. They, along with the saints of God from every age,** *are currently sleeping in their graves* (Job 3:11-19; Psalms. 6:5; 115:17; Ecclesiastes. 9:5, 10; I Corinthians 15:20; Isaiah 57:1-2; Danial 12:2; Acts 2:29, 34; 13:36]. These people await the first resurrection, to take place when Jesus returns at the sounding of the seventh trumpet (Matthew 24:30-31; I Cor. 15:51-52; I Thessalonians 4:16; Revelation 11:15-18). Even with the most skillfully imagined eisegeses, there is no way to reconcile the Scriptures above with a literal understanding of Lazarus's story and the rich man.

So, what does the death of these two men represent?

The death of the Rich Man represents the Jews. Lazarus represents the Gentile nations. They are *symbolic* of this parable. *Their expiry depicts a fundamental change in the status and reposition of the two groups.* Look at the meaning of Lazarus being *"carried to Abraham's bosom."*

The symbolic meaning of being in one's bosom is to be in a closeness position, being highly regarded; the ancient practice of having guests at a feast *recline on their neighbor's chest* gives birth to this symbolism. The place of highest honor belonged to the one seated next to the host, recalling the example of John at the Last Supper (John 13:23). Paul explains the imagery:

Abraham "believed God, and it was accounted to him for righteousness." Therefore, know that only those who are of faith are sons of Abraham. And the Scripture, foreseeing that God would justify the Gentiles by faith, preached the gospel to Abraham beforehand, saying, "In you all the nations shall be blessed." Those who are of faith are blessed with believing Abraham. (Galatians 3:6-9).

This passage, along with the fourth and ninth chapters of Romans, shows that Gentile believers become "sons of Abraham" through faith in Jesus. Through this faith, Gentiles are no longer "strangers and foreigners, but fellow citizens with the saints and members of the household of God" (Ephesians 2:19). For centuries the Jews received the benefits of being "God's chosen people" by being Abraham's physical descendants. But Jesus' sacrifice gave this place of *blessings and honor* to the people *Lazarus represented.* Therefore, you find the meaning of being "carried to the bosom of Abraham."

In contrast to Lazarus, the rich man was *buried in Hades. Earlier in this chapter, we examined the Mythological Greek origin of Hades, but let's take a closer look.* Understanding of the original meaning of the Greek word hades is fundamental to understanding the parable. Regarding Hade's etymology:

According to The New International Dictionary of New Testament Theology [12] Hades: "comes from the Greek word 'idein,' the "appearance (what is seen), form, idea" (to see) with the negative prefix, 'a', meaning the *invisible*. In the LXX hades occurs more than 100 times, in the majority of instances to translate Hebrew, she'ol, the underworld which receives *all the dead*. It is the land of darkness." Hades *originally meant* **"unseen."** As mentioned earlier, the Concordant Literal Version (CLT) chose **"unseen"** *75 out of 76 times*, replacing the incorrectly translated word hell in other translations of the Bible. Later, hades evolved to refer to the hidden state of those *buried in the earth*. This parable symbolically points to when the house of Judah becomes "**unseen**" by God, out of view, out of favor. There would come a time when the Jews would no longer be God's favored nation. Hardened hearts rejected Jesus (John 1:11).

And being in torments in Hades, he lifted up his eyes and saw Abraham afar off, and Lazarus in his bosom. Luke 16:23

What did Jesus mean when he said the rich man was in "torment in Hades"? The key to the symbolism is the Greek noun "basanos" translated "torments" above. Friberg's Analytical Lexicon of the Greek New Testament explains that basanizo is a form of the noun basanos, and means "... *strictly, a touchstone for testing the genuineness of metals by rubbing against it...*"

Basanos' etymology found in Kittel's Theological Dictionary of the New Testament [13] helps to understand this verse: In non-biblical Greek correctly, [basanos] is *a commercial or government expression*; it takes on the meaning *to check calculations*, naturally developing out of an underlying sense of [basanos, basanizein]. In the spiritual context, its reason is figurative, closely related to the original meaning: *a means of testing.* As *often happens* over time, with numerous examples in modern culture, a word undergoes an evolution of definition; over time, the original fades into the background. [Basanos] evolved to symbolize "torture" or "the rack," mainly used with slaves. [Basanos] developed in its medieval use as "torment."

"Then he cried and said, 'Father Abraham, have mercy on me, and send Lazarus that he may dip the tip of his finger in water and cool my tongue; for I am tormented in this flame." Luke 16:24

It's essential to note: **the rich man identifies Abraham as his father,** just as the Pharisees did in John 8:39. The rich man (Judah) is undergoing reproof, testing, and punishment in "this flame" (singular, not "these flames"). It's readily apparent the flame is symbolic. *Touching a wet fingertip to anyone's tongue wouldn't do anything to quench the pain of real fire.* A form of the Greek verb odunao here is translated "torment" literally—meaning "grief," "pain," or "suffering." It principally conveys the sense of *mental anguish*, not physical pain. Only four times in the Scriptures do we find some forms of this word *and all of them in Luke's writings*. It appears in verses 24 and 25. The same word describes *anxious distress* that Mary and Joseph felt when they discovered their 12-year old Jesus missing on the return home from Jerusalem following the Passover feast. It also depicts the *sorrow* the elders of the Ephesian Church felt when Paul announced his farewell, telling them that they would never see him again.

The rich man suffers in "the flame" and cries out for comfort from Hades' *symbolic darkness*. Context is required to understand the flame's symbolism. Moses defines God's part of His covenant with Israel in Deuteronomy 11 and 28. He tells them that obeying the "Eternal," will make them *the most blessed nation on Earth*. Conversely, if they *disobey, they would be cursed and eventually destroyed*. Israel's history in the Tanakh reveals that they *rarely* obeyed God. The "Eternal" was patient, and when they repented, forgave them. But He eventually cursed Israel as He had vowed to do, beginning with the house of Israel. The ten tribes composing the northern kingdom with Samaria as their capital was carried into captivity by Assyria (c. 722 B.C.). Hosea prophesied at the end of the northern kingdom: "My people are destroyed for lack of knowledge. Because you have rejected knowledge, I also will reject you from being priest for Me; because you have forgotten the law of your God, I also will forget your children." Hosea 4:6. About 135 years later, Babylon conquered and subdued Judah's southern kingdom (c. 587 B.C.). As promised, God delivered Israel to their enemies. They got another chance. The Jews were permitted to return to Judea after the Persians defeated the Babylonians (c. 538 B.C.), eventually rebuilding the Temple. Many sought to again obey God's laws upon their return to the land. But by the time Jesus appears on the timeline, unbelief once again becomes a significant problem. The religious teachers substituted the laws God had given Israel and returned to their traditions. (Matthew 15:1-9; Mark 7:1-13). They didn't believe the scriptures they professed to follow (John 5:39, 45-47). In the end, they altogether rejected Jesus and conspired with the Romans to crucify him.

When anyone looks at the history of the Jewish people from the time of Jesus until today, one theme remains constant—*persecution*. That is what "the flame" in this parable represents.

Rome suppressed the Jewish revolts (66-70 A.D. and 132-135 A.D.) The saga in the Diaspora has been persistent with harsh persecution from all directions. The Inquisition of the 15th century and the Holocaust of the 20th century are two of the more well-known anti-Semitic episodes through the bloody pages of history record many more. Their unbelief and "rejecting truth and knowledge," God cursed the Jews with the "flame" of suffering and grief down through the centuries. Unfortunately, most of that mistreatment comes from the hands of those who called themselves "Jesusians."

Quantum
Brook

The rich man represents the Jews in this parable, in their condition of wealth, political power, and unbelief, which ultimately manifests in rejecting Jesus. The parable shows that the punishment and testing they would undergo would not immediately lead them to Christ. Instead of calling on Jesus, *the rich man calls on his ancestor Abraham* **to help ease his suffering.** But Abraham said,

"Son, remember that in your lifetime you received your good things, and likewise Lazarus evil things; but now he is comforted, and you are tormented." Luke 16:25

An important note: *Abraham clearly—identifies the rich man as his descendant by calling him "son."* He tells him that things have changed. When the Jews were God's chosen people, they enjoyed the spiritual blessings associated with that status. But Abraham says to the rich man grieving in sorrow, "tormented," Lazarus now enjoys those blessings ("Tormented" here is yet another form of "odunao," the same Greek verb found in verse 24.) And besides all this, between us and you there is a great gulf fixed so that those who want to pass from here to you cannot, nor can those from there pass to us. (Luke 16:26)

In the eleventh chapter of Romans, Paul explains the "great gulf" Abraham references, is God's *blinding the Jews to the truth about Jesus.* He explains that "God has given them a spirit of stupor, eyes that they should not see and ears that they should not hear, to this very day" (Romans 11:8). Paul goes on to say that "a partial hardening would happen to Israel until the fullness of the Gentiles had come in" (Romans 11:25). In II Corinthians 3:14-15, Paul tells us the Israelites' "minds were blinded. For until this day, the same veil remains unlifted in the reading of the Old Testament, because the veil is taken away in Jesus. But even to this day, when Moses is read, a veil lies on their heart." It's not that the Jewish nation won't acknowledge Jesus; *they cannot recognize his true identity* because of God's actions! Then he said,

"I beg you therefore, father, that you would send him to my father's house, for I have five brothers, that he may testify to them, lest they also come to this place of torment." Luke 16:27-28

Yielding to his destiny, the rich man asks one more thing of father Abraham. He pleads with him to send someone to warn his brothers, so that they may escape "this place of torment" (basanou), the testing and punishment he is undergoing. The fact that the rich man has five brothers is a fundamental clue to his symbolic identity. Judah, the Jews' ancestor, was the son of Jacob through

Leah [Genesis 29:35]. He *had five full-blooded brothers*: **Reuben, Simeon, Levi, Issachar, and Zebulun** [Genesis 35:23]. The significance *seems* pointless and one often overlooked. However, you can be confident that it *didn't escape the notice of the Pharisees and scribes* to whom Jesus was speaking. They knew their history very well and incredibly proud of their heritage. **Jesus wanted those self-righteous Pharisees to know—precisely who He was referring to with this parable.** This one detail *solidifies the identity* of the rich man as *the house of Judah—the Jews.*

"Abraham said to him, They have Moses and the prophets; let them hear them." Luke 16:29

Abraham again refuses the rich man's request, telling him that the brothers already have a witness in Moses' writings and the prophets that will allow them to escape his fate. Moses, as well as the prophets, are shown several times in the New Testament, to support Jesus's identity (Luke 24:27, 44; John 1:45; 5:46; Acts 3:22-24; 7:37; 26:22-23; 28:23). Abraham tells the rich man that his brothers would have to recognize the prophesied Jesus because of the things written about him in the Tanakh. Echoing what Jesus told the Jews.

"Do not think that I shall accuse you to the Father; there is one who accuses you —- Moses, in whom you trust. For if you believed Moses, you would believe Me; for he wrote about Me. But if you do not believe his writings, how will you believe My words?" (John 5:45-47). The Jewish leaders of Jesus's day generally failed to recognize the very one Moses wrote about (Deuteronomy. 18:15, 18). And he said,

"No, father Abraham; but if one goes to them from the dead, they will repent.' But he said to him, 'If they do not hear Moses and the prophets, neither will they be persuaded though one rise from the dead." Luke 16:30-31

Jesus prophesizes his resurrection from the dead in the last two verses of the parable. The rich man explains that his brothers will not accept scriptures evidence of who Jesus is but—they will accept the testimony of his resurrection. But Abraham tells him that anyone who rejects God's word about Jesus will also refuse to acknowledge the resurrection. *Jesus ends this parable abruptly, with no real resolution.*

Paul's soliloquy in Romans 11:1 asks if God has cast away, Israel. He answers his question saying, "by no means!" God did not throw away the people He foreknew. Paul compares the remnant of Israel to the seven thousand reserved to God in Elijah's time that God has elected by grace (I Kings 19:18). God hardened the remainder to include the Gentiles in salvation through grace. Verse 26 offers the resolution.

"For I do not desire, brethren, that you should be ignorant of this mystery, lest you should be wise in your own opinion, that blindness in part has happened to Israel until the fullness of the Gentiles has come in. And so, all Israel will be saved, as it is written: The Deliverer will come out of Zion, and He will turn away ungodliness from Jacob; for this is My covenant with them, when I take away their sins. Concerning the gospel, they are enemies for your sake, but concerning the election they are beloved for the sake of the fathers. For the gifts and the calling of God are irrevocable." (Romans 11:25-33) For God has committed them all to disobedience, that He might have mercy on all.

Conclusion

Mainstream, evangelical Fundamentalism has *long used* the parable of Lazarus and the rich man to teach the "reality of hell," which ironically— has nothing at all to say *about punishment or reward* in the afterlife. Jesus told the story in a way that fit the common misconception about the afterlife in his day. He used the misunderstanding to prophesy the fate awaiting the Jewish nation, which culminated in rejecting him as the Messiah. That was his message, *and his only message* in the parable.

The following are *spine-chilling* quotes from early philosophers and Church Fathers, proving where the brutal concept of a "Hell of everlasting punishment" originates. These *alarming quotes* expose distressingly sanctimonious, narcissistic egos through their own brazenly poetic words:

Polybius, the ancient historian, says: *"Since the multitude is ever fickle, full of lawless desires, irrational passions and violence, there is no other way to keep them in order but by the fear and terror of the invisible world; on which account our ancestors seem to me to have acted judiciously, when they contrived to bring into the popular belief these notions of the gods, and of the infernal regions." B. vi 56.*

Strabo, the geographer, says: *"The multitude are restrained from vice by the punishments the gods are said to inflict upon offenders, and by those terrors and threatenings which certain dreadful words and monstrous forms imprint upon their minds...For it is impossible to govern the crowd of women, and all the common rabble, by philosophical reasoning, and lead them to piety, holiness and virtue - but this must be done by superstition, or the fear of the gods, by means of fables and wonders; for the thunder, the aegis, the trident, the torches (of the Furies), the dragons, etc., are all fables, as is also all the ancient theology. These things the legislators used as scarecrows to terrify the childish multitude."* Geog., B. I

Tertullian (Considered by many to be the father of modern church doctrine) *"At that greatest of all spectacles, that last and eternal judgment how shall I admire, how laugh, how rejoice, how exult, when I behold so many proud monarchs groaning in the lowest abyss of darkness..."*

Gerhard *"The Blessed will see their friends and relations among the damned as often as they like but without the least of compassion."*

John Calvin (Who had some of his theological enemies burned to death in green slow-burning wood) *"Forever harassed with a dreadful tempest, they shall feel themselves torn asunder by an angry God, and transfixed and penetrated by mortal stings, terrified by the thunderbolts of God, and broken by the weight of his hand, so that to sink into any gulf would be more tolerable than to stand for a moment in these terrors".*

Charles Spurgeon (Commonly called the "Prince of Preachers" a preacher of great eloquence) *"I further believe, although certain persons deny it, that the influence of fear is to be exercised over the minds of men and that it ought to operate upon the mind of the preacher himself."* The Soul Winner Pg. 111

Saint Thomas Aquinas *"That the saints may enjoy their beatitude more thoroughly, and give more abundant thanks for it to God, a perfect sight of the punishment of the damned is granted them."* Absolute Recoil Pg.218

Jeremy Taylor *"Husbands shall see their wives, parents shall see their children tormented before their eyes...the bodies of the damned shall be crowded together in hell like grapes in a wine-press, which press on another till they burst..."*pg. 514 A Critical History of the Doctrine of a Future Life

Richard Baxter *"It is not a terrible thing to a wretched soul, when it shall lie roaring perpetually in the flames of hell, and the God of mercy himself shall laugh at them; when…God shall mock them instead of relieving them; when none in heaven or earth can help them but God, and he **shall rejoice** over them in their calamity ."* (The Saint's Everlasting Rest" 1846)

"Reverend" E.B. Pusey, D.D. *"Gather in one, in your mind, an assembly of all those men and women, from whom, whether in history or in fiction, your memory most shrinks, gather in mind all that is loathsome, most revolting * * * conceive the fierce, fiery eyes of hate, spite, frenzied rage, ever fixed on thee, looking thee through and through with hate * * * hear those yells of blaspheming concentrated hate, as they echo along the lurid vault of hell; everyone hating everyone * * * Yet a fixedness in that state in which the hardened malignant sinner dies, involves, without any further retribution of God, this endless misery."* (Quoted from Christ Triumphant by Thomas Allin)

*"What will it be like for a mother in heaven who sees her son burning in hell? **She will glorify the justice of God.** "* —Pamphlet from the late 1960s, part of a catechismal teaching [cited in an essay by the English poet, **Stevie Smith,** "Some Impediments to Christian Commitment"

"THOSE WHO CAN MAKE YOU BELIEVE ABSURDITIES CAN MAKE YOU COMMIT ATROCITIES." VOLTAIRE

Chapter 8

A Universal Loss

The trick to missing the big picture entirely—- is to always be looking at everything—- up close.

This chapter will be the only place I devote to "doctrine." As I've made clear in previous chapters, I firmly believe that hundreds of years of arguments over scripture's jot and tittle have done more to harm the advance than any "weapon" outside the faith. Christianity's wounds are self-inflicted. Using the Bible to settle doctrinal disputes is like asking people who speak thousands of languages to decide on—a single tongue. Each will argue their language is the one everyone must choose. None are willing to relinquish the system around which they have built their economy. The only thing I know of that may be more subjective than agreeing on scripture is getting agreement on how good—or bad, is a piece of modern art. It is highly subjective. The evidence suggests that *there will never be a consensus.* So far, how well has the millennia-long fray served Christendom? It is not the solution. It is—the problem.

As I've stated previously, it doesn't escape me, that in unavoidable ways, I will here be doing what I most detest. I will be *judging the judgmental for which admittedly, I have great contempt.* To clarify, it's not judging an individual or a specific group. I am sympathetic to the plight and the blessing of being human. You will observe the disrespect I direct at petty indoctrination and groupthink at those who long ago abandoned the *big picture.* I invite my readers, to the extent possible, to consider rethinking. Like one of my 1970s era motivational heroes, Zig Ziglar once said: *"From time to time we all need a little check-up from the neck up."*

Quantum
Brook

Most of Christianity accepts that Jesus' mission on the earth was singular and simple: He came "not to judge the world but to save it," not just part of it—but all of it! (John 12:47) Church history is replete with those who've had the faith and courage to make the bold declarations of Christ's purpose and triumph seriously and—literally. Yet, over the past few hundred years, this inclusive perspective, has been increasingly scorned and ridiculed, why? It's *straightforward*. It puts the power back into—God's hands and removes it from the doctrine manipulators who all *have much on the line professionally*. In modern theological circles, many (probably most) label a belief in universal salvation as heretical, *ignorantly* alleging that it is was imported into Christianity from pagan philosophies. Ironically, *the exact opposite is in evidence as the truth.* So—in light of the apparent limitations of working with error-ridden manuscripts (Chapter 6,) Evangelical Fundamentalism has no other way to characterize *their choice* to ignore the corroborating abundance of unambiguous, impossible to twist or reinterpret, plainly stated scriptures regarding Jesus' purpose, and his declaration of that purpose.

What does the word ignore, and ignorance have in common? But, to be fair to the unaware: When you are pre-convinced to view church history—and particular scripture through a specific lens, you see only—that which denomination's colored glasses permit you to see. If the lens creates distortion, then what you see is also colored, and its appearance misrepresented. When you read, as in the story of David and Goliath, it reads as taught. Doctrinal filters warp perspective and color meaning. Week after week, month after month, and year after year, its interpretation is laid down and reinforced until it becomes difficult, if not impossible, to read it any other way. For example, why do most denominations today, who are ignorant of the thousands of errors we learned about in Chapter 6 *Quoting Misquotes,* prefer to ignore *the hundreds of Scriptures*, which declare and redeclare that when Jesus completes His work on Earth, He will "reconcile *all things* unto Himself? So, when did all things, whether they are in Heaven or on Earth (Col. 1:20) fail to include *all things*? Ironically, many of these same people also profess *supernatural faith for health, wealth, and—their salvation*—yet they cry heretic at those who believe in the singular and primary proposition of the entire Biblical message!

What Christian, regardless of the denomination, would embrace this Levitical commandment to advance a pet doctrine?

"No man who has any defect may come near: no man who is blind or lame, disfigured or deformed; no man with a crippled foot or hand, or who is a

hunchback or a dwarf, or who has any eye defect, or who has festering or running sores or damaged testicles. No descendant of Aaron, the priest who has any defect is to come near to present the offerings to the Lord. He has a defect; he must not come near to offer the food of his God." (Leviticus 21:18-21)

There are no words for the sound of—clearing my throat. Yet, to ancient Israel, *this was "scripture"* and for them, and as commonplace as breathing. Now, indeed most Christians with even basic knowledge of the Bible know this commandment was Old Testament, Levitical Law. Most Christian will agree that Jesus fulfilled the law, and the Levitical law is no longer applicable. But what is also relevant in this day and age, is **applying common sense that has sadly become so rare, even coming from civilized human beings,** regardless of religious belief. Why is enlightened, common sense used for some things—and not to others? Who among my readers would today voice support for such a shocking commandment? In retrospect, is it conceivable *that such an uncivilized thought ever existed at all?*

How many contemporary Christian ideologues advocate their interpretation of the scripture *as perfection*? How many of those same people argue the deformity, of other versions of the faith and the deformity, the falsity of different beliefs outside their faith as if Leviticus 21:18-21 was describing them? Aren't they judging themselves as being whole, complete, worthy, informed, quite extraordinary, unique, and deserving before God—while painting those who are not of their faith as spiritually crippled, deformed and defective? If I had a dollar for every time I've heard "false doctrine" and "false religion," I would be set for life.

Selah

The hypocrisy carousel keeps going "round and round."

Do even the most secular parents decide to love one child and destroy the other? If the choice is killing the child, could mercy, (at the very least), step in and—allow it to be over—quickly vs. the so-called, predestined *eternal torment?* The answer is clear and self-evident to even *the most fallen human mind* yet, the more religious the discourse, the less evident the obvious becomes. Christianity's *cornerstone doctrine* is that Jesus' ultimate purpose was to become the sacrifice for sin. In light of the preceding chapters, why does virtually every denomination,

Quantum
Brook

champion their doctrine, their version of **The Gift**, rather than **shout an Inclusive declaration from the mountaintop**, should one exist.
It does.

     Exclusive, by definition, **excludes** anyone who does not agree to agree. Does **exclusivity**, by any reasonable explanation or measure, demonstrate unconditional Love? If so, how? If God IS Love, as "He" is rumored to be (although in specific context and with numerous caveats), can *Love Rise Up* and cut through the obnoxious noise in the religious marketplace? The majority of the "Good News" seems to be that God's "Love" will destroy the vast majority of his creation, all of those born in the wrong place at the wrong time, to the wrong parents, into the wrong tradition. Can this possibly build confidence, demonstrate Love to any—*thinking*—person and advance the gospel message?

How?

     Did Christian Fundamentalists *first* learn to ride the metaphorical "backward bike" [Chapter 2], *breaking their mind* and now find themselves unable to ride a—regular bike? Have we considered how backward our "normal" view may be to even the most basic civility? How have we so readily accepted the idea that God said: "*dash their little ones to pieces and rip open their pregnant women,*"; and "*The little child is in the red-hot oven. Hear how it screams to come out; see how it turns and twists itself about in the fire...*"

     Since the time of the Protestant Reformation, thousands of written arrangements, rearrangements, mistranslations, and retranslations have emerged, arguing scripture with scripture. These arguments—create, procreate, recreate and dominate, *dogmatic doctrine* that gives birth to yet more variations which then competes with the parent and sibling doctrines.

     For something (which claims to be) so spiritual, purpose-driven, and purposely immaterial, it has emerged as one of the most divisive and exhausting topics in human history. [1] What drives the territorial protectionism? What happens to a person when the lens so colors what they see that it reshapes everything entering the eyes, the ears, and exiting the mouth? There is once again, neither time nor space to adequately cover this one topic—alone. This one example demonstrates—that which somehow takes over and malforms the mind's ability to—*Think.*

I know of no better case to illustrate the point than the very words of one of Christendom's most well-known protestant reformers, better known for his Predestination doctrine. John Calvin:

"Forever harassed with a dreadful tempest, they shall feel themselves torn asunder by an angry God, and transfixed and penetrated by mortal stings, terrified by the thunderbolts of God, and broken by the weight of his hand, so that to sink into any gulf would be more tolerable than to stand for a moment in these terrors. "I am persuaded that it is not without the special will of God that, apart from any verdict of the judges, the criminals have endured protracted torment at the hands of the executioner." [2] Read carefully and follow closely:

John Calvin had his doctrinal competitor, Spanish physician Michael Servetus, burned-at-the-stake just outside of Geneva on October 27, 1553, for his *competing* doctrine. [3] Calvin contemplated this event long before Servetus' capture, *clearly* a case of *premeditated manslaughter of a fellow believer*- just— not one who believed in Calvin's brand of The Gift. *How messed up is that?*

February 13, 1546, seven years before Servetus' arrest, Calvin wrote his friend, Farel, saying: "If he [Servetus] comes [to Geneva], I shall never let him go out alive if my authority has weight."[4a] Evidence suggests that Calvin's authority [in Geneva, Switzerland] had ultimate "weight," causing some to begin to refer to Geneva as the "Rome of Protestantism" [4b] and to Calvin as the "Protestant 'Pope' of Geneva."[5] During Servetus' trial, Calvin writes:" <u>I hope that the verdict will call for the death penalty.</u>" [6][7] It did. Servetus was burned at-the-stake.

How about a reasonable and compassionate "solution" to the *impossible rationalization* that GOD will send babies, children, and 75% of earth's population to hell just because they happened to be born somewhere that Christianity is not the dominant faith; born human! What if the scriptures say Jesus accomplished what He came to do; to save the world, all the world, all of Humankind? *Why wouldn't every* **believer** *on earth be eager to share and cheerlead that version of the "Good News" with everyone? Why?*

A fundamentalist icon's change of heart

In his elder days, having wrestled lifelong with his fundamentalist programming, the world's most famous evangelist, the Rev. Billy Graham said this in an interview with Dr. Robert Shuller: [8]

Schuller: Tell me, what do you think is the future of Christianity?

Billy Graham: Well, Christianity and being a true believer—you know, I think there's the Body of Christ. This comes from all the Christian groups around the world, outside the Christian groups. I think everybody that loves Christ, or knows Christ, whether they're conscious of it or not, they're members of the Body of Christ. And *I don't* think that we're going to see a great sweeping revival, that will turn the whole world to Christ at any time. I think James answered that, the Apostle James in the first council in Jerusalem, when he said that God's purpose for this age is to call out a people for His name. And that's what God is doing today, He's calling people out of the world for His name, *whether they come from the Muslim world, or the Buddhist world, or the Christian world or the non-believing world, they are members of the Body of Christ because they've been called by God. They may not even know the name of Jesus but they know in their hearts that they need something that they don't have, and they turn to the only light that they have, and I think that they are saved, and that they're going to be with us in heaven.*

Schuller: What, what I hear you saying that it's possible for Jesus Christ to come into human hearts and soul and life, even if they've been born in darkness and have never had exposure to the Bible. Is that a correct interpretation of what you're saying?

Graham: Yes, it is, because I believe that. I've met people in various parts of the world in tribal situations, that they have never seen a Bible or heard about a Bible, and never heard of Jesus, but they've believed in their hearts that there was a God, and they've tried to live a life that was quite apart from the surrounding community in which they lived.

Schuller: [R. S. trips over his tongue for a moment, his face beaming, then says] "I'm so thrilled to hear you say this. There's a wideness in God's mercy."

Graham: There is. There definitely is.

"The unifying theme of Graham's new thinking is humility."

It's interesting to hear evangelical Fundamentalism's foremost leader emerge from the marinade and endorse a doctrine called "inclusivism," which teaches that people can come to saving faith through general revelation. That means one does not have to hear of Christ nor of the Bible to be "saved." Yet, many denominations consider this view to be heresy. ***For God's sake—Why?***

The prophets, Jesus and the apostles, ratify one single fact which is central to the Gospel. Yet an endless parade of self-serving, religious "authorities" has seemingly done everything possible to divert attention into the divisive theological weeds rather than marvel at the breathtaking vista of *this single unifying doctrine.* Jesus "… came not to judge the world but to save it," not just a part of it, but *all* of it! (John 12:47) Church history is replete with those who once had the faith to make bold declarations of Christ's triumph seriously *and-literally.* Yet, over the past several hundred years, this doctrine has been ridiculed when the fact is, it **is more outrageous** *not to believe* in the numerous scriptures which make this case. But that is what programming does. It robs you of the ability to see what is right there in front of you. The indoctrinated choose instead to embrace the Old Testament God which, we examined in previous chapters—more thoroughly than most will ever dare to do.

Modern Christians, drowning in doctrine, prefer conditional love over unconditional love. They prefer a God who loves those he has *chosen and predestined.* Likewise, they prefer his hatred for those he did not want, or rather, *the ones he **predestined** to be **unchosen**.* They prefer to ignore hundreds of Scriptures *(not just a few that skew)* but the many which clearly states that Jesus finished His work on earth. The many that say that He will "reconcile all things unto Himself where all things in the original languages mean—*ALL things whether they are in heaven or on earth.*" (Colossians 1:20) Ironically, numerous evangelical fundamentalist Christians who profess to have such great faith for virtually everything else, criticize those who believe in the *overarching, primary promises*, which is ***The Whole Point*** of the Biblical message. It is the Central Message. It is the reason. *"This is a faithful saying and worthy of **all** acceptance. To this end, we both labor and suffer reproach, because we trust in the living God, who is the **Savior of all men** especially those who believe. These things command and teach."* (1 Timothy 4:9-11)

That—is Carlton Pearson's *"Doctrine of Inclusion,"* THAT message is what caused Carlton to lose it all. It is plain. It is simple. It is straight forward. It is *not complicated.* Is that the problem? Is it too simple to gain enough support to build a career and pay the bills? It's NOT exclusive to a few but Inclusive of all.

Quantum Brook

The Doctrine states that Christ is indeed and in fact, the Savior of the whole world and "especially" ones, that is, the church. (John 4:42; 1 John 4:14)

If——there is a Gospel—this is the Gospel. If there is a Biblical message, *this is it.* It's the only Gospel that can give real hope *to all* because it knows—no limit. The *traditional—and now numerous, competing* Christian doctrines are NOT good news for anyone—but them. These Doctrines fail most of humankind, leaving those in condemnations' profound hopelessness. In 1 Timothy, Chapter 2, Paul encourages: *"pray for all men."* *If we pray in faith according to God's will, will we not receive that for which we ask?* (Mark 11:24) According to the "little faithers," Jesus will instead save *the few* for which He died, *maybe,* one or two out of ten. Why do most in the Church not **want to believe these and a whole lot—of other supportive scriptures?** It is not as if they are cryptic. It is not as if they are a "strange saying" and hard to understand. But I find it particularly interesting that the apostle Paul warned that the vast majority of the Church would fall away from this one central truth, the whole point of the entire New Testament message! He warned there would be those in the Church who would draw disciples after themselves. And yes: Even while reading Paul's warnings *not* to divide.

As we have covered repeatedly, there are tens of thousands of denominations "dividing the body of Christ." We prove that most Christians "honor Christ with their lips, but their hearts are far from Him." (Isaiah 29:13; Matthew15:8.) *Numerous scriptures* support the teachings that all humankind will be restored to God. [9] This "falling away" has not been confined to the last 150 years, but for millennia.

By the turn of 5th century AD, the Church had all but abandoned the Scriptures. Saint Jerome, which some consider the second most voluminous writer after Augustine of Hippo, translated the Scriptures into Latin, *introducing numerous errors to the thousands that already existed from the manuscript copyist and scribes* (The "lying pen of the scribes" Jerimiah 8:8, NIV). In later years, adherents were prohibited from reading Scripture in any language, including Latin. During this period, the Church integrated thousands of pagan doctrines, rituals, and traditions, which Jesus said, "made the word of God of no effect." (Matt. 15:6-9) The Protestant Church would later discard many of these traditions, yet even today, much of the Dark Age baggage remains. Too many of these distortions made their way into English translations adding Dark Age theology to our modern versions of the Bible. Mythological creatures like satyrs and unicorns appear in translations like the KJV. There is no archeologic evidence that suggests these creatures ever existed. However, the 17th century England King James translators believed in them. They were a few of the many things, including "hell" not found in original Hebrew or Greek text, something we explore in-depth in the previous chapter, "A Hell of an Idea."

An honest look at history shows that most of the early Church believed all would "be saved." Volume 12, page 96 of *The Encyclopedia of Religious Knowledge by Schaff-Herzog* says, "In the first five or six centuries of Christianity there were **six theological schools, of which four** (Alexandria, Antioch, Caesarea, and Edessa, or Nisibis) were **Universalist;** and one (Ephesus) accepted conditional mortality; one (Carthage or Rome) taught endless punishment of the wicked." [10]

It's important to understand that early Christians and the church leaders taught—universal salvation. St. Basil the Great writes in the fourth century: "The mass of men (Christians) say that there is to be an end of punishment to those who are punished." In the same period, St. Jerome writes: "I know that most persons understand by the story of Nineveh and its king, the ultimate forgiveness of the devil and all rational creatures." St. Augustine (who taught eternal torment), wrote, "There are very many (imo quam plurimi, *translated "majority"*) who though not denying the Holy Scriptures, *do not believe in endless torments."* (Enchira, ad Laurent)

Rome is the seat of the Roman Catholic Church, where the doctrine of eternal torment served them well. [11] Priests selling Indulgences for the forgiveness of sin during the Middle Ages and early Italian Renaissance, *leveraging fear, ignorance, and misunderstanding* lead to the abuse of indulgences and bringing them to the forefront in Martin Luther's Ninety-five Theses, the disputation on the Power and Efficacy of Indulgences (a.k.a. Luther's Ninety-five Theses) and the subsequent Reformation. [12] There is considerable upside. Indulgences, in part, funded the 100-year construction of St. Peters Basilica in Rome. (Personal Note [13]) So, for what possible reason would the later Church adopt an emphasis on a tyrannical God of eternal damnation? A most crucial point in church history was Emperor Constantine militarizing and politicalizing the Church. Teaching the fear of Hell was a far more powerful of control than the previous traditions that taught a God who loved all humankind, which, through severe persecution, began stamping out the teaching of universal salvation. The result? The Church created what we now know as "The Dark Ages." Before the Dark Ages, the Church taught God's Love for all humanity.

Quantum
Brook

The second major church council met in Constantinople in AD381, where hundreds of bishops from the entire Church elected Gregory of Nazianzus, an avowed Universalist, as president. What better proof that the immense majority of the church leaders believed in universal salvation at the end of the fourth century? Clearly—the early Church was far better versed in Scripture's original languages and certainly much closer to the apostles' original teachings. So again. Why is universal salvation considered heresy in most denominations? Could it be the more straightforward the message, the less maintenance required, and the less profitable?

Amid the divine madness, let's permit the voice of reason to speak if but only on rare occasions. Who is more likely to have, at least something closer to the truth? The early Church or the tens of *thousands of divisions* serving individual interest, each building astonishingly profitable fiefdoms today? "Drawing disciples after themselves" (Acts 20:30) *What is a plausible argument?* One which, at least, holds water? There are none. But when taught to believe, after a while, it's easier to stop thinking and let someone else think for us— regardless of facts.

Well-known, great men and women embraced the "larger hope" some which became known as the teaching of the salvation of all humankind. Perhaps Abraham Lincoln's belief in *the salvation of all humanity* was the primary influence on his ending slavery. A signer of the Declaration of Independence, Benjamin Rush, also believed it. Many famous theologians like Karl Barth, B.F. Westcott, and William Barclay, among others, also embraced it. *Those embracing Universalism today are usually more versed in church history and the Bible's original languages than the average Christian.* They believe Jesus is the way, the truth, and the life and are very Scripture-centered. But when it is about God's Love, not the heavy hand of judgment, it is not *as "effective"* as preaching eternal damnation, which subconsciously promotes the teacher-preacher and— demotes the parishioner.

Universalists have greater faith in God's Love, mercy, and power to ultimately save humanity than God's permanent disposal of most of humankind. Jesus promising to save the world is (ironically) the source of great persecution at the hands of doctrinal siblings. Some believe that Love *never* fails—some believe it WILL fail most of humankind. (1 Corinthians 13:8) Some believe nothing is impossible with God, while most believe that man's will is stronger than God's will to save the world. (Luke 1:37) Some have great faith in God's promises that *all the families and nations on earth will be blessed* and—some don't.

(Genesis 12:3; 12:18) Why would everyone not jump at the chance to believe Jesus when He said, "And if I am lifted up from the earth, will draw *(drag in the Greek)* all mankind unto Myself." (John 12:32) Some Christians beam with delight when they read Scriptures like: "And being found in appearance as a man, he humbled himself and became obedient to death—even death on a cross! They smile when they read: "Therefore God exalted him to the highest place and gave him the name that is above every name, that at the name of Jesus every knee should bow, in heaven and on earth and under the earth, and every tongue confess that Jesus Christ is Lord, to the glory of God the Father." (Philippians 2:8-11)

The Center for the Study of Global Christianity at Gordon-Conwell Theological Seminary estimated 34,000 denominations in 2000, rising to an estimated 43,000 in 2012. There was only 1,600 in the year 1900. Some argue that these estimates exaggerate; that it represents many of the same denominations in other countries. Okay, for argument, let's say that is true. Pick a number. If it is more than one, it is still divided! We only have two, maybe three political parties in American politics, yet can the USA possibly be more divided and around things we can touch, feel, verify, and in which we live our lives every day. Yet the Church divides around *what they think is informed and most surely are vastly uninformed views of the 2000-year-old manuscripts* which have produced numerous error-ridden translations. Yet, as it is in politics, it is more profitable to divide ideologies into their (not so) neat little silos and dilute the original message. The Church ignored Paul's warnings not to divide yet- we did it anyway, proving that most Christians prefer to "honor Christ with their lips, but their hearts are far from Him." (Isaiah.29:13; Matthew 15:8)

Numerous scriptures support the teachings that all humankind will be restored to God. [Genesis. 12:3; 1 Timothy. 2:4-6; 4:9-11; John 4:42; 12:32; 12:47; 1 John 4:14; Romans 5:18; Romans 11:32; Colossians 1:16-20; 1 Corinthians 15:22; Philippians 2:9-11; Acts 3:20, 21; Revelations 5:13; Ad infinitum; footnote and index]. [14]

Chapter 9

The End of the World—Again.

Conditional salvation, the devil, "end times; the rapture," and eternal torment were the four pillars of the "Good News" when I was growing up. The great tribulation was one leg of the fear motif, and hell was the other— and the ultimate consequence for missing the rapture. All of this was, and still is, known as literalist, "dispensational eschatology."[1]

I have *surprisingly* vivid memories, somewhere around the age of five, of a visiting evangelist displaying an oversized chart. The banner must have been four feet by fifteen feet, but, at that age, judging scale is challenging. Everything is large to a five-year-old. It contained a timeline with Genesis on the left and Revelation on the right. The preacher talked of the rapture and the battle of Armageddon. His eisegesis [2] *and exegetics*) [3] tied Gog and Magog to Russia. Modern Russia now occupies the land formerly known as Magog.[4] *Eisegesis is a systemic problem within Fundamentalism's Christendom.* As a grade school-age child, I reasoned that if Ezekiel (or any other prophet) prophesies something *as important as the end of the world—thousands of years in the future, shouldn't they know and prophesy the new names?* Wouldn't that one thing alone remove all doubt? Humm. If they can see into the future, then why do they not—know the future's new names? With something *so vitally important*, remove the ambiguity, eliminate the confusion, remove the guesswork. Then—there would be *much* less to debate, less foggy *revisions* to fill the steady stream of *revised* books to sell that tell us about the *revised* predictions.

If Gog is the leader of Russia and Magog is Russia's land, why not just say—Putin and Russia? When I was of the age to ask that question, it was not Vladimir Putin and Russia, it was Nikita Khrushchev and Russia. When prophets name names, it leaves zero wiggle room and "lots of explaining to do." Russia *(as a part of the former Soviet Union)* was a *much* bigger deal in the 50s than it is today. Today's tweaks always have and always will involve the hotspots. Russia, Iran, North Korea, and China.

Dispensationalism began in earnest in the 1830s with Classic Dispensationalism and evolved through Ultra, Classic Pauline, Mid-Acts, Revised, Progressive, and the Hyper Dispensationalism of the 1980s. [Exhibit-Evolution of Dispensationalism] The eisegesis changes as quickly as the most current prediction fails to materialize—*the end of the world.* "Blood will flow out of the press up to the horses' bridles for about 180 miles" [5] (a mathematical impossibility of volume and containment, but that shouldn't matter.) My mind of a child wondered why they would use something so inefficient as horses in modern warfare. Still, horses also serve as rides for the four horsemen of the apocalypse [6] and myriad scary other things.

I am restating that my purpose is not to dive into the weeds and build a brand. Instead, it is to overview this crucial portion of Fundamentalism's product and provide a baseline for the reader who may be unfamiliar with the origins. Suffice it to say; this is yet another area of *many competing views of "the end."* At a summary level, here are different (and elaborate) eschatological renderings. There are various scenarios as to what will happen in "the last days" the "end-times" primarily divided into the camps known as Pre-Tribulation, Mid-Tribulation, Post-Tribulation, Pre-Millennialism, Millennialism, Post-Millennialism, or Amillennialism. The dispensational (Tribulations) schools of thought seek to time the rapture as happening before, in the middle or—at the end of the seven-year "great tribulation" where the Antichrist rules, (1 John and 2 John.) The Millennialist versions (at a high level) look for a literal second coming of Christ (without a rapture) and a thousand years of peace before the great judgment. You will typically find Millennial views in Catholic and traditional, mainline protestant camps. Evangelical Fundamentalists are, *by in large*, dispensational in their "end times views."[7]

Dispensationalism emphasizes the threading of various passages in 2 Daniel, Ezekiel, Matthew, and Revelation. The different tribulation camps package the most fear and regularly compare the "end-times" or apocalyptic prophecies in the Bible with *current events* in an ongoing attempt to timeline "the rapture of believers" before, during or after the great tribulation, or—the Second Coming of Christ to establish Jesus' thousand-year (i.e., millennial) Kingdom on Earth.

When I was a child, the threat of nuclear war from the former Soviet Union was real. We had fallout shelters and air raid sirens signaling drills where we practiced

Quantum
Brook

crawling under our desk in case of an attack. They were all just "window dressing." It was an exercise of complete futility if a nuclear bomb was incoming. Furthermore, the tumultuous 1960s and early 1970s *were every bit as turbulent* as events current to this writing. The US population was then *half of what it is* today, and only three networks were covering the news. In those days, social media was sharing some news or a magazine with a friend, and email wouldn't arrive for a half-century. Civil Rights era marches, Vietnam riots, and antiwar protests were regular fixtures on the evening news. The high school I attended too often found its way onto the local news for knife fights and an occasional gun brought to school. Of course, there was the inevitable war with the Iron Curtain's Soviet Union, all of which provided fertile ground for an idealistic rapturous escape.

Jesus was **an apoplectic preacher**, and (authors word,) Rapturest often cites Jesus' extensive apocalyptic language in the book of Matthew, when building a case for the end of the world. In Matthew 24:34, Jesus said: *"Truly I tell you; this generation will certainly not pass away until all these things have happened."* Since the rapture (as Fundamentalism packages it) didn't happen within the 40-year biblical generation, they now suggest "generation" was referring to the nation of Israel. Verse 32 says, *"Now learn this lesson from the fig tree: As soon as its twigs get tender and its leaves come out, you know that summer is near."* Rapturest *exceptionally creative eisegesis* uses the fig tree as a reference to modern-day Israel's reestablishment in 1948. But it troubled many Fundamentalists when Jesus says in verse 36, *"But about that day or hour no one knows, not even the angels in heaven, nor the Son, but only the Father."* It takes yet another, very creative, interpretive dance to explain why Jesus, as God wouldn't know about an event of such great importance and the very one motivating all of his apocalyptic preachings. Yet, he also tells those listening in verse 28*, "Truly I tell you, some who are standing here will not taste death before they see the Son of Man coming in his kingdom."* Calling for yet another creative explanation since none of those listening to him that day are left standing 2000 years later.

In AD70, the Temple in Jerusalem and 1.1 million perished during *a total annihilation of Hebrew people.*[8] The Jewish historian Josephus attributes this high number lost due to Passover's celebration at the time of the attack. The 97,000 armed and elderly that survived the siege are later forced to become gladiators, and eventually, all remaining are slaughtered in the arena. Israel was annihilated. This time, the destruction *did not—Passover.*

Flavius Josephus converted to Christianity after witnessing, firsthand, Jesus' prophecies materialize about the destruction of Jerusalem and the complete annihilation of the Judahite Hebrews. He says: *"Now the number of those that were carried captive carried during the whole war was collected to be ninety-seven thousand; as was the number of those that perished during the whole siege, 1.1 Million, the greater part of whom were true of the same nation, [with the citizens of Jerusalem,] but not belonging to the city itself; for they were come up from all the country to the feast of unleavened bread, and were suddenly shut up by an army, which, at the very first, occasioned so great a straightness among them, that there came pestilential destruction upon them, and soon afterward such a famine as destroyed them more suddenly." "Caesar exhibited all sorts of shows in Cesarea Philippi. There, the captives were destroyed, many thrown to wild beasts, and others in multitudes forced to kill one another as if they were enemies." "Caesar gave orders that they should now demolish the entire city and temple, but should leave as many of the towers standing as were of the greatest eminency; that is, Phasaelus, and Hippicus, and Mariamne; and so much of the wall as enclosed the city on the west side. This wall was spared, in order to afford a camp for such as were to lie in garrison, as were the towers also spared, in order to demonstrate to posterity what kind of city it was, and how well fortified, which the Roman valor had subdued; but for all the rest of the wall, it was so thoroughly laid even with the ground by those that dug it up to the foundation, that there was left nothing to make those that came thither believe it has ever been inhabited."* [9] The Apocalypse completely wiped out the Hebrews, except for those who converted to Christianity and fled beforehand.

This—was *the desolation* in AD70 Jesus foretold. *"Jesus turned and said to them, 'Daughters of Jerusalem, do not weep for me; weep for yourselves and your children.'"* Luke 23:28, *"But he responded, 'Do you see all these buildings? I tell you the truth, they will be completely demolished. Not one stone will be left on top of another!'"* Matthew 24:2, *"But when you see Jerusalem surrounded by armies, then recognize that her desolation is near. Then those who are in Judea must flee to the mountains, and those who are in the midst of the city must leave, and those who are in the country must not enter the city."* Luke 21: 20,21, *"Truly I tell you this generation will certainly not pass away until all these things have happened."* Matthew 24:34, *"They will be killed by the sword when all of them are made captives by the Gentiles. And Jerusalem will be trampled down by the Gentiles until the period of the Gentiles is fulfilled."* Luke 21:24, *"And their dead bodies will lie in the street of the great city which mystically is called Sodom and Egypt, where also their Lord was crucified."* Revelation 11:8. The 12 Hebrew Tribes were decimated. They can't and won't be "found" either because they're not lost, they are dead. *"Jerusalem will become a heap of rubble, the temple hill, a mound overgrown with thickets."* Micah 3:12, *"And I will silence in the cities of Judah and in the streets of Jerusalem the voice of mirth and the voice of gladness, the voice of the bridegroom and the voice of the bride, for the land shall become a waste."* Jeremiah 7:34, *"From the time that the daily sacrifice is abolished and the abomination that causes desolation is set up..."* Daniel 12:11, ***"Behold, your house is being left to you desolate!"*** Matthew 23:38

Hal Lindsey, a significant name on Fundamentalism's stage in the 1970s, originally suggested these climactic events that already occurred, would occur again in the 1980s. Hal's prediction counted one generation (forty years in Biblical terms) from **1948**, establishing modern Israel. According to evangelical, fundamentalist eschatology, this was a significant event. Lindsey wrote a book, Countdown to Armageddon, predicting that "the decade of the 1980s (**1948 + 40** years) would be the final decade of history as we know it". He also wrote The Late, Great Planet Earth, the first Christian prophecy book published by a secular publisher, selling **28 million copies** (do you have to sell fear to be so fortunate?) by 1990, all of which was a treatment of literalist, dispensational, eschatology. It, too, as it always does, compared end-time prophecies in the Bible *with, then-current events,* in an attempt to predict future scenarios that would result in the rapture of believers. One reader's review of Lindsey's book on *Amazon, put it this way:*

"This book [The Late Great Planet Earth] contains incontrovertible proof that Christianity is the one true way. Everybody should read it. Every 3 years Hal Lindsay [sic] writes a new book denoting how the world will end in 5 years. Each subsequent book [Lindsay] explains how he WASN'T wrong in the previous book and the world will really end in [the next] 5 years. . . He has followed this pattern for 3 decades and is now acknowledged as "the foremost authority on Biblical prophecy in the world today." I'm an electrician. If I had been doing my job [this] poorly and wrong for 30 years, I doubt I would be "the foremost authority." In fact, I dare say I would have ceased to make a living in my chosen profession in the first 10 years." [10]

Fear has again sold millions of <u>the not-yet dated</u>, six books, "Left Behind" for author's Tim LaHaye and Jerry B. Jenkins, all of which build their case around the same primary eschatological recipe but graciously add a few new sprinkles and wrinkles for updated contemporary goodness. Let's take a look at some of the other more notable notables over the past couple of hundred years.

History is replete with numerous proclamations of Jesus' imminent return, but none, stranger than a hen (yes, a chicken) in the English town of Leeds in **1806** that began laying eggs, on which the phrase "Christ is Coming" was written. News of this "miracle" quickly spread convincing numerous people that doomsday was just around the corner until— a curious, and somewhat skeptical local, who took the time to watch the hen laying one of the prophetic eggs. He discovered the only thing that hatched was a hoax. [11]

In February **1835**, Joseph Smith, the founder of the Mormon church, called a meeting with his church leaders. He said that he had spoken to God, and during their conversation, he learned that Jesus would return within the next 56 years (1891) and on February 14 *"the Savior of the world would make his appearance again upon the earth, and the winding-up scene take place."* The End Times would promptly begin.[12] Then there was The Millerites, April 23, 1843.

William Miller, an American Baptist preacher, New England farmer, and founder of Millerism, carefully studied his Bible for many years. Like the many who would follow the next 175 years, convinced he could divine the destruction of the world through a literal interpretation of the scripture, Miller explained that the world would end between March 21, **1843**, and March 21, **1844.** Eventually, he convinced thousands of Millerite *followers to sell or give away all their possessions*, which they would leave to the Apocalyptic world. Of course, April 23 arrived, but—Jesus did not. [13] The group eventually dispersed, some of whom formed the Seventh-day Adventists. Miller's tail bore an up-close and somewhat embarrassing resemblance to my own experience.

In 1881, spectral analysis revealed that a comet's tail contained a deadly cyanide gas called cyanogen. No one outside the scientific community showed any interest until astronomers realized Earth, in **1910**, would pass through the tail of Haley's comet, The New York Times and other newspapers predicted the comet would bath the Earth in the toxic gas spelling the End for humankind. The news caused widespread panic in the USA and around the world. The End was here. [14]

In May **1980**, televangelist and Christian Coalition founder Pat Robertson alarmed a lot of people when he informed his worldwide "700 Club" TV audience, that he knew when the world would end. *"I guarantee you by the end of 1982 there is going to be a judgment on the world."* I'm guessing he now wishes that videotape didn't exist. [15] Let's take a further step back into the 1980s, with Edgar Whisenant (1932-2001).

Many of my readers may recall what will probably go down in history as the rapture prediction *generating pure pandemonium* in fundamentalist circles. Whisenant, a *former NASA engineer* and Bible student, was best known for

writing *88 Reasons Why the Rapture Will Be in **1988**. (88 is a lot of reasons)* My favorite part of Whisenant's quote: *"Only if the Bible is in error am I wrong; and I say that to every preacher in town"* and "If there were a king in this country and I could gamble with my life, I would stake my life on Rosh Hashana 88."

The book was all the rage in Christian bookstores and the Trinity Broadcasting Network during August and early September 1988. Coupled with another essay: *On Borrowed Time*, the booklet, published by the World Bible Society, had a sudden rise on the Christian book market best-seller lists, and, no surprise, just as rapid a fall—once the fateful weekend had come and gone. Trinity Broadcasting Network preempted their regular programming during the three-day window running PSA spots with "what to do if you just missed the rapture." Whisenant quickly claimed he got a number wrong. **He revised his math *and issued a new book,*** [16] *"The Final Shout: Rapture Report."* The original title proposed *(believe it or not)* 89 Reasons Why the *Rapture Will Be in 1989.* [17]

Circa **1987**, our beloved pastor (a genuinely wonderful, deeply loving, well-intended but also a thoroughly-indoctrinated man with a million-dollar personality) convinced the END was any day. From the pulpit of a 1500-member church, he told the parishioners to *"...max out all of your credit cards and leave the Antichrist's debt."* After years, weary of the rapture doctrine, it was soon after that specific ill-advice that I would leave the church I had attended for almost thirty years. Our tradition had always been rapture centric, but our pastor (clearly) bought into Jesus' **1988** imminent return. When an escape is what you are looking for, all you need to do is keep repeating the mantra: "Just any day now" because— the statement is current—in perpetuity. The End is Near—any day of any month of any year of any decade of any century you choose to consume the news. See Notes: **Sidebar**

When the Hale-Bopp comet appeared in **1997**, rumors surfaced that an alien spacecraft was following the comet, facts "covered up" by NASA and the astronomical community. Though astronomers refuted the claim, it was one that could be denied by anyone with an excellent telescope. Art Bell's "Coast to Coast AM" radio talk show, about the paranormal, publicized the claims inspiring the San Diego UFO cult, "Heaven's Gate," to determine that the world would end. The world did—indeed end for 39 of the cult's members, who committed suicide on March 26, **1997**. [18]

The End of the world **2012** included a variety of eschatological beliefs from cataclysmic to transformative. In any event, either would occur around December 21, 2012, the Mesoamerican Long Count calendar's 5,126-year-long cycle end-date. Various theories emerged for numerological formulae and astronomical alignments, including a New Age interpretation for the beginning of a period in which the Earth and humankind would experience a positive physical or spiritual transformation. The 21st was said to be the beginning of a new era. However, others said the date marked a catastrophic end of the world. [19]

Most people are at least vaguely familiar with the murky, metaphorical writings of Michel de Nostrdame. Nostradamus has provided the world with much intrigue for more than 400 years. His prophecies' accuracy relied heavily upon *very flexible interpretations* and have been translated and re-translated in dozens of different versions. [20] One of his most contemporaneous and therefore famous: "The year **1999**, seventh month / From the sky shall come a great king of terror.", seeming, by some to be a reference to the book of Revelation. Many Nostradamus devotees were concerned that this was a vision of Armageddon. I remember it well. Its timing added fuel to the looming—doom and gloom rhetoric of Y2K. As the last century drew to a close, many speculated that a computer problem might usher in doomsday. A challenge, first observed early in the 1970s, expressed potential for many computer programs to crash with the "rollover" of xx99 to xx00. Most computer's "date field" in those days only used two places; it *assumed* the 19 and, therefore, only required the last two digits_ _, all of which worked well until the final hours of the 1900s became history. No one was sure what would happen, but disaster forecasts ranged from catastrophic problems ranging from massive blackouts to nuclear holocaust. Gun sales jumped, and survivalists prepared to live in bunkers (a dear friend of mine was one of them), but the new millennium began with a few, very manageable glitches.

Yet, in the unlikely event that the Y2K bug didn't result in the end of the world, Richard Noone, author of The Ultimate Disaster, promised a catastrophe of global proportions in his book "5/5/2000: Ice, The Ultimate Disaster, [21] Noone predicted that on May 5, **2000**, an enormous Antarctic ice mass would be three miles thick at the time Mercury, Venus, Mars, Jupiter, and Saturn aligned with Earth the first time in six thousand years. Forces from this planetary alignment would shift Earth's orientation on its axis, causing ice to build up at the South Pole to such a great extent that it would release trillions of tons of ice and water to cover Earth's surface.

In fall **2008,** according to "God's Church Ministry's," Ronald Weinland, the End Times were upon us—yet again. In his book entitled "2008: God's Final Witness," [22] Weinland writes *"...by the End of 2006, only a tiny percentage of human life will continue on into that new era that will begin after the return of Jesus Christ as King of kings over all the Earth— will be a maximum time of two* *years remaining before the world plunges into the worst time of all human history. By the fall of 2008, the United States will have collapsed as a world power, or will have begun its collapse and no longer exist..."* In the book, Weinland places his reputation on the line as the end-time prophet of God." This author must admit that "the great recession" was challenging for my wife and me, but we lived through it like most of us. Meanwhile, Weinland discovered like all those who had gone before; it was not God's Final Witness. As usual, the sun came up the following day. Ninety-nine percent of humanity was unaware the world was supposed to have ended, but Weinland sold some books.

American Christian radio host Harold Camping trumpeted that May 21, 2011, was Rapture and Judgment Day, and the end of the world would take place five months later on **October 21, 2011**. Camping, then president of the Family Radio Christian network, cited the Bible as his source. May 21, Camping said, *"it is beyond the shadow of a doubt the Rapture and the day of judgment."* Camping suggested that it would occur at 6 p.m. local time, with the Rapture sweeping the globe time zone by time zone. Some of his supporters claimed that around 200 million people (approximately 3% of the world's population) would be 'raptured'. Camping had previously claimed that the Rapture would occur in September **1994.**

Following the prediction's failure, media attention shifted to the response from Camping and his followers. On **May 23,** Camping stated that **May 21** had been *a "spiritual day of judgment"* and that the physical Rapture would now occur on **October 21, 2011**, simultaneously with **God's *destruction of the universe***. However, on October 16, Camping admitted in an interviewer that he didn't know when the end would come and made no public comment after his October 21 apocalypse failed to materialize. [23] [24] [25]

"just any day now."

As I write: There are significant and disturbing things currently on the world stage. A third-generation nut job who has access to nuclear weapons runs North Korea. Iran's aspirations are to develop or acquire nuclear weapons, chanting Death to America and Death to Israel. China and America are now in a cold war, and Wuhan China is ground zero of a pandemic and the Chinese Communist Party's greatest attempted coverup of all time. The Corona Virus continues to threaten. The economic fallout has been "cage rattling," taking the most exceptional economy in American history to 40 million unemployed Americans in a matter of months. Riots break out in the streets of numerous cities, protesting George Floyd's murder under the knee of a brazenly arrogant, narcissist—knowing the murder is being recorded. Months later, organized "wolves in sheep's clothing" pose as legitimate protesters at 3 AM, emboldened morning after morning to pillage, plunder, burn, destroy, and kill as spineless "leaders" in some of America's greatest cities allow the anarchy to continue. Yet,

Every minute of every waking day, there are *multiplied millions of good things* happening around the world that goes unseen, unreported. The press will never report them—because Fear Sells. "If it bleeds it leads." The continuous coverage emboldens the anarchy. All the while, America just returned to space after a long absence. As of this writing, America launched our Mars Rover to touch down on the red planet in February 2001 in preparation for putting four Astronauts on Mars by 2025. America returns to space after a nine-year absence via SpaceX rockets, which after launch, return to earth landing feet first for reuse in future flights. Astonishing discoveries in medicine and technology pave the way for a prosperous 2020 decade. As always, same modern-day prophets tiresomely prophesize the end of the world as they have in my forty-year memory [26] while others foresee the 2020 decade as reformative, transitional, and prosperous.[27] Whatever suits your taste, positive or negative, it's out there. Where will you choose to place your focus?

Five years, a decade, 20 years from now, will the world have ended, or will we look back at 2020 and wonder how we got through "this one too;" one of the more significant tests in our country's history? Will humanity face a new set of challenges as history reflects how we overcame or failed to overcome the ones we face today? One thing we know for sure. Time—will tell.

Quantum Brook

Conclusion

I must emphasize how I am bewildered by the tenacity with which so many good people, 60 years later, continue to champion the ongoing; *"the sky is falling, end of the world narratives."* It invites the question—why? It sells books and fills the pews on Sunday, but why would *anyone* fight so hard to believe the vast majority of humankind will be "left behind" and doomed to an eternal hell? For many, it must somehow be comforting to think that they are more special to God than—others. My empathy is genuine. It bubbles from the swamp of past regret. As I said to one friend predicting a fiery, nuclear, end of the world: *"If you know where ground zero will be, text me. I want to be there to say goodbye to this dimension. I know where my loved ones and I will be the second after it blows. 'Throw me in the briar patch"'* [28]

"Loving people live in a loving world. Hostile people live in a hostile world. Same world." — Wayne W. Dyer

Chapter 10

Gob Smacked

A Conscious Universe

Many years ago, my daughter Nicole was home from college for a few days. I was eager to share some of the astonishing things I had learned from David Hawkins' MD, Ph.D.'s book "Power vs. Force." Commanding evidence of (and another practical application for) a *conscious universe*.

A few years earlier, I was mesmerized reading Lynne McTaggart's book, "The Field." At the time, her work was (for me), an overview of the results of numerous experiments in the quantum field conducted over the last century. It was also a possible explanation to *the innumerable things* we call mysterious, unexplainable, or supernatural that should be—less uncommonly supernatural and—more commonly natural.

Scientists loosely define the field, or the *zero-point field* as kind of (mathematically) reimagined, theoretical generalizations of Maxwell's classical electromagnetic field and Einstein's gravitational field. Physicists began to *reformulate the classic definition* with equations that describe the "nonsensical" and bewildering behavior they observed *contradicting Newton's natural laws.* Yet numerous scientists watching experiments in labs around the world *repeatedly validate* this strange subatomic behavior. One of the most astonishing findings is that *the presence of an intelligent observer*, causes subatomic *waves* to collapse into *particles*. When no observer is present, *the energy remains—as waves*. We will delightfully delve into this in greater depth in Volume II, "A Glimpse Beyond the Spin."

Wayne Dyer, another teacher whom I greatly admired, *(rest in peace, Wayne)*, described the book "The Field" as "…a magnificent job of presenting the hard evidence for what spiritual masters have been telling us for centuries." McTaggart, Hawkins, Dyer, and a host of other philosophy of science thinkers like Joseph Selbie and Amit Goswami in their book "The Physics of God," fell in love with the magnificent, propositions of quantum mechanics.

Quantum Physics is for me, in all of its depth and breadth, the most exciting subject on planet Earth. Why? It is not only the underpinning of all that is—it is part and parcel of all there is. In reality, it is a sea of pure potential. Like the great Physicist, Niels Bohr said: "Those who are not shocked when they first come across quantum theory cannot possibly have understood it." For this author, it's a peek behind the curtain of everything valuable. It is a fantastic look into everything that is anything—discovering a sea of energic potential waiting to take form. It is like gazing into the mind of God and realizing we've yet to see even a "Glimpse" of this astonishing reality—although—intellectual materialist zealously distances themselves from such interpretations.

Simply put, all of the things that average Joe Citizen once thought to be material—is not. The world around us that we perceive as tangible, at a subatomic level—is not. What can be more thrilling? *(But I'm told that I'm a bit quirky.)*

Max Plank -Nobel Prize Winner, Physics put it this way: "As a man who has devoted his whole life to the most clearheaded science, to the study of matter, I can tell you as a result of my research about the atoms this much: **There is no matter as such!** All matter originates and exists only by virtue of a force which brings the particles of an atom to vibration and holds this most minute solar system of the atom together. **We must assume behind this force the existence of a conscious and intelligent Mind.** This Mind is the matrix of all matter." Physicist Amit Goswami said it this way: **"Consciousness is the true reality, and matter is an epiphenomenon bordering on trivial."** Max Plank also said: "I regard consciousness as fundamental. I regard matter as a derivative of consciousness. We cannot get behind consciousness. Everything that we talk about, everything that we regard as existing suggests consciousness. Sir James Jeans- Physicist writes: "The stream of knowledge is heading towards a non-mechanical reality; **the universe begins to look more like a great thought than a machine.** Mind no longer appears to be an accidental intruder into the realm of matter—we ought rather [to] hail it as the creator and governor of the realm of matter. Get over it and accept the inarguable **conclusion the universe is immaterial, mental, and spiritual."**

In her book, "The Field," Lynne reveals how various scientists were each on a quest for the secret force of the universe. Around the globe, they were often doing dissimilar research yet, all working towards a common goal and—getting confirmative, supportive, repeatable results, some of which Einstein would later call *"spooky at a distance"* when describing quantum entanglement.

These are results which, more than a century later, still have physicist scratching their collective heads. When you read about and understand *the implications* of these experiments' outcomes, you have to work—*hard* to devise an explanation that does not involve consciousness. A 2009 Pew research revealed that only 41% of the scientist polled consider themselves atheists, while 51% believe in God, a universal spirit, or a higher power. [1] More than half embrace consciousness as an architect and builder. I think that the documented evidence is *so compelling that* you must be on a mission, which itself is a statement of faith in a Godless universe, to advance the narrative that we and all there is, is a mechanical accident. But clearly, I too am on a mission to gaze into "the eyes and mind of God."

"I went through the standard scientific atheist phase when I was about 14. I bought into that package deal of science equals atheism. For more than 200 years, materialists have promised that science will eventually explain everything in terms of [classic] physics and chemistry. Believers are sustained by the faith that scientific discoveries will justify their beliefs." Rupert Sheldrake, Ph.D. and self-described "science heretic."

Explaining to my daughter Dr. Hawkins' astonishing discovery of how to connect to universal consciousness would be more easily demonstrated than trying to describe it. My excitement was evident, given that my extraordinary experience a few years earlier when Dr. Albury Gardner delivered a natural solution to a personal health crisis. That one experience opened my eyes to possibilities unknown in the circles of my fundamentalist upbringing. These things were universally spiritual but not in the sense religious Fundamentalism describes as spiritual. Yet, it was Universal in size and Infinite in its scope, something orders of magnitude (like God) too large to fit in *anyone's* "Box."

For my demonstration, I gathered ten identical plain white #10 envelopes, ten 8.5" x 11" pieces of paper. I searched the internet for a "picture of Jesus" who was holding a little Lamb and a picture of Adolf Hitler. I printed both in color on separate pieces of paper. On the remaining paper, in a huge, bold font, I typed the words: Good, Evil, Love, Hate, Light, Darkness, Death, Life, printing (from my computer) each separately on a piece of paper. I then tri-folded each page and placed it in a separate envelope, blinding both Nicole and me to the contents. I shuffled the ten envelopes and asked her to stand up facing me, extending her right arm to the side, palm down, and parallel to the floor. Taking the first envelope from the stack, I asked her to hold it against her solar plexus (just below her navel) as I applied a firm, but not aggressive, downward pressure to her extended wrist. We repeated this procedure with each of the ten envelopes. [2] When her arm remained strong, locked, unyielding to the downward pressure, I placed the envelope we "tested" in stack "A." When her arm collapsed under the slightest downward pressure, I put the envelope in stack "B." Two of the ten demonstrated neither a complete lock nor complete collapse; but rather a vague "in-between result' which went into pile "C." After testing all ten envelopes, we first opened the arm stays strong, stack "A." There we found: Love, the picture of Jesus, the words Light, and Life. In stack "B" (the arm went weak), we found Hate, Darkness, and Adolf Hitler. In pile C, we found, Death and Good. I mused briefly about the ambiguity in both words, the result and set the mystery aside to chew on later. Was this a double-blind study with multiple subjects, in numerous locations, conducted by many testers with the same result? No. Was its evidence anecdotal? Yes, of course. Was this exciting for me! You bet! But Hawkins had already published the "clinical method" basis of his research, and I quote:

"Research done over a 20-year period, involving millions of calibrations on thousands of test subjects of all ages and personality types, and from all walks of life. By design the study is clinical in method and has widespread, pragmatic, implications. Because the testing method is valid in application to all forms of human expression, calibrations have successfully been taken for literature, architecture, art, science, world events, and the complexities of human relationships. The test space for the determination of the data is the totality of the human experience throughout all time. Mentally, test subjects ranged from what the world calls "normal" to severely ill psychiatric patients. Subjects tested were from Canada, United States, Mexico and throughout South America, Northern Europe, and the Far East. They were all nationalities, ethnic backgrounds and religions, ranging in age from children to elders in their 90s and covered a wide spectrum of physical and emotional health. Subjects were tested individually and in groups by many different testers and groups of testers. But in all cases, without exception, the results were identical and entirely reproducible, fulfilling the fundamental of the scientific method: Perfect experimental replicability. Subjects were selected at random and tested in a wide array of physical and behavioral

settings: on top of mountains and at the seashore, at holiday parties, and during the course of everyday work, in moments of joy and in sorrow. None of the circumstances had any effect on test results, which were found to be universally consistent irrespective of any extraneous factor with the singular exception of the methodology of the testing procedure itself." [3]

But this simple demonstration for my daughter was the tip of the iceberg. Hawkins's work stood on the shoulders of a definitive study on muscle testing conducted in 1971 [4] that inspired him to begin his paradigm-shifting work, a discovery that would catapult a *connection* to The Field when he develops "The Map of Consciousness." [5] George Goodheart, DC, of Detroit, MI, studied muscle testing techniques extensively and made a breakthrough discovery that the strength or weakness of every muscle in the human body **connects to the health or pathology of a specific organ**. Goodheart also discovered that each muscle was associated with an acupuncture meridian. [6] Psychiatrist Dr. John Diamond began using what he labeled—"behavioral kinesiology" to diagnose and treat his patients. Diamond's test was "easy to perform and highly decisive." All of the researchers confirmed the *absolute replicability* of the test results. [7]

Hawkins describes how the reliability of the "testing experience" amazed the public, the patients, and practitioners on his lecture tours. In his audiences of ~1000 people, Hawkins' team randomly passed out 500 envelopes, all containing artificial sweeteners. They then passed out another 500 containing organic vitamin C. He would then divide them into groups and have them *test each other*. Universally, all of those who had the envelopes with the artificial sweetener *went weak*, and those with vitamin C *stayed strong*. This experiment was the same principle as my ten envelopes. The difference is the energy signature, the frequency that accompanied the artificial sweetener. (artificial sweetener is now known to have adverse health effects with long term use.) It was akin to the one with the picture of Hitler. Both made the test subject go weak. [8] He describes how "in the early 70s the medical profession, generally—and psychiatry specifically, was *"highly resistant if not outwardly hostile"* to the idea that nutrition had much if anything to do with health, let alone emotional health or brain function." He adds that" twenty years later, the concepts he presented in Power vs. Force, are now *fundamental to the current treatment of mental illness*." [9] An essential KEY was that practitioners and researchers observed that the test responses **"were completely independent of the test subject's belief systems, intellectual opinions, reason, or logic."** The story of Astronaut Edgar Mitchel's mother's healing later in this chapter illustrates the importance of this "complete independence." It was also observed that the cerebral hemisphere desynchronization accompanied the test response where the subject went week. [10]

Years before I read any of Hawkins's work, of which I have now read nine of his books, I had already been *a first-time and unwitting benefactor*. It was my first exposure to connecting answers to questions via consciousness alone. There was no label for me at the time, and I didn't have a nook to put it all comfortably. I was unaware that chiropractors used AK (applied kinesiology) during every visit, in ways so subtle, I didn't know that it was a regular part of their diagnostic modality. I was unaware that the series of pulls or pushes against my legs, arms, etc., before the spinal adjustment, would enable the clinician to determine misalignment. All I knew, when I left, I felt better than when I arrived. But it would be the following connection to the field that would *permanently open my eyes* to one of the most astonishing discoveries of our time.

Many years ago, Dr. Albury Gardner [11] would diagnose and treat a *severe,* stress-related medical condition, pull me from the brink. There was *no one*—like him or, will there ever be. He is missed, and unfortunately, irreplaceable. RIP Albury. The things he studied, the innovative alternatives he used in his practice, were, at the time, far outside the mainstream. I'll never forget how ill I was before my first visit. In the months following, he would tell me, "You were days away from landing in the emergency room and—maybe worse."

In December 2006, I went to his office for the first time. When I walked through the door, my beleaguered, pale face began to tell the story of a mostly incoherent mind and a body wracked with pain. Peripheral neuropathy engulfed me like a wet suit plugged into an electrical outlet. I was no stranger to stress; I lived a high-stress career for decades. But my condition that day was, in my experience, unprecedented, unsustainable. I was on tilt.

Around four years earlier, I flew to Detroit, MI to have dinner with the CEO of a small company that had developed a cutting-edge, Laboratory Information System (LIS) built for Hospitals, Reference Labs and Public Health Labs. The previous year the company had done less than a half-million $ in revenue. After meeting to watch a demonstration the following day, I was impressed with the numerous advancements. I saw what appeared to be a significant opportunity to have a lot of fun marketing something that few of our competitors could touch. I called a dear friend and former colleague to tell him about what I found. Mark was playing golf at the time and expressed little interest in taking the time to investigate. I've never been too good at taking no for an answer and insisted he agree to meet with the CEO and see for himself. That got me a yes. Over the next several weeks, Mark and I convinced Mike, another of our former teammates to join us. Mike had been the Laboratory Director of a 1000 bed Texas Hospital, and a natural entertainer when presenting to a crowded room. His credentials meant instant credibility, his skills demonstrating complex systems, coveted in the industry. We knew, as a team, that we had a potential home run. Over the following three years later, Mark, Mike, and I would take the company from $500,00 to almost $16,000,000 in annual revenue.

The problem we ran into, far too soon, was too much success, too quickly. We flourished so rapidly that we outgrew our ability to hire, train, install, and support the systems we had already sold. LIS systems perform the mission-critical functions that manage hundreds, even thousands of confirmatory medical tests a day. It manages the chain of custody for each specimen, pathogen typing, disease monitoring, research, and immediately disseminating test results back to the clinician, equipping them with the vital information they need to make quality clinical decisions for treating the patient. To shorten a much longer story, our reputation, once on a trajectory to the stars, plummeted to Earth like a rocket run out of fuel. Our references and revenue begin to dry up. Even though the company continued to pay my salary, they owed me $100k in commissions and stonewalled my efforts to get a palatable answer when I saw the money. I rightfully began to worry that I would never recoup a dime. Months later and bleeding cash, the company was on the verge of Chapter 11, and soon, they "let me go,"—and within a year filed for bankruptcy.

While these kinds of things are never desirable, under any conditions, it's life and something from which we can always recover. But, four unique events converged to make these circumstances an unusual challenge. First of all, I lost my income. Secondly, my daughter was engaged to be married five months later and—in her "dream wedding." A year earlier, my wife and I had scheduled a two-week vacation to Europe, departing *the day after the wedding*. Reserving first-class seats using FF points, required booking all legs of the multipart round-trip flight a year in advance. It had been three years since she or I had taken some badly needed time off, and to cancel would have been unthinkable. We purposely scheduled the departure to coincide with the conclusion of *everything wedding*, which the expense was fast approaching half what I was owed and unable to collect. Contemporaneously, I was trading Stock Options hoping to close the gap. One particular day I had four Call positions open, and the Federal Reserve announced a quarter-point rate increase; the kind of news the market never likes to hear. The value of the underlying stock dropped precipitously. The bids opened below my contingent stop-loss triggers—meaning my sell orders didn't activate. The value of Options, unlike Stocks, embodies "time decay." They rapidly lose value, the closer they get to their expiration. Moves up in value for "Calls" and down in value for "Puts" are magnified. That is the appeal to trading Options. That is also the danger in trading Options. All four positions never recovered; I lost a lot of money, which I could least afford to lose.

In the weeks leading up to my near collapse, the accumulated stress from *this series of unfortunate events* caused my body to become dangerously acidic. My saliva tasted acidic, and chronic sweaty palms started to also smell of acid and began to eat away at the metal plating on my laptop computer where I rested my hands during regular use. I was alarmed. The evening before I would see Dr. Gardner, I was in immense pain. My feet burned—severely as I lay in a fetal position between my wife and daughter; not a good look for any man. Their faces painted with concern as they applied ice packs to the bottom and sides of my feet, trying to comfort me. I sobbed—uncontrollably. I felt incoherent. Desperate. The tears were not from the intense pain but the sense of total exhaustion, desperation and hopelessness. The compounding stress scrambled my endocrine system causing estrogen to skyrocket and testosterone to plummet, fueling the emotion. The delicate dance of my body's hormones in their healthy interaction with proteins and amino acids was confused and misdirected. In conflict with itself, my body was unable to orchestrate the cacophonous chain of numerous internal chemical events up and downstream. I was disoriented, unable to think; to reason; to take action. Before I knew what had happened, I was in full collapse. The "logical" thing would be the emergency room. But I stubbornly resist tranquilizers or any drugs of any kind in my system. Pharmaceuticals are a distant—*last resort*. After spending decades in conventional healthcare, I was too aware that the side effects are often worse than the disease they are treating. In retrospect, there could have been only a few things worse than what I was suffering at the time.

The following morning, Ronda drove me to Dr. Gardner's office, where I would soon lay face up on an exam table. He stood to my right and told me to extend my right arm straight up. In the following minutes, I wondered in silence, "What manner of voodoo is this?" Nothing of the sort from this fundamentalist Christian man whom, over the years to follow, would become a dear friend. I would learn that Albury was *very* conflicted about many of the things he had learned and could do to bring healing—to restore health. The imagined conflict was quite real to him as it grew in the fertile soil of his indoctrination—his programming. He struggled in silence for years, mentally dancing in the eisegesis shadows to explain away many things that were more "Eastern in nature," to keep his guilt in check. Over a rare lunch together, he told me that "it was the first time he had admitted these things to anyone."

During the exam, Aubrey's left hand did a quick dance from one touchpoint on my body to another. He first touched his right thumb and middle fingers to my closed eyes, then, the cheekbones beneath each eye; the center of my forehead, *connecting to my brains' frontal lobe*, the center top of my head *connecting (through intention) to my hypothalamus*, then the right and left hemisphere of my brain. Slightly lifting my head to connect to the amygdala, he broke into a mischievous grin. "Missing our brain today, huh? We will fix that," he said confidently. That was something I was desperate to hear. Missing my brain was an understatement. But—exactly how did he know? Aubrey proceeded, placing thumb and middle fingers to each side of my throat *(my thyroid)* then to my heart, to my liver, and my spleen before sliding an open palm up, between my back and the table, first on the right, then on the left connecting with each kidney. He then went back to my stomach, my small, then large intestine. Taking my left hand, placing it over my groin, he touched the top of my hand before again ending with my heart.

For over four decades, he practiced each of these moves thousands of times, and they had become second nature as if his hands had a mind of their own. One touchpoint to the next with his right hand while *the fingers of his left hand lay together as if they were in a mitten*, pulling lightly against my extended wrist as if to sideways motion for someone to "come here." In a final pass, he reached beneath me again, touching the tip of my spine (the coccyx) before then pressing his fingertips (almost painfully) into the top of my pubic bone, then against my navel, my heart, my throat, between my eyebrows and ending with the crown of my head. The first pass connected with all my vital organs along the energy meridians (sometimes called acupuncture meridians). The second pass connected to each of the body's seven major energy centers, known in Eastern traditions as Chakras. [Image, next page.] We will explore this subject in depth in Volume II, A Glimpse Beyond the Spin.

My extended arm "went weak" on the first and second pass. "Everything in your body is offline," he told me." I wasn't sure what that meant, but then, nothing felt close to "online"—in any context. All of these procedures were foreign to my experience. I didn't know that my arm was "going weak." I had no reference point between weak and strong or what "strong" meant or— how it felt. I was experientially incapable of quantitative or qualitative judgment. I was just a willing patient, coming by faith to see a man, whom people I trusted, said to be the best there was in the world of alternative and complementary medicine.

There was silent yet crystal clear language between Dr. Gardner and my body, one requiring no words. "The requisite language?" *Intention*. His intention to diagnose and treat my condition required no pomp and circumstance, no ritual or words in any *spoken* language. My presence in his office *implied the need*. He was there in his exam room, responding to my *implied request for help*.

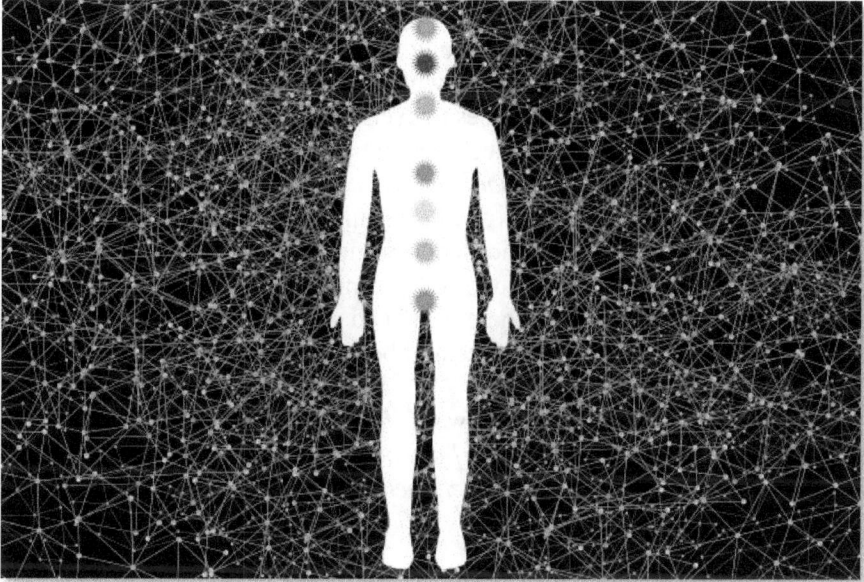

Access to knowledge for anything—is universal. Information is available Everywhere— *from Anywhere*. A conscious universe enables and facilitates this *nonverbal conversation*. Dr. Gardner's purpose was to restore to me, in me, the *universal life force* that animates every living thing. "How" you accomplish this feat is fascinating (no—utterly mesmerizing) to people like me, but the "how" it performs its directive is for now relatively unimportant. What is important is that it is possible for everyone and available to everybody. While the internal combustion engine also fascinates me, it is unnecessary to know how the numerous parts interconnects before it takes me from point A to point B— successfully. I just get in and—drive.

We naturally conceptualize the separation of any two things as— *distance* (of separation) *over time* (the time required to make the trip.) Two—way communication is the time needed for the conversation to make—a round trip: *The ask, The answer*. For example:

From Earth, it takes 2.564 seconds for a laser, moving at the speed of light, to make a trip to the moon and back. If I am working with nonlocal consciousness, I don't need 2.564 seconds. It isn't required. What I need to know is *Now-Here*. If *I am on* Alpha Centauri, 4.37 *light-years* from Earth, and need the same information, the same is true. That same information is also still *Now-Here* on Alpha Centauri. The data is nonlocal; it is omnipresent. It is everywhere at the same time. Non-locality is a phenomenon still baffling scientist. It is relatively easy to conceptualize everything as being everywhere. It is another thing entirely to explain how, and even with a modern-day Einstein as my mentor and best friend, I remain on my tiptoes to even begin to grasp the underpinnings of "the how." Regardless of how much fun that may be for quirky people like me, it is of little importance to *vast useable, universal implications*, and overarching thesis of this book. The universe is a sea of quanta. Energetic "substance" from which we are all made at the physical and spiritual levels, is pure energy—without regard to cultural, ethnic, or any discriminating label. The information Dr. Gardner needed to treat me was "here-now" and with no "respecter of person" regardless of doctrine, religion, a system of belief, or non-belief.

Scientific American put it this way: *"In everyday life, distance and location are mundane absolutes. Yet [quantum] physics now suggests that the universe is nonlocal. At the most fundamental level, there is no such thing as place or distance."* [12]

For decades, Dr. Gardner studied the body's skeletal, chiropractic neurological system, acupuncture meridians, and considered which modalities would be most efficient under various conditions. All of which ultimately restore health by replenishing the body of depleted energy. Each approach is different, yet it relies on a similar path to restore the dwindling universal life force known in numerous cultures and traditions by approximately 90 different names like Chi (qi), pneuma, energeia, prana, Ki, manitou, etc. To avoid confusion, and for our discussions here, we will use the more commonly used term Chi, also spelled "qi" when discussing this circulating, animating, quickening, universal life force. Chi is not a figment of hopeful imaginations, regardless of the narrative mechanistic materialism may wish to advance. It is—tangible. It is measurable *(within the limits of current technologies' ability to provide measurement)*, and in many ways, it is quantifiable. It embodies bio-electromagnetic properties but also contains other constituents that cannot yet be measured. The instruments do not exist (*except for*—a one of a kind which my friend James West invented, and is sadly now in the hands of the Department of Defense. Yes, I'm urging him to build another.)

Chi is *far more* than just *electromagnetic energy*, though that is the component (at this time) that is most directly tangible and measurable in cultivating and moving/directing Chi. The recipient experiences the benefits of the parts known and those who are yet unknown and unmeasurable. So— measured or not, the results speak for themselves. Until that time comes, it will be *the* **corollaries** *of Chi*, which are observable and measurable. Thunder is a corollary of lightning, but it is not itself, lightning. However, where there is lightening, there is thunder, and where you hear thunder, you are not far away from the lightening.

In his book *Energy Medicine, The Scientific Basis*, James L. Oschman, PhD., observed: "[…] I noticed similarities between the discoveries of modern medical researchers and the daily observations of *'hands-on' energy therapists.* […] To be specific, […] oscillating magnetic fields are being researched at various medical centres for the treatment of bone, nerve, skin, capillary, and ligament damage. *Virtually identical energy fields can also be detected around the hands of suitably trained therapists*. There is an inescapable conclusion. Medical research is demonstrating that devices producing pulsing magnetic fields of particular frequencies can stimulate the healing of a variety of tissues. *Therapists from various schools of energy medicine can project from their hand's fields with similar frequencies and intensities*. Research documenting that these different approaches are efficacious is mutually validating. Medical research and hands-on therapies are confirming each other. The common denominator is the pulsating magnetic field, *which is called a bio-magnetic field when it emanates from the hands of a therapist."*

This author knows about Chi first-hand (pun intended). After becoming an astonished and profoundly grateful beneficiary of universal and nutritional Chi, I learned to "cultivate it" years ago. It is now so natural, to the point of being ordinary, that I find myself occasionally (and absently mindedly) "playing with it, shining a beam" from the palm of one hand to the other. When *I intend* the Chi to flow, the palm of the motionless hand feels the subtle, wave-like movements coming from the opposite hand; the typical separation is one to three feet. It feels as if each palm is a transmitter, (and they are) emitting this bio-magnetic beam of energy *in a spectrum invisible* to the naked eye, yet one which is surprisingly tactile to the hands, tangible in varying degrees depending on the amount of focus given to intention. Imagine if you will, each of your hands is the same magnetic "pole." It feels akin to placing the same pole of a magnet opposite the same pole of another magnet. We all know from elementary science that "like" poles repel each other. Placing the palm of one hand opposite the palm of the other hand, with intention—causes the Chi to flow. It turns on the spigot, and the energy flows from each palm. It's also akin to feeling the subtle internal pressure of a giant beach ball without feeling the ball's surface.

Conversely, a slight separation from the center point of the repelling, a small further separation, creates an attraction, pulling the palms back to the original position. It is as if the movement reverses the polarity. Much like a spring pulled or pushed beyond its resting position, there is a neutral "sweet spot" where there is neither a push nor a pull. That is consciously observing the flow of Chi. That is also cultivating the Chi in real-time, focusing on the Universal Force that animates all life. Regardless of the tradition or the vehicle, the practice that moves Chi, from SOURCE is the same. Generally speaking, we haven't even a vague idea about what the Infinite Source of Consciousness makes available.

"One teacup of empty space contains enough energy to boil all the world's oceans." Richard Feynman, *Theoretical Physicist*

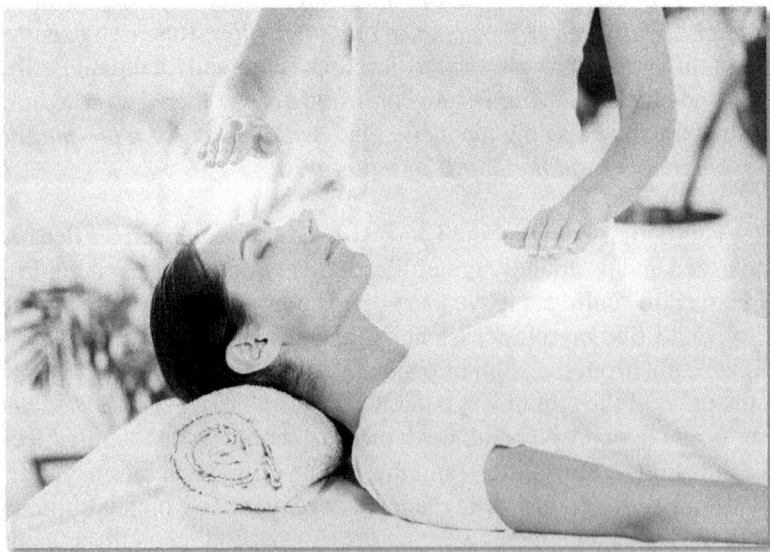

Acupuncture is one of the better-known, "not invented here" energy healing modalities. It works by eliminating blockages in the body's energetic meridians, enabling the Chi to flow freely again. The needles used in acupuncture are much like an (indicative) tool to clear a beaver dam of the stagnant, bacteria-ridden, swampish debris that blocks a stream's natural flow. When the block clears, the water flows again. Likewise, when the block in the meridians cleared of the obstruction, the Chi again flows freely. It flushes the stagnant pools with clear, fresh chi filling the hollows and restoring hemostasis to all life downstream.

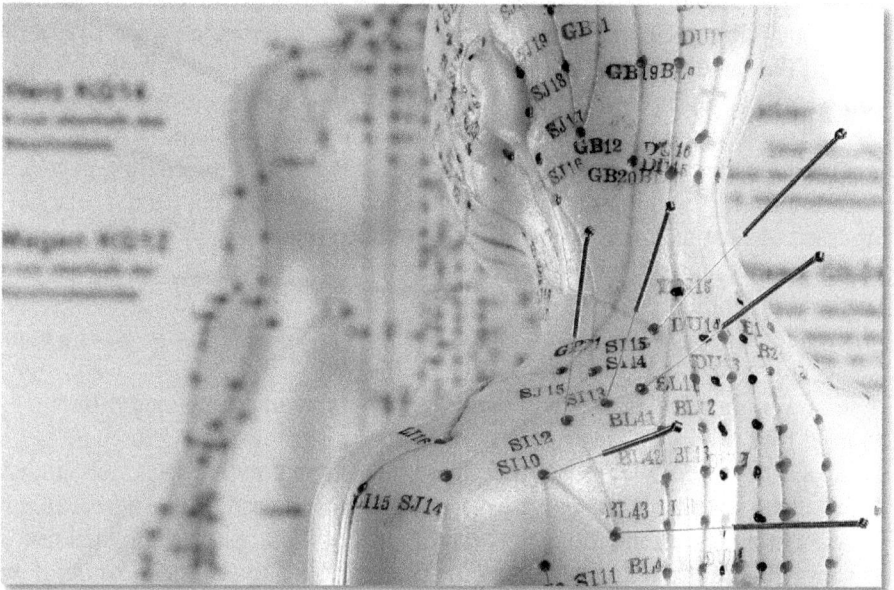

Acupuncture Meridians

Back in the exam room, Dr. Gardner made a final round, connecting to each of my organs verifying the initial results and, without a word, left the room, my hand still in the air, and my mind in a daze. A short time later, he returned with a bag full of a variety of nutritional supplements. What he would usually carry in one hand, this day required—a bag. As with any physician, it's necessary to diagnose the problem, but it's essential to know precisely how to fix it and prepare the body to heal. Albury inventoried hundreds of possibilities on his floor to ceiling shelves, lined with things the likes of which I had never heard. He knew from experience and a resonate intuition which of supplements in his inventory would likely "test" on me, a term with which I would soon become quite familiar. Reentering the exam room with the bag, he said four words: "Hold this for me." He handed me a non-descript Dixie Cup (high-tech, huh?) sitting it upright over my solar plexus (the navel area) while positioning my left hand to hold the cup upright comfortably. Before opening the first bottle, he laid the whole jar against my body near the cup and, as before, pressed against my outstretched arm. It went strong! For the first time, I understood the difference. All—till now "went weak." "Oh! THIS is what strong feels like", I thought to myself. I was amazed at what just happened. No doubt my raised eyebrows reflected my surprise. He poured several capsules into his hand before setting the jar on the adjacent counter and began to take first one capsule then another and drop it into the cup. With each add, he connected the specific organ that the supplement was designed to treat. First one pill in the cup, then a light pull (against my extended wrist.) Weak. Now two of the same type pills in the cup. Pull. Weak. Three, weak, four, Strong! Since my body was completely "offline," until my health was restored, each organ required a targeted supplement in a specific amount. I would have to take the required amount each day for a time to restore the health and energy, eventually "testing strong" without the supplement. Each time he connected to the organ and pressed against my arm. It locked! He continued making the rounds, adding the supplement's necessary quantity, each supporting me to go strong. Each capsule worked individually, and in most cases, synergistically with all the others, for my arm to lock strong on—all of them. All organs and—all Chakra's were a lock.

Within a few days, I was back "online" I felt an astonishing difference. I would follow Albury's instructions to the letter over the coming three to six weeks. Three weeks later, he reran the same test, and my body had rebounded 75%-80%. Within six to eight weeks, I was almost completely restored, requiring dramatically less of the product. Overall, most of the organs would then test strong without the aid of any supplements at all. He adjusted the quantity down on some, eliminated others, and added a few new ones, tweaking the mix.

"Consciousness, rather than being an epiphenomenon of matter, is actually the source of matter. It differentiates into space, time, energy, information, and matter. Even though this view is an ancient view, an ancient world view, it is now finding some resonance amongst a few scientists." – Deepak Chopra

---

When Dr. Gardner placed the correct number of nutritional supplements in the cup, why did the strength immediately return to my arm? The plant/herb/

mineral/in that supplement *provided the depleted energetic frequencies of nutritional Chi to resonate with the cells in my body.* "There are three main sources of Chi (qi): breath, food, and constitution." The three mix to form *the nutritive qi* that travels through the acupuncture meridians to all tissues. [13]

Dr. Gardner became the knowledgeable, Conscious Conduit between the supplement's energetic frequency and the energy frequency of my body's organs. He knowledgeably and skillfully applied what a Conscious Universe told him, sometimes down to ½ of a capsule between my arm going weak or strong. Consciousness welcomed the question and hastened to provide him with the answer at a fantastic granularity. His unspoken questions connected with Consciousness, the Quantum field. With God. By his actions and intention alone, he asked the Universe what was needed to heal me. If my arm remained strong under his light pressure, nothing was required. If my arm went weak while his fingers connected with a specific organ, that part of my body was depleted and needed help. Consciousness processed the implied question and provided an accurate answer as to accurately how much of each to prescribe. The result? In just a few short weeks, I was healed. Amazed.

Note: Today, as I write, (now in my mid-sixties), I just a very a few weeks ago qualified for a sizeable life insurance policy with a premium available only to those who pass a series of test documenting—exceptional health. I am on zero prescriptions, only nutritional supplements. And, then—

There is *the energy of belief* in its form. If I had known then what I know today, I would have been far less likely to have gotten so sick and less likely to have needed Dr. Gardner's help to make the journey back. Today I practice regular, deep mediation and connecting to the source, to God who revitalizes and sustains my body and mind. In Fundamentalism's words:

"For in him we live and move and have our being.' As some of your own poets have said, 'We are his offspring." Acts 17:28

Would Dr. Gardner's or a similarly skilled physician's process only work for fundamentalist Christians? Or, would it work on Buddhists, Muslims, Jews, Hindus, Agnostics, etc.? Another rhetorical question—of course. Yes, by the thousands over the decades that he practiced. It worked for everyone, regardless of their religious tradition or belief system. Their belief did not change the fact that all are God's children. Their relationship with Consciousness was no different than mine. The stuff from which they are made, their spirit, body, soul (their memories and experiences), is the "stuff," all of which is part of that Consciousness. At a quantum level, it is ALL inexplicably intelligent energy. But here is an exciting twist. What if a fundamentalist Christian experienced healing through what was *(for a Christian)* a nontraditional means; through an instrument (a vessel), which was perhaps something other than the Christian tradition's "laying on of hands?" Would a Christian entertain a healing modality that was not western medicine, was not fundamentalist sanctioned, of fundamentalist origin as is "divine healing?"

That which follows is one highly creditable, real-life occurrence. It happened with the mother of the sixth man to walk on the Moon, Astronaut Edgar Mitchell. Mitchell was also the founder of the "Institute of Noetic Sciences" (INS). The following excerpt from his book "The Way of the Explorer" is reprinted here, word for word, under a license with the publisher. Mitchell was organizing a conference for his newly created INS. Like many astronauts, he had a life-changing awakening, a heightened awareness when he returned from the moon. He brought together people whose skills and gifts may complement the goals and objectives of the new organization. *Mitchell writes*:

"During the conference, I met several remarkable men and women, one of whom was a man by the name of Norbu Chen. Norbu was an American who had studied the earliest form of Tibetan Buddhism, a form that was liberally infused with ancient Tibetan Shamanistic practice. He was a small man of quick movements, graying beyond his years, inscrutable, and always in the midst of controversy. He also purported to be a healer. One evening after an entire day of speechmaking, I introduced Norbu to my mother, who was at the time in her early 60s. My interest was twofold. I wanted to find out whether Norbu Chen was real or just talk, and to help my mother if that was possible, though I was skeptical. My mother, being a fundamentalist Christian all her life, had definite and traditional ideas as to how the mind was capable of influencing matter through healing—either by the hand of God, or by that of Satan. There was no middle ground. Norbu did not think of himself as either but was quite convinced he could help. Making no promises, he merely suggested that we try and see what would happen. I was intensely curious, and my mother was at least a good sport about the whole thing. She agreed that something good might come of it. The following day Norbu and I met my mother in the seclusion of my suite, where he asked her to sit in a chair, remove her thick glasses, and relax. I watched from across the room as this strange Asian - trained man did what he claimed to have done for so many years. Then I witnessed my mother settle deeply into a relaxed state. After placing himself in a meditative trance (he claimed) through singing his strange mantra, his hands floated over my mother's head, pausing over the eyes. There seemed to be an unspoken acceptance on her part, a silent trust in this man she had never met until this weekend. After a few minutes of this, Norbu gently announced that he was finished and suggested she go to bed, sleep well, and treat herself kindly, as though she had been through major surgery. His prescription for nourishment was grape juice and broth. As I sat there in the chair observing, there was the hope that I'd just witnessed the extraordinary. I wanted something to have happened, but at the same time, I tried to be the detached, clinical observer, and not let my expectations soar. In any case, I didn't have to wait long for the results. At 6 o'clock the following morning, my mother came rushing to my room, exclaiming, "Son, I can see, I can see!" Without pausing to let me come to my senses, she proceeded to demonstrate her claim by reading from her thumb - worn Bible with glasses in hand. Then once again, she said more quietly, "I can see. Praise the Lord, I can see!" Dropping her glasses to the floor, she ground the thick lenses into shards under the heel of her shoe. Needless to say, I was impressed. I am not, by this account, nor with any other anecdotal story, attempting to convince the doubtful. That can only happen when the open-minded skeptic sets out for himself or herself to view (or better, to experience) such peculiar phenomena (at least peculiar to the Western mind), and conducts a careful investigation, unbiased by traditional interpretations. This wasn't science, but as far as I was concerned, it indicated where I personally needed to probe more thoroughly. All I can say is that it absolutely did happen in just this way Afterward I experienced the deep - down astonishment that arises from witnessing the extraordinary. This was an event I couldn't explain, but I couldn't deny it either. I knew my mother's reaction was authentic, and she hadn't been duped about her own sight. She proceeded to drive home alone, several hundred miles, without her glasses. After this episode I was sufficiently impressed, so I invited Norbu to Houston for a visit so that I might learn a few things from him myself. He arrived a few weeks later to stay many months, during which time I came to know not only Norbu the healer, but Norbu the man. What I learned was notably unremarkable. He wasn't especially complex, just a fellow with a peculiar capacity to heal that he couldn't adequately explain. A few days after returning home I learned another lesson that I wouldn't soon forget. After going about her routine for several days with nearly perfect vision, unassisted by contacts or eyeglasses, my mother called one day to ask whether or not Norbu was a Christian. His name was clearly derived from an Asian culture, which she suspected didn't likely coincide with her beloved faith. Though I didn't want to tell her, she was adamant. She absolutely wanted to know the faith of the man who'd allowed her to see again. Reluctantly, and perhaps ominously, I told her Norbu was in fact not a Christian, and the moment I did, the deep pain of regret was clear in her voice. Her new sight was not the work of the Lord, she insisted, but that of the darker forces of this world. She was absolutely certain that Norbu, being of another faith, must be an instrument of evil. No matter what I said to her, no matter how I explained my own secular understanding of such phenomena, she would not be convinced. Her vastly improved eyesight was the work of Satan. Hours later, the gift slipped away, and thick new glasses were required. I was both distressed and intrigued by this incident — distressed that such an incredible healing would be dismissed, and by my mother's agony in making this personal decision. But the intrigue, the fact that the sequence of events could occur at all, left an overriding impression. How could I have been so ignorant of something so important? It set me on the search for other persons similar to Norbu and gave me clear indication that I needed to learn something more about the role and power of belief in our lives. Whatever the clinical implications, it was clear to me that one's internal life, the subjective life, had fundamental importance. This was something science didn't address; I had paid little attention myself. But at the same time, I recognized a need for caution. Though I subsequently encountered many healers with similar capabilities, I also encountered many frauds. I've learned through years of experience that health and well - being are a product of total lifestyle. There is no panacea for illness in healers, allopathic medicine, naturopathic medicine, chiropractic, nutrition, and the like, though all can help. 2 Looking back on these times, I see how naïve I was. For several years I would continue to underestimate the power of belief in our lives because of the pervasiveness of my classical scientific training. It still puzzled me that belief could affect anything at all. But I suppose naïveté was also in large measure the impetus behind my founding an institution where research I thought important could be carried out. I believed that if other scientists witnessed such legitimate phenomena in controlled environments, they would see that it was at least worthy of further study and become excited by the prospects. But there were invisible veils that such unbridled idealism could not

Quantum Brook

see. As it turned out, disbelief was one of them. It was my opinion then, and it is my opinion today that disbelief prevents one from seeing what one wishes not to. My belief in the rationality of science blinded me to the equally rational consequences of disbelief. At the time, I still suspected there might be a nonphysical component to consciousness, capabilities that cannot be attributed to physical laws. But more likely, there were physical principles yet to be discovered. Whatever the answers, they would surely be revealed one day by a rational, thorough approach to the issues. These were natural, not supernatural events, well within the domain of scientific inquiry, and when validated, the impact on science would be revolutionary. But it should also change the way we addressed religion, philosophy, government, the way we saw ourselves in the universe, and the values we adhered to in daily life. Unfortunately, there were precious few who took the field of study seriously, as a number of eminent men of science had blunted their swords on these issues during the past century. But again, synchronicity would arise in my own exploration."

Selah

Conclusion:

This intensely personal and profound experience with Dr. Gardner opened my eyes to the vast implications of a Conscious Universe. Additionally, I continue to study various *energy healing* modalities like Qigong, Reiki, Acupuncture, and different similar interventions, each one exciting in and of itself. Yet, it is not so much they are all useful; it is how that experience laid a foundation and receptivity to Hawkins' discovery. Looking at all that we have examined in this chapter through a Biblical lens, the question is: Where can you go, in this dimension, or any other aspect or realm—that God is not there? My favorite and (*to me the*) most profoundly beautiful Psalm of them all…

Psalm: 139: 1-18

"You have searched me; Lord and you know me. You know when I sit and when I rise; you perceive my thoughts from afar. You discern my going out and my lying down; you are familiar with all my ways. Before a word is on my tongue you, Lord, know it completely. You hem me in behind and before, and you lay your hand upon me. Such knowledge is too wonderful for me, too lofty for me to attain.

Where can I go from your Spirit? Where can I flee from your presence? If I go up to the heavens, you are there; if I make my bed in the depths, you are there. If I rise on the wings of the dawn, if I settle on the far side of the sea, even there your hand will guide me, your right hand will hold me fast. If I say, "Surely the darkness will hide me and the light become night around me," even the darkness will not be dark to you; the night will shine like the day, for darkness is as light to you. For you created my inmost being; you knit me together in my mother's womb. I praise you because I am fearfully and wonderfully made; your works are wonderful; I know that full well. My frame was not hidden from you when I was made in the secret place, when I was woven together in the depths of the earth. Your eyes saw my unformed body; all the days ordained for me were written in your book before one of them came to be. How precious to me are your thoughts, oh God! How vast is the sum of them! Were I to count them, they would outnumber the grains of sand— when I awake, I am still with you."

Through a nuanced, more "Eastern" lens:

Can the wave that rises from the ocean say it is separate from the sea? It cannot. It is but a transient expression of that from whence it came. Can the cloud say it is not a part of the sea? It, too, is a momentary expression of the ocean. This vapor which has risen from the vast waters returns to the ground as rain. It flows into the brook, to the stream, into the river, and once again it returns to that which it is:

The Sea.

Quantum
Brook

Chapter 11

Conclusion &

A Glimpse Beyond the Spin

One of the things that I always loved about Star Trek's half Vulcan half-human, Mr. Spock, initially played by the late Leonard Nimoy, was his cool-headedness, something I rarely (if ever) enjoy. I am either passionate or completely indifferent. There is not a lot of in-between.

Spock's Vulcan-half tempered his human-half. His human-half sometimes softened his Vulcan-half. He was almost machine-like in his logic, but when needed most, empathy found a voice in situations where black and white answers are elusive. Humanness is more intuitive and emotional for some, while more logical and data-driven for others. Some are more artistic and "right-brain," while others are more "left brain" and analytical. Regardless of which "brain" dominates, we are mostly unconscious of the lengths our ego will go, to defend its viewpoint. Numerous studies show that ***the more evidence to the contrary, the more we will dig in to protect our position, regardless of what that position may be.*** The tendency to embrace information that supports our beliefs and reject information that contradicts our viewpoint is well known as "*confirmation bias.*" Copious, well-documented experiments on this subject have become the content of entire textbooks.

Harvard cognitive scientists Mercier and Sperber [1] concluded that it's hard to conceive of a more severe flaw than confirmation bias. They muse that a mouse, "bent on confirming its belief that there are no cats around," would quickly—be dinner. To the extent that confirmation bias leads people to dismiss the evidence, it doesn't change the fact that the cat is—right around the corner.

For us, humans (what has come to be known as) "myside bias" is skillful at spotting the weakness in someone else's argument while almost invariably being utterly blind to their own, and so it is with matters of faith. Other studies show that there is a release of dopamine when we find information that supports our bias. It makes us feel good. The point is, far more goes into changing our mind than just saying, *"I didn't know that. I've never thought of it that way."* The subconscious editor stands vigilant, rarely accepting, and largely rejecting any revisions to our operating system. The ego's pushback and that rush of dopamine make objectivity and change—difficult. The reality is: Regardless of the science, the evidence, logic, and reason are immaterial when it comes to how we *feel* about something. When it affects how we *feel*, it goes to the core of our very identity.

As an evangelical fundamentalist, I liked the idea of being exclusive, chosen, predestined, set apart, and separate from my eight billion brothers and sisters—*until* I had decades to digest—and fully process *the egoic implications, the inequity, the myopic absurdity, the total impossibility* of such a proclamation that God loved me—more than everyone else he created. That realization became as bright as the noonday sun. There is nothing more human than wanting to be daddy's favorite. But maturity brings empathetic imagining of being in my brother or sister's shoes. If God would predestine me to be his exclusive child, and predestine someone else from Tibet, India, Iran, Africa, China, Catholics, (or—the fundamentalist brand not quite measuring up) to hell, how could I possibly view that God as Love? If my Dad told me he loved me yet built a fire out back to dispose of one of my Buddhist playmates, how could I realistically see my Dad as loving and therefore Love my Dad? Could there be room for anything but utter contempt for such actions towards—*another human being?* Would he even do that to—a dog? Could there be anything more undivine? How *much more hatred* would I have for a deity who would condemn my friend to eternal hell—just for being born at the wrong place and wrong time? These descriptions are more befitting a lower life form that needs to fulfill a sadistic thrill.

If for some, the Bible is entirely inspired, totally infallible, and altogether inerrant. If it doesn't contain mistakes for others and there are no contradictions, if "it's very words remain truly—verbal, plenary inspiration," how excellent, for the rest of humankind would an utterly simple, pristine proof be? Yes, I know the response. "That wouldn't require faith."

The same who believe that God who created all there is possesses the *unparalleled ability to communicate effortlessly in a clear—single, inarguable, uncontested truth to ALL.* The endless exegetical dancing is threadbare.

God—has not *Self Revealed* in a manner that is remotely clear and unmistakably true. Instead, we have a confusing array of mixed messages emanating from more than 4,000 religions and *tens of thousands of perspectives— just within Christianity.*

The facts stand, unassailable. While argued emotionally, intellectually, they are indisputable. So, what shall we say then? If the beautiful story of Jesus, birth, death, and resurrection demonstrates that God so loved *the world*, could we— make an effort to once and for all, leave the doctrinal weeds or—is Humpty Dumpty irretrievably broken? Is it still possible to ascend the mountain and endeavor to look at *the whole world*, through an entirely new lens?

A Brief Glimpse Beyond the Spin.

Seeing Through the Spin, in part, spotlights the conflicts, flaws, inconsistencies, and the inhumanity of that which is said to be good news for the 25% and terrible news for the 75%. But what about the things common to all humankind rather than those which have divided us for millennia? Are there some things which may be demonstrably less elusive and consistently more inclusive? We have touched on briefly, if at the quantum level everything in the universe is energy, including you and me, did God instill the ability to reconfigure and realign misaligned energy or remove the blocks to the natural flow of the universal life force that animates us all? Jesus (clearly) knew how and said we would do more extraordinary things than he did (John 14:12). Did he give us tools that would (literally) enable us to determine truth from falsehood? Volume II—A Glimpse Beyond the Spin explores remarkable, little-known examples of "unexplainable" phenomena. If energy doesn't just contain information, but the information is itself energy, everything in the known universe, in the quantum state, is pure information-energy, which creates observable matter. [2] Let me restate that again. ***Energy is intelligent information, and all information is smart energy.***

Our thoughts and beliefs are also information-energy, which, literally, (not figuratively), creates our physical reality. The human brain emits energy in various wavelengths readable with EEG. The heart emits a field of electromagnetic energy 100 times more potent than the energy from the brain. The Heart Math Institute [3] suggests that if we had the instruments sensitive enough, we might be able to detect heart energy hundreds of feet away, perhaps miles away. With our current technology, we can detect toroidal field heart energy radiating 360 degrees from over five feet away.

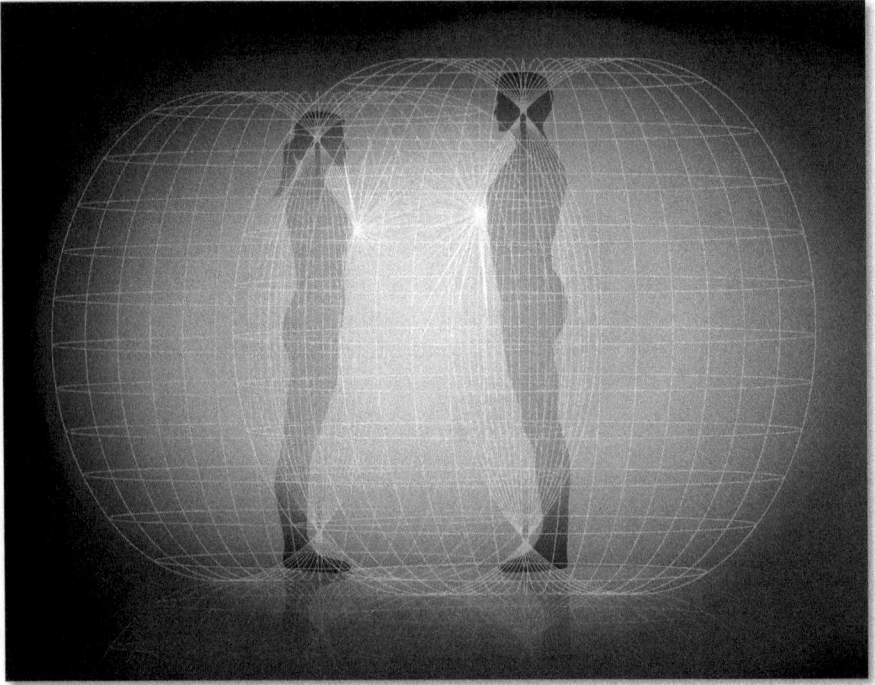

"EVERYTHING IN LIFE IS VIBRATION" – **ALBERT EINSTEIN**

Could it be that Jesus knew how to restructure, clean, realign that which was misaligned, reorder that which was out of order, and therefore he "healed many?" In Mark 6:5-6 where *"He could not do any miracles there, except lay his hands on a few sick people and heal them. He was amazed at their lack of faith."* Did the inharmonious conflict (vibrational dissonance) created by their lack of faith, affect His ability to rearrange, restructure, restore, and heal? When the Bible speaks of faith as being "substance and evidence," does that suggest that belief may be a Biblical word for *getting into a state of knowing* where the feeling of surety becomes a conductor [4] enabling faith-energy (a current) to flow instead of the lack of faith creating a resistance (resistor) [5] which diminishes the flow or stops the energy's movement entirely? What did Astronaut Edgar Mitchel's mother's healing reversal demonstrate? What does the astonishing results of the placebo effect in highly sophisticated double-blind studies suggest? What does it intimate when Jesus said, *"...they will do the works I have been doing, and they will do even greater things than these..."*[6]

Our bodies are third-dimension expressions of pure energy. The average size body is a compilation of 32.7 trillion individual cells. [7] Millions of cells are dying every second. Millions of cells are dividing, regenerating every second. Billions x billions of chemical reactions are happening between the cells *every second. Each cell* is comprised of 100 trillion atoms, and the protons in each atom are connected to all the other protons in the Universe [Nassim Haramein equations], *and— all of the information in the Universe is present in every proton.* Each cell [8] has approximately 100,000 protein receptors, like a tiny television antenna. That means 32.7 quintillion (32,700,000,000,000,000,000) total receptors. Each cells' 100,000 receptors are tuned to a different frequency. Our thoughts, **positive, negative, and mediocre all have a resonance** that effects and programs every cell in our body. Research in cell biology shows how our cells respond to nutritional frequencies, thought, music, visual images, **and the frequencies of communication—words of love or hate, self-talk, affirmations, or self-loathing.**

There is something commonly known as the placebo effect. In big pharma's double-blind studies, there are active efforts to **weed out those most affected by the belief** that the pill they are taking in the study may be the real drug. The efficacy for the group getting the actual drug is **often so small;** *the results are little more than "statistically significant"* when compared with the results of the group getting the placebo. *The sugar pill returns virtually the same result.* As it turns out, "You are not healed by the pill, you are healed by the belief that the pill heals you." According to Dr. Bruce Lipton, in a laboratory test, Prozac is no better than the placebo. Yet, millions of dollars are spent worldwide, everyday advertising Prozac. If Prozac works, it is because the person taking the pill believes it will work; it is the Placebo effect.

There is also something called the Nocebo effect. It is the belief that something is wrong. A feeling that you are going to contract a disease or get this cancer and die. *If you believe you will or will not,* **either way—you are correct.** If we take a drug and it is effective, it is because the receptor to that drug **already exists in our biology**, meaning the natural equivalent to that drug is already a part of us. The hypothalamus region of our brain is a magnificent, comprehensive, did I say incredible pharmacy ready and able to dispense whatever it is that we need—whenever we need it. We have to learn how to access it. (And mechanist believes all of this was a complete accident and fundamentalist believe it is complete heresy)

Ho'oponopono

Years ago, I listened to Dr. Joe Vitale's recorded series "The Missing Secret" and learned about a therapist who worked at a mental hospital for the criminally insane in Hawaii. This therapist used the ancient Hawaiian Huna *practice of forgiveness*, "Ho'oponopono," astonishingly healing *virtually all*—of his patients. The exciting thing is, he never once met with any of them over the four years that he worked at the hospital.

Joe learned of "self-identity Ho'oponopono," through a friend at a convention that they were both were attending. The story sounded so farfetched that he "blew it off" as impossible. The following year, his friend asked again if he pursued investigating the phenomenon. His friend retelling the story this time planted a seed of curiosity that Joe "had to act on," one which resulted in a phone interview and—eventual face to face with Dr. Ihaleakalá Hew Len.

Dr. Len explained that he had been the therapist on staff at the hospital. He asked the administration to agree that he *would not see the patients individually*; he would not see or visit them in his office. Instead, Dr. Len would walk the halls, seeing them in passing, but—Len wouldn't talk to them. When he went back to his office, he would close his door and think about each patient or, sometimes, first reading their file, then using the Ho'oponopono technique to "clean" what he was feeling *within himself.* Over the coming weeks, the patients started to get better.

Traditional Psych therapy requires a one on one. Dr. Hew Len's approach was highly unorthodox. In his interviews, Joe asked him to explain. Dr. Len's response was very "matter of fact." "Whatever I found in their file or intuited as I passed them in the halls, I would focus *and "clean on it."* To "clean on it" means that he would ask: "What is going on *in me,* that he/she/or what in my presence *is creating this behavior, and producing this outcome?* When he sees it, he says: *I'm sorry, please forgive me, thank you, I love you."* Joe asked, "what do those four phrases have to do with the patient?" Dr. Len said. "What I notice in the other person, *is first in me.* I am unable to see it in the other person *if it is not in me* (this is very similar to the Essene Mirrors.) What I am doing, Dr. Len said, "is petitioning divinity to erase it in me. It is erased in the other person **when it is erased first in me.**"

Dr. Len explained that the hospital ward he went to was so bad that the patients were shackled and-or sedated and put into isolation. When he started working there with the criminally mentally ill, he said they had three or four significant attacks between patients a day, maybe 30 patients at a time. If you worked there, you walked down the hall, with your back against the wall because you were afraid of being attacked. That is how dark, depressing, and scary it was. Most of the nurses and support staff would quit their job in less than thirty days. They couldn't keep a staff therapist. The therapist would also leave. When Dr. Len agreed to join them, they gave him free rein to do whatever he wanted. Rather than a traditional approach to therapy, he would use Ho'oponopono instead that he had been doing for 25 years. Dr. Len explained that Ho' oponopono was about "taking 100% responsibility for everything in *your world*," taking the phrase "you create your own reality" to a whole new level. If someone or anything shows up in your world, *you—caused it to happen. You co-created it.* Whatever or whoever is in your perception, there must be something *in you*—that created that creation. Ho, oponopono, asks that "whatever you observed, to be erased. Dr. Len described that "When it is erased—in him—it is deleted in the other person or persons in his personal or professional world.

"Your outer world is essentially a projection that doesn't exist outside of what is inside of you." When you experience something within yourself that you see in another person, anger, fear, rage, jealously, envy, you have to take it to the Divine-to God, and ask help in erasing (whatever he was holding in mind) by saying: "I'm sorry, please forgive me, thank you, I love you."

Dr. Len explained that "you are running, *entirely off of programs installed in your subconscious (unconscious) mind over time*, and—to such an extent that you do not even realize the effect they are having on you." (Does this mirror the material we covered in Chapter 1?) So, the things that are in our lives, we attract. At the unconscious level—We co-create.

"They must be 'cleaned'" as he quotes scientific studies that reveal how our conscious mind is aware of about 50 bits of information a second. Our unconscious mind is aware of 11 million bits of information at any given moment time. There is no contest as to which "mind" wins. Dr. Len worked at the Hawaii State hospital for four years. Just a few months after he started to work there, the patients began to get better. The patients previously requiring sedation, no longer needed sedation. The patients requiring shackles no longer had to be shackled. The employees that worked there started to come to work every day. They began to enjoy their work. They wanted to be in the mental ward, where Dr. Len was doing his job. However, most of the employees didn't know what he was doing— at all. When he went into his office, he would browse the patient's records, documentation, and notes.

Dr. Vitale went on to interview many people who worked at the hospital and found everything Dr. Len said to be true. In one interview, a former nurse said: "When Dr. Len first came here, he didn't do evaluations, assessments or diagnosis. Dr. Len provided no therapy or psychological testing. He often came late and didn't participate in case conferences or in the mandated record keeping. He instead practiced a 'weird' process of self-identity healing called Ho' oponopono which had something to do with taking 100% responsibility for yourself, looking only at yourself, and allowing the removal of harmful and unwanted energies within you." She cited numerous examples of the progress she observed with all the patients, but two, in particular—stood out for her.

An ex-marine was admitted to the unit as criminally insane. He later had to go to court for the heinous crime of the molestation and murder of a four-year-old girl—the crime that put him into the institution. Several psychologist and psychiatrists provided an array of diagnoses that would have *virtually guaranteed that* he would get a verdict of NGRI (not guilty because of insanity.) After Dr. Len's work, this ex-marine instead *dismissed his attorney*—and in court, faced the Judge saying "Your Honor. I am responsible for what I did, and I am sorry." The Judge granted his request to work out his sentence in a federal prison in his home state to be closer to his wife and children.

On another occasion, there was a relentlessly paranoid delusional patient with a history of violence who had seriously hurt people in public and the hospital. He had been admitted to this hospital many times. On this occasion, they sent him to the CISU (closed intensive security unit) for murder. She said the hair on her neck and back would stand up whenever he was close. A year or two after Dr. Len came, she saw this patient escorted in restraints. This time the hair *did not stand up*. She said it was if she was noticing him without judgment. Even when she would pass him, almost touching shoulder-to-shoulder, there was no longer an "I have to run away reaction." He appeared calm. She found out that the staff had been doing the Ho'oponopono that Dr. Len taught them. [9]

Dr. Len says, the way to clean, the way you erase the negative programming that dominates the subconscious is *to go to the Divine; go to God and ask that it "be cleaned," that the database in your unconscious "be erased."* It appeals to Love to delete the "bad data" in the psyche that is resonating-vibrating-with and attracting all of the things *you do not want*. You erase it by saying: ***I love you, I'm sorry, please forgive me. Thank you.***

Whatever I see in another person that I don't like; it exists in me and— needs cleaning. —Dr. Ihaleakalá Hew Len

It was assumed and accepted that the mentally ill, criminally insane patients, once admitted to the hospital, *would never be released*. Nevertheless, within months, of Dr. Len's arrival, restoration began, so much so that eventually, the hospital released all but two of them. The standard accepted, seclusion rooms, and need for physical restraints evaporated. The need for regular medication dwindled—all on its own. "...patients left the units for recreation and work activities without needing medical approval." The volatile, crazy, and very tense ward transformed into *one of peace*. The same chronically understaffed ward became overstaffed without effort.

How would evangelical Fundamentalism characterize this story; these results? Is this documented outcome desirable? Is this "a work of the devil" or—a *universal spiritual law? When **Love is put into motion, does it work**—regardless of the label? Identifying the blocks in ourselves removes blocks outside ourselves.

Conclusion

Something which became glaringly apparent over recent years is how often religious and academic indoctrination appears to paralyze the ability to think beyond the box it builds for itself. But then, when looking in the rearview mirror, building boxes seems to be the idea.

My perspective remains limited to what I've been able to reprogram and open my mind to see. I am also keenly aware that it is light years beyond where it used to be. I am just as aware that I have so much yet to learn. The plight of self-imposed limited vision is not only an affliction of the religious; it is often just as prevalent among academic elites who become too smart to contemplate that they may be missing the bigger picture. Their map from *here to there* becomes final, and the idea of other roads no longer exist—perceptions once open to new thought, quickly close to all, but self-serving groupthink. Thinking becomes the echoes of the silo. There is now too much to lose to think *outside the box.*

If only for a moment, break free and go where the noise is unable to obstruct the view. Stop doing. Stop thinking and—BE. Go beyond an intellectual understanding of the words on the page where "teacher" applied *their meaning*. Purposely escape Finite's programming and reach to *connect with the Infinite*. Contemplate your comparative smallness to *The Infinite* that created us. *You* are an eternal part of all there is.

I hope we will meet here again in volume II, and journey into some startling, spine-tingling discoveries that take *A Glimpse Beyond the Spin.*

Blessings

Open my eyes that I may see,
Open my ears—that I may hear,
Open my mind, so that I may—understand,
Open my heart—to unconditional Love,
So that I too, may love unconditionally.

EXHIBITS

Wright Brothers Telegram to their Father

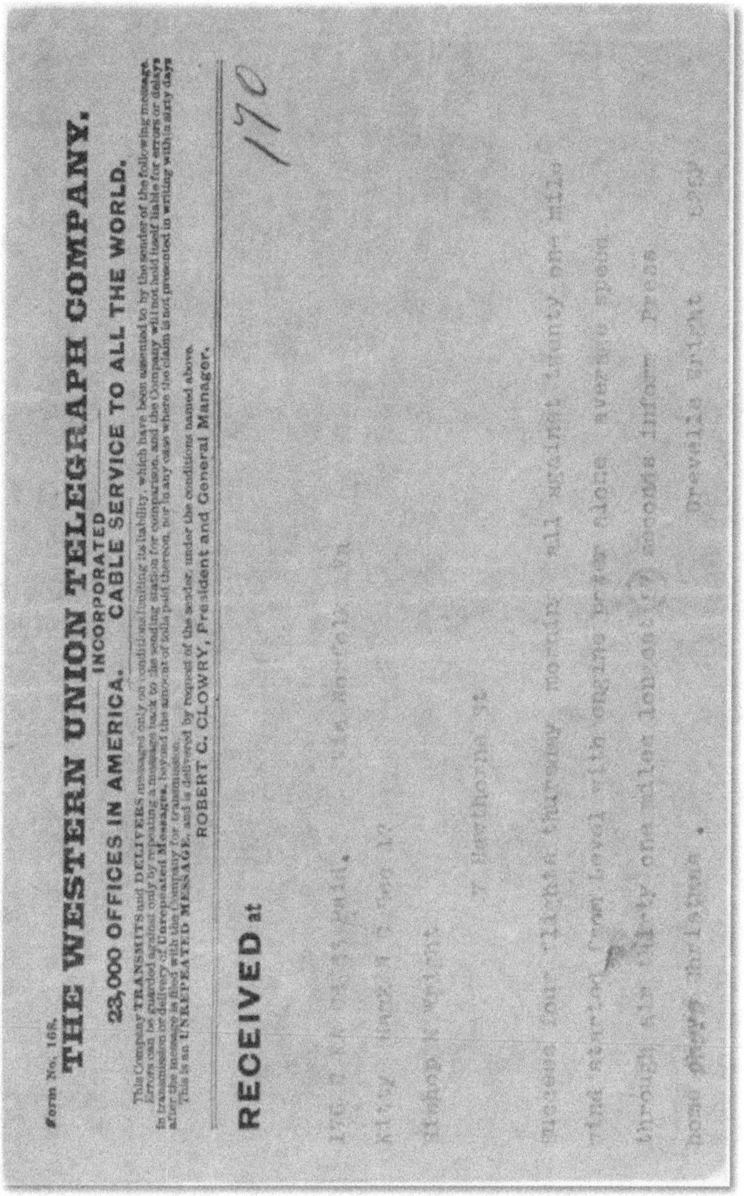

Form No. 168.

THE WESTERN UNION TELEGRAPH COMPANY.

INCORPORATED

23,000 OFFICES IN AMERICA. CABLE SERVICE TO ALL THE WORLD.

This Company TRANSMITS and DELIVERS messages only on conditions limiting its liability, which have been assented to by the sender of the following message. Errors can be guarded against only by repeating a message back to the sending station for comparison, and the Company will not hold itself liable for errors or delays in transmission or delivery of Unrepeated Messages, beyond the amount of tolls paid thereon, nor in any case where the claim is not presented in writing within sixty days after the message is filed with the Company for transmission.
This is an UNREPEATED MESSAGE, and is delivered by request of the sender, under the conditions named above.

ROBERT C. CLOWRY, President and General Manager.

RECEIVED at

170

176 C KA CS 33 Paid. Via Norfolk Va

Kitty Hawk N C Dec 17

Bishop M Wright

7 Hawthorne St

Success four flights thursday morning all against twenty one mile

wind started from Level with engine power alone average speed

through air thirty one miles longest 57 seconds inform Press

home Christmas . Orevelle Wright 525P

Granddaughters

Quantum
Brook

1956 Hammond B3 with a 147 Leslie

Ronda, my "steady" girlfriend Circa 1974

Yearbook Photo by Gary S. Chapman

Wedding Day

The Potter

Photograph by Joe Garland

NOTE: Matthew formats Jesus' genealogy begins with "Abraham, the father of Isaac."
Luke's inverts and flips his format and starts with "Joseph the son of Heli" and goes back
to Adam. To make it an easier read, I've made both consistent. Matthew and Luke now
begin with Joseph and go back to Abraham. Luke starts with Joseph and goes only to
Abraham to conserve space.

Matthew 1	Luke 3
1 This is the genealogy of Jesus the Messiah the son of David, the son of Abraham:	23 Now Jesus himself was about thirty years old when he began his ministry. He was the son, so it was thought, of Joseph,
Joseph son of Jacob,	**Joseph son of Heli**
Jacob son of Matthan	**Heli** the son of **Matthat**
Matthan son of Eleazar	**Matthat** son of **Levi** vs. 24
Eleazar son of Elihud	**Levi** son of **Melki**
Elihud son of Akim	Melki son of Jannai
Akim son of Zadok	Jannai son of Joseph
Zadok son of Azor	Joseph son of Mattathias
Azor son of Eliakim	Mattathias son of Amos
Eliakim son of Abihud	Amos son of Nahum
Abihud son of Zerubbabel	Nahum son of Esli
Zerubbabel son of Shealtiel	Esli son of Naggai
Shealtiel son of Jeconiah	Naggai son of Maath
Jeconiah son of Josiah	Maath son of Mattathias
Josiah son of Amon	Mattathias son of Semein
Amon son of Manasseh	Semein son of Josek
Manasseh son of Hezekiah	Josek son of Joda
Hezekiah the son of Ahaz	Joda son of Joanan
Ahaz son of Jotham,	Joanan son of Rhesa
Jotham son of Uzziah	Rhesa son of Zerubbabel
Uzziah son of Jehoram,	Zerubbabel son of Shealtiel
Jehoram son of Jehoshaphat	Shealtiel son of Neri
Jehoshaphat son Asa,	Neri son of Melki
Asa son of Abijah	Melki son of Addi,
Abijah son of Rehoboam	Addi son of Cosam,
Rehoboam the father of Abijah,	Cosam son Addi
Solomon son of David	Addi son of Elmadam,
David son of Jessie,	Elmadam son of Er,
Jesse son of Obed,	Er son of Joshua,
Obed son of Boaz,	Joshua son of Eliezer,
Boaz son of Salmon,	Eliezer son of Jorim,
Salmon son of Nahshon	**Jorim** son of **Matthat,**
Nahshon son of Amminadab,	**Matthat** son of **Levi,** vs 29
Amminadab son of Ram,	**Levi** son of **Simeon,**
Ram son of Hezron,	Simeon son of Judah,
Hezron son of Perez,	Judah son of Joseph,
Perez son of Judah,	Joseph son of Jonam,
Judah son of Jacob,	Jonam, son of Eliakim,
Jacob son of Isaac.	Eliakim son of Melea,
Isaac son of Abraham,	Melea son of Menna,
	Menna son of Mattatha,
	Mattatha son of Nathan,
	Nathan son of David,
	David son of Jesse,
	Jesse son of Obed,
	Obed son of Boaz,
	Boaz son of Salmon,
	Salmon son of Nahshon,
	Nahshon son of Amminadab,
	Amminadab son of Ram,
	Ram son of Hezron,
	Hezron son of Perez,
	Perez son of Judah,
	Judah son of Jacob,
	Jacob son of Isaac,
	Isaac son of Abraham,

Jesus' Genealogy

"The Dress"

If you purchased the black and white version of the book, Go to:
https://en.wikipedia.org/wiki/The_dress
to discover what color, it is that- *you see.*

Quantum
Brook

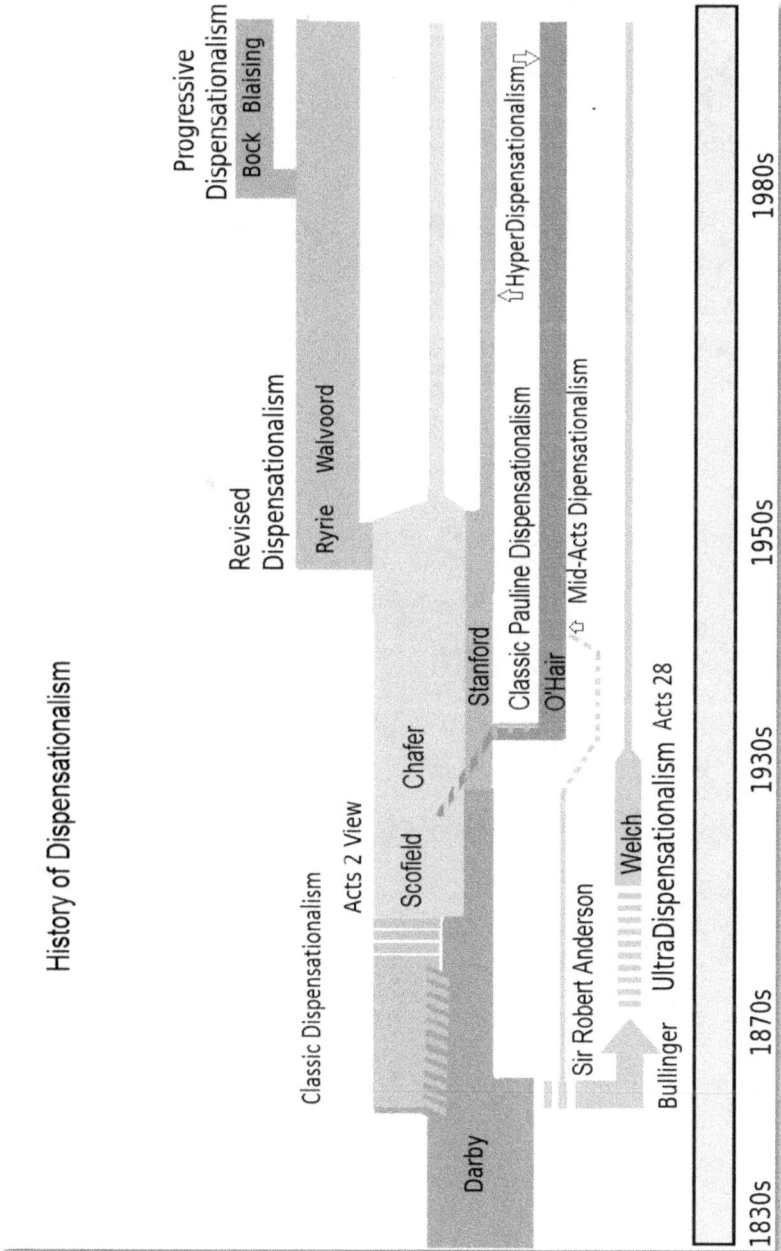

History of Dispensationalism

Classic Dispensationalism

Progressive Dispensationalism

Revised Dispensationalism

Bock Blaising

Ryrie Walvoord

⇧HyperDispensationalism

Acts 2 View

Stanford

Classic Pauline Dispensationalism

O'Hair

⇦ Mid-Acts Dipensationalism

Scofield Chafer

Darby

Sir Robert Anderson

Welch

Bullinger   UltraDispensationalism Acts 28

1830s   1870s   1930s   1950s   1980s

APPENDICES

May 18, 1920. You are born in Wadowice, Poland.

Your mother dies when you are nine years old. Your older brother will die when you are twelve. Growing up, you will be athletic. You will attend Krakow's Jagiellonian University where you will show interest in theater and poetry. The following year the Germans occupy Poland and Nazi troops will shut down your school. It is your desire to become a priest. You study at a secret seminary run by the Archbishop of Krakow. When WWII ends you spend two years in Rome and complete your doctorate in theology. You are ordained in 1946 and well regarded by your peers for your contributions to the church. You are made Cardinal in 1967. In 1978, you will make history by becoming the first non-Italian Pope in more than four hundred years. As the leader of the Catholic Church, you travel the world, visiting more than 100 countries to spread a message of faith and peace yet—an assassin will shoot you twice in attempt to take your life. Fortunately, you recover from your injuries and later forgive your attacker.

You are Pope John Paul II

The year is 1703. You are born in Epworth, England.

You are Twenty-three miles north-west of Lincoln. You are the fifteenth of nineteen siblings— only nine of which will live beyond infancy. Your parents became members of the Church of England as young adults. They purpose to give you an early education. You and your siblings will be taught to read as soon as you can walk and talk. They will expect you to become proficient in both Latin and Greek and to learn major portions of the New Testament by heart. Your mother will test your progress each day before lunch and before your evening prayers. Your mother will individually interview you and your siblings one evening each week for the purpose of intensive spiritual instruction. At age eleven, they will send you to the Charterhouse School in London where you will live a studious, methodical and religious life as you were trained at home. You will become known as an English cleric, theologian and evangelist, a leader of a revival movement within the Church of England. The societies you found will become the dominant form of an independent movement that continues to this day. You will be educated at Charterhouse and Christ Church, Oxford, Wesley and be elected a fellow of Lincoln College, Oxford in 1726. You will be ordained as an Anglican priest two years later. You will lead the "Holy Club," a society formed for the purpose of study and the pursuit of a devout Christian life. You will be unsuccessful in a two-year ministry in Savannah Georgia before returning to London to join a religious society led by Moravian Christians. May 24, 1738 you experience what will become known as evangelical conversion, when you feel your "heart strangely warm". You subsequently leave the Moravians and begin your own ministry. A key step in developing your ministry is to travel and preach outdoors. In contrast to Calvinist doctrine, you will embrace Arminian doctrine. Although you will not be a systematic theologian, you will argue the notion of Christian perfection, against Calvinism—and, in particular, against the doctrine of predestination. Throughout your life, you will remain within the established Church of England, insisting that your movement is well within the Church's tradition. Early in your ministry, you will be barred from preaching in many parish churches and will be persecuted. Later you will become widely respected and, by the end of your life, described as "the best loved man in England." You are the founder of the Methodist Church.

You are John Wesley,

July 10, 1509. You are born in France.

You are the first of four sons that will survive infancy. Your mother is the daughter of an innkeeper. She will die while you are still a child after giving birth to your brothers. Your father will have a prosperous career as the cathedral notary and registrar to the ecclesiastical court. He will die in 1531 after suffering with testicular cancer. Your father intends that you and your brothers enter the priesthood. You more so than your brothers are precocious and by age twelve, the bishop will employ you as a clerk. You soon receive the tonsure, a ceremony cutting your hair symbolizing your dedication to the Church. You will also win the support of a very influential family and, through their assistance, you will be able to attend the Collège de la Marche, in Paris where you will learn Latin from the great teacher, Mathurin Cordier. When you complete your studies, you will enter the Collège de Montaigu as a philosophy student. You will go on to become a theologian, pastor and reformer in Geneva during the Protestant Reformation. You will be a principal figure in developing the system of Christian theology later to be called Calvinism. These doctrines will emphasize predestination and the absolute sovereignty of God in granting salvation of the human soul from death or to eternal damnation. You will be a tireless polemic and apologist creating a lot of controversy. You will write commentaries on most books of the Bible, confessional documents, and various other theological treatises. Around the year 1530 you will break from the Roman Catholic Church. You will flee to Basel, Switzerland after religious tensions erupt in widespread and deadly violence against Protestant Christians in France. When you return, you will introduce new forms of church government and liturgy despite opposition that will come from powerful families in the city who will attempt to curb your authority. A Spaniard regarded by both Roman Catholics and Protestants as having a heretical view of the Trinity, will arrive in Geneva. You will denounce him, and the city council will burn him at the stake. An influx of supportive refugees will make way for new elections to the city council and your opponents will be forced out shifting the balance of power. You will spend your final years promoting the Reformation in Geneva and throughout Europe.

You are John Calvin

July 6, 1935. You are born in Taktser, mainland China.

Taktser is also known as Hongya Village, a village in Shihuiyao Township, Ping'an District, Haidong, in the east of Qinghai province. Taktser is the home of Tibetan, Han and Hui Chinese. Taktser was long ago pastureland for the larger village of Balangtsa, a two-hour walk from the valley. Your birth name is Lhamo Thondup. You are the fifth of sixteen siblings—seven of which die at a very young age. Religious officials search several months and following numerous significant spiritual signs, find you. You are now two years old. The officials identify you as the reincarnation of the 13th Dalai Lama. They rename you Tenzin Gyatso. Your tradition believes Dalai Lamas are the reincarnation of Avalokitesvara, an essential Buddhist deity, and the personification of compassion. According to the centuries-old your tradition, Dalai Lamas are enlightened beings who have postponed their own afterlife and chosen rebirth to benefit humanity. "Dalai" means "ocean" in Mongolian. "Lama" is the equivalent of the Sanskrit word "guru," or spiritual teacher. The title, Dalai Lama, is translated "Ocean Teacher," meaning "a teacher as spiritually deep as the ocean." You grow to become the head of state and spiritual leader of Tibet, a government-in-exile based in Dharamshala, India.

You are—the Dalai Lama

It was on October 2, 1869. You are born in Sudamapuri, India,

It is a coastal town on the Kathiawar, a part of Porbandar's small princely state in the Kathiawar Agency of the Indian Empire. At age 9, you enter the local school in Rajkot, near your home. You study the rudiments of arithmetic, history, the Gujarati language, and geography. When you turn 11, you go to the High School in Rajkot. You are an average, but a shy and tongue-tied student. You are not interested in games. Instead, your interests are books and school. At the age of 13, you will marry 14-year-old "Kasturba" in an arranged marriage according to the local customs.

You will grow up in a Hindu and Jain religious environment in your native Gujarat, which will become your primary influences. But you will also be influenced by your reflections and the literature of the Hindu Bhakti saints, Advaita Vedanta, Buddhism, Christianity, Islam, and thinkers such as Tolstoy, Ruskin, and Thoreau. Your devout Vaishnava Hindu mother will influence you the most. The local Hindu temples and saint tradition co-existed with Jain tradition in Gujarat. Your thoughts will evolve; your initial ideas will become the framework for your maturing philosophy. Early on, you commit yourself to truthfulness, temperance, chastity, and vegetarianism. In November 1887, when you are age eighteen, you graduate high school and enroll at Samaldas College in Bhavnagar State, which is the only degree-granting institution of higher education in the region. You drop out and return to your family in Porbandar.

In August 1888, you will leave Porbandar for Bombay. You will stay with the local Modh Bania community while waiting for the ship travel arrangements. After learning of your plans, the elders will warn you that England will tempt you to compromise your religion and eat and adopt Western ways. You will tell them about your promise to your mother and her blessings. You will sail from Bombay to London and attend University College, London, at UCL; you will study law and jurisprudence. You will be invited to enroll at Inner Temple with the intention of becoming a barrister. The burdensome shyness and self-withdrawal you experienced through your childhood, and teens will persist through your arrival in London. But you will join a public speaking practice group and overcome your handicap to practice law. During your future stay in South Africa, along with scriptures and philosophical texts of Hinduism and other Indian religions, you will read translated texts of Christianity, including the Bible and Islam's Quran. A Quaker mission in South Africa will attempt to convert you to Christianity. You will join them in prayer and debate Christian theology with them, but you will refuse conversion explaining that you cannot accept their theology that Christ was the only son of God. Your comparative studies of religions and interaction with scholars will lead you to respect all faiths and develop many concerns about the imperfections in them all, troubled by their frequent misinterpretations. You will become fond of Hinduism and refer to the Bhagavad Gita as your spiritual dictionary and the most considerable single influence in your life.

You are Mahatma Gandhi

Excerpts from a Letter to Georgia's Governor, Brian Kemp

COVID-19

Governor, I need your help in getting the following information to the right person. I have made *Numerous* attempts over the past several months, to connect with government officials and high-profile media, all of which have failed to connect with anyone *who will stop—and listen*. I am asking for nothing more than an opportunity to— validate legitimacy. Anyone genuinely interested *(and who wouldn't be)* in stopping COVID-19 and preventing its reemergence, *PLEASE take this request seriously.*

Our nation's current COVD-19 strategy is equivalent to using a metaphorical BB gun when we have available to us a metaphorical B1 Bomber to stop this Pandemic— **dead in its tracks**. But what I have to say is "impossible to believe" so therefore I'm little more than a voice crying in the wilderness. The war on COVID would be over—- in a day if this technology had been in place before COVID19. It *would have never reached our shores*.

Whatever the reason or God forbid, sinister intention behind this scourge, "We the People" would be protected. This technology would not only eliminate COVID19 but cold viruses, influenza, COVID-XX, SARS-Co-V, Hanta virus, Lassa virus Legionnaires, and diseases born bacteria. In other words:

The need for all the medications and vaccines to treat these threats to our health would evaporate and—That became the problem. For many years, the inventor made strenuous attempts to get it into the market after receiving his patent, but it would all but put big pharma out of business; at the very least cost them Trillions…

The inventor and patent holder, *whom I am privileged to call my best friend*, has an Einsteinian IQ and two PhDs. He was awarded a Ph.D. in physics for generation, manipulation and shaping "E" fields and "H" fields. He was awarded Ph.D. EE for the methodology in reading and translating "E" fields and "H" fields. He is a prolific inventor who holds more 600 national and international Patents in Physics, Luminary, Chemistry, Medical, Molecular Physics, and numerous additional subcategories and the Moxy molecule I will describe. Early in his career, he worked at Schlumberger and Scientific Atlanta. He served, and still serves as a highly sought-after international consultant and problem solver. He enjoyed a distinguished military history as a *member of Seal Team One*.

Approximately 9 years ago, *the USPTO issued the only multi-patent ever awarded— for a molecule.* The patented mechanism generates waves of Moxy in real-time where it seeks airborne and surface born viruses and bacteria, killing them instantly, all the while creating oxygen-rich environments, which dramatically improves the health of those who may suffer from upper respiratory challenges. The side effects are *Higher Oxygen levels. Oxygen* would saturate homes, airplanes, offices, business, restaurants, stadiums, malls, places of worship, and—*hospitals*, making it necessary to calibrate or dial back an "always-on" condition. It would have to be timed to an, "occasionally on" condition, in order to regulate saturation. Otherwise, everyone would be high on Oxygen as if they were hyperventilating. Moxy is a programmable molecule (as hard as that may be to understand) for the *very desirable, and purposely highly unstable* state of as high as O14 but usually programmed for O6 before it quickly degrades to O2.

There are presently only two facilities in the world that can build the mechanism that generates Moxy in the required tolerances (10 to 7th). Thankfully, it is not China. One of the primary Moxy generating components is a Single-Electron Gate Technology (SEGT) diode that contains a tuned resonate junction, which was also granted *four separate patents on this one unique component alone.* This technology is real, tested, and demonstratable.

I need to connect with my Governor and—- my President and let them know there is a solution but— *one which* BIG PHARMA will do everything in their power to stop. Enough is enough.

The following is an excerpt from my personal email conversation with him several years ago, which summarizes the crux of the challenge, one which led to his frustration, complete exhaustion, and abandoning potential ongoing efforts.

"...after I ran out of money from the endless chase. I partnered up with [...] for five years jumping through hoops, demonstrating how Moxy killed every airborne, surface borne virus, and bacteria we put to it. $5million later, countless hours of special lab test, meetings over and over— and over again to present results; testimonies by doctors, scientists, and still—- we were not any closer to getting past the FDA than when we began. In our final meeting at [...], we had hired a special investigator whose specialty was the FDA. After paying him $35,000, his conclusion was:

Quantum
Brook

'Gentlemen, isn't it obvious that Big Pharma owns the FDA lock, stock, and barrel? What you have here could cost big Rx $Trillions. How much do you think it would cost them to instead, exterminate this whole problem? A whole lot less than a $Trillion! Gentlemen, the President of the United States, can't help you. It's way beyond him too! Bury it and go on with your lives!'"
Jerry Bush

The Great Flood

The Gilgamesh Epic

In 1853 archeologists discovered several fragments of a different ancient text in the palace ruins of ancient Nineveh. George Smith deciphered the text written in the cuneiform script. The discovery is one of the great epics of ancient literature, named for its lead character *Gilgamesh*, the king of Uruk, a city in southern Mesopotamia. Numerous additional fragments of the legend have since been discovered and assembled. They tell the story of this great hero, Gilgamesh (the Noah character), especially in his relationship with a once very uncivilized, but now tamed, companion Enkidu. The epic is highly episodic, quickly going from one adventure to the next. Still, there are many striking parallels to what can be found in the ancient history of Genesis, for example in the tale of the Garden of Eden. One part of the epic was immediately found to be particularly significant: a story of the flood with unmistakable similarities to the account in Genesis. At one point in the narrative, *Gilgamesh* meets with a man who had become immortalized, named *Utnapishtim*. Utnapishtim tells Gilgamesh how he survived a flood sent from the gods to destroy all the living things on earth. The gods instructed him to "Put aboard the seed of all living things, into the boat, the boat that you are to build." [1] They instruct him as to how to build the boat and what dimensions to make it. They tell him to take his relatives onboard as well. The rains descend, the massive flood occurs; all the peoples of the earth are destroyed. The boat comes to rest on a mountain. As the waters dry up, Utnapishtim sends out a dove, which returns when there is no dry place to perch; then a swallow with the same result; and a raven, which does not return. After leaving the boat, Utnapishtim makes a sacrifice to the gods. All of these points parallel the Genesis story of the flood cannot be accidental, nor could Genesis have influenced this Mesopotamian myth. The earliest accounts of Gilgamesh date from before 2000 BC, *many centuries before the J and P (historical) sources of the story of Noah.*

The Story of Atrahasis

Stories from around the world about a flood destroying the human race isn't limited to Genesis and Gilgamesh. Another from ancient Near Eastern text tells of "Atrahasis" (the main character). An old version of the story comes from Babylon. It was written on clay tablets dating to the beginning of the 17th century BCE, *many centuries before the J and P sources for the book of Genesis*. In this

224

account, the gods are upset that the earth is overpopulated. It's so overpopulated that the noise the masses are creating is so disturbing, the gods decide to destroy them by the flood. They instruct Atrahasis to build a boat. The boat is to have upper decks, lower decks, and bitumen (most likely for waterproofing.) Atrahasis then gathers all the animals and his family on board before sealing the door shut. The flood "roars like a bull. The winds scream and howl like a wild ass." There is total darkness; no sun. [2] In this version of the story, the flood only lasts seven days and nights, but it kills most of the population. Atrahasis makes a sacrifice to the gods.

Some apologist suggests that multiple ancient texts containing flood stories make a case for a worldwide flood that destroyed the entire human race. The problem is, which one? Who was the real hero? If all of these stories are true, which man, his family, and animals were saved? Noah? Utnapishtim? Atrahasis? If it was more than one flood, was Noah's flood the last one? Regardless, covering the entire globe in water over five miles deep, and for it to ever recede, is *physically impossible*. Add that there is not a bit of geological evidence to support the fantasy. [3] In fact, quite the opposite: there is undeniable evidence that nothing like this (on a worldwide scale) happened. [4] It is wiser to think that these various texts arose in cultures rooted in areas prone to severe floods, some so severe that they became the stuff of legend.

Portions of this appendices taken from eharmanblog.com

[1] Translations made by Stephanie Dalley, *Myths from Mesopotamia: Creation, The Flood, Gilgamesh,* and Others (New York: Oxford University Press, 1989), p. 110.
[2] Dally, Myths from Mesopotamia, p. 31.
[3] biologos.org/articles/flood-geology-and-the-grand-canyon-what-does-the-evidence-really-say
[4] *The Grand Canyon, Monument to an Ancient Earth;* Carol Hill, Gregg Davidson, Wayne Ranney, Tim Helble

Appendices

	NIV	NKJV	KJV	1611 KJV	YLT	CLT	Latin Vulgate
Gn. 37:35	grave *2	grave	grave	graue	Sheol	unseen	infernum
Gn. 42:38	grave *2	grave	grave	graue	Sheol	unseen	inferos
Gn. 44:29	grave *2	grave	grave	graue	Sheol	unseen	inferos
Gn. 44:31	grave	grave	grave	graue	Sheol	unseen	inferos
Nu. 16:30	grave *2	pit	pit	pit	Sheol	unseen	infernum
Nu. 16:33	grave	pit	pit	pit	Sheol	unseen	infernum
Dt. 32:22	death	hell	lowest hell	hell	Sheol	unseen	inferni
1Sa. 2:6	grave	grave	grave	graue	Sheol	unseen	infernum
2Sa. 22:6	grave *2	Sheol	hell	hell	Sheol	unseen	inferi
1Ki. 2:6	grave *2	grave	grave	graue	Sheol	unseen	inferos
1Ki. 2:9	grave	grave	grave	graue	Sheol	unseen	infernum
Job 7:9	grave *2	grave	grave	graue	Sheol	unseen	inferos
Job 11:8	grave *2	Sheol	hell	hell	Sheol	unseen	inferno
Job 14:13	grave *2	grave	grave	graue	Sheol	unseen	inferno
Job 17:13	grave *2	grave	grave	graue	Sheol	unseen	inferus
Job 17:16	death *2	Sheol	pit	pit	Sheol	unseen	infernum
Job 21:13	grave *2	grave	grave	graue	Sheol	unseen	inferna
Job 24:19	grave *2	grave	grave	graue	Sheol	unseen	inferos
Job 26:6	Death *2	Sheol	hell	hell	Sheol	unseen	infernus
Ps. 6:5	grave *2	grave	grave	graue	Sheol	unseen	inferno
Ps. 9:17	grave *2	hell	hell	hell	Sheol	unseen	infernum*11
Ps. 16:10	grave *2	Sheol	hell	hell	Sheol	unseen	n/a
Ps. 18:5	grave *2	Sheol	hell	hell	Sheol	unseen	n/a
Ps. 30:3	grave *2	grave	grave	graue	Sheol	unseen	n/a
Ps. 31:17	grave *2	grave	grave	graue	Sheol	unseen	n/v
Ps. 49:14	grave *2	grave	grave	graue	Sheol	unseen	n/a
Ps. 49:14*5	grave *2	grave	grave	graue	Sheol	unseen	n/a
Ps. 49:15	grave	grave	grave	graue	Sheol	unseen	n/a
Ps. 55:15	grave *2	hell	hell	hell	Sheol	unseen	n/v
Ps. 86:13	grave *2	Sheol	hell	hell	Sheol	unseen	n/v
Ps. 88:3	grave *2	grave	grave	graue	Sheol	unseen	n/a
Ps. 89:48	grave *2	grave	grave	graue	Sheol	unseen	n/v

Quantum Brook

	NIV	NKJV	KJV	1611 KJV	YLT	CLT	Latin Vulgate
Ps. 116:3	grave *2	Sheol	hell	hell	Sheol	unseen	n/v.
Ps. 139:8	depths *2	hell	hell	hell	Sheol	unseen	n/a
Ps. 141:7	grave *2	grave	grave	graues	*6	unseen	n/a
Pr. 1:12	grave *2	Sheol	grave	graue	Sheol	unseen	infernus
Pr. 5:5	grave *2	hell	hell	hell	Sheol	unseen	inferos
Pr. 7:27	grave *2	hell	hell	hell	Sheol	unseen	inferi
Pr. 9:18	grave *2	hell	hell	hell	Sheol	unseen	inferni
Pr. 15:11	Death *2	hell	hell	hell	Sheol	unseen	infernus
Pr. 15:24	grave *2	hell	hell	hell	Sheol	unseen	inferno
Pr. 23:14	death *2	hell	hell	hell	Sheol	unseen	inferno
Pr. 27:20	Death*2	hell	hell	hell	Sheol	unseen	infernus
Pr. 30:16	grave *2	grave	grave	graue	Sheol	unseen	infernus
Ec. 9:10	grave *2	grave	grave	graue	Sheol	unseen	inferos
SS. 8:6	grave *2	grave	grave	graue	Sheol	unseen	inferus
Is. 5:14	grave *2	Sheol	hell	hell	Sheol	unseen	infernus
Is. 14:9	grave *2	hell	hell *9	hell	Sheol	unseen	infernus
Is. 14:11	grave	Sheol	grave	hell	Sheol	unseen	inferos
Is. 14:15	grave	Sheol	hell	hel*10	Sheol	unseen	infernum
Is. 28:15	grave *2	Sheol	hell	hell	Sheol	unseen	inferno
Is. 28:18	grave	Sheol	hell	hell	Sheol	unseen	inferno
Is. 38:10	death*2	Sheol	grave	graue	Sheol	unseen	inferi
Is. 38:18	grave *2	Sheol	grave	graue	Sheol	unseen	infernus
Is. 57:9	grave *2	Sheol	hell	hell	Sheol	unseen	inferos
Ez. 31:15	grave *2	hell	grave	graue	Sheol	unseen	inferos
Ez. 31:16	grave	hell	hell	hell	Sheol	unseen	infernum
Ez. 31:17	grave	hell	hell	hell	Sheol	unseen	infernum
Ez. 32:21	grave *2	hell	hell	hell	Sheol	unseen	inferni
Ez. 32:27	grave	hell	hell	hell	Sheol	unseen	infernum
Ho. 13:14	grave *2	grave	grave	graue	Sheol	unseen	mortis
Ho. 13:14*5	grave *2	grave	grave	graue	Sheol	unseen	inferne
Am. 9:2	grave *2	hell	hell	hell	Sheol	unseen	infernum
Jon. 2:2	grave *2	Sheol	hell *9	hell	Sheol	unseen	inferni *12
Hab. 2:5	grave *2	hell	hell	hell	Sheol	unseen	infernus

	1611 KJV	KJV & NIV &	Geneva	NASB	YLT	Vulgate
Gehenna translated in the New Testament						
Mt. 5:22	hell fire	hell	hell *3	hell *6	Gehenna	gehennae
Mt. 5:29	hell	hell	hell	hell	Gehenna	gehennam
Mt. 5:30	hell	hell	hell	hell	Gehenna	gehennam
Mt. 10:28	hell	hell	hell	hell	Gehenna	gehennam
Mt. 18:9	hell fire	hell	hell fire	hell	Gehenna	gehennam
Mt. 23:15	hell	hell	hell	hell	Gehenna	gehennae
Mt. 23:33	hell	hell	hell *4	hell	Gehenna	gehennae
Mk. 9:43	hell	hell	hell	hell	Gehenna	gehennam
Mk. 9:45	hell	hell	hell	hell	Gehenna	gehennam
Mk. 9:47	hel fire*1	hell	hellfire	hell	Gehenna	gehennam
Lk. 12:5	hell	hell	hell	hell	Gehenna	gehennam
Js. 3:6 *2	hell	hell	hell *5	hell	Gehenna	gehenna

*1 spelled with one L in the original
*2 Other than Jesus, the only other person in the N.T. who uses the term Gehenna.
*3 Margin reads: "Whereas we read here, Hell, it is in the text itself, Gehenna, which is a Hebrew word made of two, and it as much to say, as the Valley of Hinnon, which otherwise Hebrews called Tophet: It was a place where the Israelites cruelly sacrificed their children to false gods, whereupon it was taken for a place appointed to torment the reprobates in Jeremiah. 7:31.
*4 Margin reads: "Look Chap 5. Verse 22."
*5 Margin reads: "So the Grecians called the deep dungeons under the earth, which should be appointed to torment the souls of the wicked in."
*6 note says Gr., Gehenna

Quantum Brook

Hades translated in the New Testament							
	1611 KJV	KJV	NIV	Geneva	NKJV	CLT	Vulgate
Mt. 11:23	hell	hell	depths	hell	Hades	unseen	infernum
Mt. 16:18	hell	hell	Hades	hel *4	Hades	unseen	inferi
Lk. 10:15	hell	hell	depths	hell	Hades	unseen	infernum
Lk. 16:23	hell	hell	hell *7	hell	Hades	unseen	inferno
Ac. 2:27	hell	hell	grave	grave	Hades	unseen	inferno
Ac. 2:31	hell	hell	grave	grave	Hades	unseen	inferno
1Cor. 15:55**	grave*2	grave	death	grave	Hades	death	mors
Rv. 1:18	hell	hell	Hades	hell	Hades	unseen	inferni
Rv. 6:8	hell	hell	Hades	Hell *5	Hades	unseen	inferus
Rv. 20:13	hell *3	hell	Hades	hell	Hades	unseen	inferus
Rv. 20:14	hell	hell	Hades	hell	Hades	unseen	inferus

*1 prop. unseen {Strong's #86}

*2 margin "Or, hell"

*3 margin "Or, hell" in some 1611 printings. Some printings had "grave" in the text and "Or, hell" in the margin. Choices clearly advance a biased narrative

*4 spelled with one L in the original

*5 Capitalized in the original

*7 footnote says Greek Hades

*8 Hades] The unseen World, the adobe of departed spirits, In the A.V. both this word and 'Gehenna' are rendered 'Hell.' Each occurs twelve times. In this translation the two words are consistently kept distinct.

**In the King James Version, 1 Corinthians 15:55 reads: "O death, where is thy sting? O grave (hades), where is thy victory?"

This is a reference to the Old Testament: Hosea 13:34: "I will ransom them from the power of the grave (she'ol); I will redeem them from death: O death, I will be thy plagues; O grave (she'ol), I will be thy destruction: repentance shall be hid from mine eyes."

Appendices

	1611 KJV	KJV, NKJV	Geneva	NIV	NRSV	YLT & CLT	Roth	Vulgate
Tartarus translated in the New Testament								
2 Pt. 2:4*1	hell	hell	hell	hell *2	hell *3	Tartarus	lowest hades	tartarum

*1 The only places in the Bible where this term appears
*2 note says Greek tartarus
*3 note says Greek tartaroo

End Notes & Bibliography

Introduction

[1] Webster defines Eisegesis as the interpretation of a text by **reading into it one's own ideas.** It defines Exegetics as **the science of interpretation** especially of the Scriptures.

[2] nytimes.com/2015/05/10/books/review/the-wright-brothers-by-david-mccullough.html

[3] *The Physics of Spirituality* | Nassim Haramein with Vishen Lakhiani

[4] Galileo was made to recite and sign this formal abjuration: *(quoted in Shea and Artigas 194)* "I have been judged vehemently suspect of heresy, the is, of having held and believed that the sun is the centre of the universe and immoveable, and that the earth is not at the center of same, and that it does move. Wishing however, to remove from the minds of your Eminences and all faithful Christians this vehement suspicion reasonable conceived against me, I abjure with a sincere heart and unfeigned faith, I curse and detest the said errors and heresies, and generally all and every error, heresy, and sect contrary to the Holy Catholic Church.

[5] *en.wikipedia.org/wiki/Orlando_Ferguson*

[6] **Perspective** refers to a point of view whereas **Perception** refers to an interpretation an individual develops through their awareness.

[7] *wiki.tfes.org/The_Flat_Earth_Wiki*

[8] Abu Umama narrated: "*The Messenger of God said,* 'Everyone that God admits into paradise will be married to 72 wives; two of them are houris and seventy of his inheritance of the [female] dwellers of hell. All of them will have libidinous sex organs and he will have an ever-erect penis.' " - Sunan Ibn Majah, Zuhd *(Book of Abstinence) 39* "Each time we sleep with a Houri we find her virgin. Besides, the penis of the Elected never softens. The erection is eternal. The sensation that you feel each time you make love is utterly delicious and out of this world and were you to experience it in this world you would faint. Each chosen one [i.e. Muslim] will marry seventy [sic] houris, besides the women he married on earth, and all will have appetizing vaginas." - Al-Suyuti, Al-Itqan fi Ulum al-Qur'an, p. 351. Two noteworthy points: 1) there is no mention in the Koran of the actual number of virgins available in paradise, 2) the dark-eyed damsels are available for *all Muslims*, not just martyrs. It is in *Islamic Traditions* that we find the 72 virgins in heaven specified [...](*Tafsir) of Surah Al-Rahman (55), verse 72:* "The Prophet Muhammad was heard saying: *'The smallest reward for the people of paradise is an abode where there are 80,000 servants and 72 wives,* over which stands a dome decorated with pearls, aquamarine, and ruby, as wide as the distance from Al-Jabiyyah [a Damascus suburb] to Sana'a [Yemen]'." Modern

apologists of Islam attempt to downplay the materialism and sexual implications of such descriptions, but, as the Encyclopedia of Islam says, even orthodox Muslim theologians such as al Ghazali (died 1111 CE) and Al-Ash'ari (died 935 CE) have "admitted sensual pleasures into paradise." One of the reasons Nietzsche hated Christianity was that it "made something unclean out of sexuality," whereas Islam, many would argue, sex was positive. One cannot imagine any Church fathers writing ecstatically of heavenly sex as al-Suyuti did, except St Augustine before his conversion. But surely to call Islam sex-positive is to insult all Muslim women, for sex is seen entirely from the male point of view; women's sexuality is admitted but seen as something to be feared, repressed, and a work of the devil. **Warraq, *The Guardian: Special Report. Religion in the UK Jan. 2002***
[9] Joseph Selbie, Amit Goswami, The Physics of God

Chapter 1, From There to Here

[1] Many preachers were illiterate and asked a congregate to read the chosen text out loud. The preacher would expound on the phrase and, when finished, shout, "Read on!"
[2] The nature of Ham's transgression and the reason Noah cursed Canaan when Ham sinned have been debated for Millennia. The story's original purpose may have justified the subjection of the Canaanite people to the Israelites; however, in later centuries, the narrative was reinterpreted by some Christians, Muslims, and Jews as an explanation for black skin, as well as a justification for slavery. Most Christians, Muslims, and Jews now disagree with such interpretations. The biblical text never mentions Ham as being cursed or race or skin color.
[3] Leslie's two-speed rotating horns (treble frequencies) and two-speed *counter-rotating* drum beneath a woofer (down-firing bass frequency speaker).

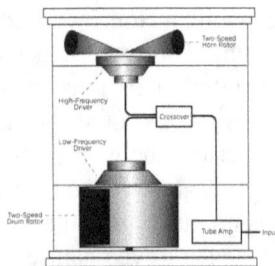

Diagram provided by Strymon Engineering

FIG 1. SCHEMATIC DIAGRAM OF LESLIE' TWIN-ROTOR SPEAKER SYSTEM

[3] Search YouTube for: Cory Henry & Yoran Vroom - Gotcha Now Doc (live @Bimhuis Amsterdam) Easily observe the top speaker rotating in the Leslie cabinet. The artist changes speed between slow and fast. Listen to the difference. The Hammond sound *is nothing but a dull organ*—without the Leslie.

Quantum Brook

[4] pg. 75 Classic Keys: *Keyboard Sounds That Launched Rock Music;* By Alan S. Lenhoff, David E. Robertson
[5] For musical classics resting on the foundation of the Hammond B3 sound, Search YouTube:

> Brook Denton, - Rainy Night in Georgia
> Procol Harum - Whiter Shade of Pale (quintessential B3 song)
> Cory Henry - The Revival Project
> Billy Preston - You Can't Beat God Giving
> Billy Preston- That's the Way God Planned It
> Steven Stills - Love the One You're With
> Steve Winwood - Gimme Some Lovin
> Billy Preston - You Are So Beautiful (on the Hammond B3)

[6] Genesis 9:18–27, Ephesians 6:5-7, Colossians 3:22-24
[7] 1 Corinthians 11:3-16, 1 Timothy 2:11-15, Ephesians 5:22-24, 1 Corinthians 14:33-35, Colossians 3:18, Peter 3:1-6, Titus 2:4-5
[8] Romans 7:15-20NIV "I do not understand what I do. For what I want to do I do not do, but what I hate I do. 16 And if I do what I do not want to do, I agree that the law is good.17 As it is, no longer I myself who do it, but it is sin living in me. 18 For I know that good itself does not dwell in me, that is, in my sinful nature. [a] For I have the desire to do what is good, but I cannot carry it out. 19 For I do not do the good I want to do, but the evil I do not want to do— this I keep on doing. 20 Now if I do what I do not want to do, it is no longer I who do it, but it is sin living in me that does it."
[9] 1Thessalonians 4:17NIV "After that, we who are still alive and are left will be caught up together with them in the clouds to meet the Lord in the air. And so we will be with the Lord forever."
[10] 2 Corinthians 5:19 that God was reconciling the world to himself in Christ, not counting people's sins against them. And he has committed to us the message of reconciliation.
[11] 2 Corinthians 5:21 God made him who had no sin to be sin for us so that in him, we might become the righteousness of God.
[12] [Isaiah 1:18] "Though your sins are like scarlet, they shall be as white as snow; though they are red as crimson, they shall be like wool."
[13] [Micah 7:19] "You will again have compassion on us; you will tread our sins underfoot and hurl all our iniquities into the depths of the sea."

Chapter 2, Perspective from a Different Perspective

[1] Beta waves (12 to 38 Hz)
  Alpha waves (8 to 12 Hz)
  Theta waves (3 to 8 Hz)
  Delta waves (.5 to 3 Hz)

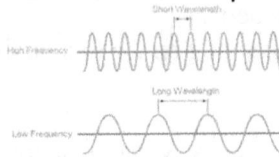

[2] Frequency is the number of wave cycles that are completed in one second. Amplitude measures the height of the crest of the wave from the midline. The wavelength measures the horizontal distance between cycles. Wave speed is found by multiplying the wavelength and the frequency.

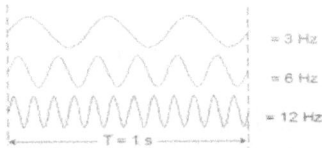

= 3 Hz
= 6 Hz
= 12 Hz
T = 1 s

[3] healyourlife.com/are-you-programmed-at-birth; BruceLipton.com; Bruce H. Lipton Ph.D.; *The Biology of Belief*: "The predominant delta and theta activity expressed by children younger than six signifies that their brains are operating at levels—below consciousness. Delta and theta brain frequencies define a brain state known as a hypnagogic trance—the same neural state that hypnotherapists use to directly download new behaviors into the subconscious minds of their clients. In other words, the first six years of a child's life are spent in a hypnotic trance! A child's perceptions of the world are directly downloaded into the subconscious during this time, without discrimination and without filters of the analytical self-conscious mind which doesn't fully exist. Consequently, our fundamental perceptions about life and our role in it are learned without our having the capacity to choose or reject those beliefs. We were simply programmed. The Jesuits were aware of this programmable state and proudly boasted, "Give me the child until it is seven years old, and I will give you the man." They knew the child's trance state facilitated a direct implanting of Church dogma into the subconscious mind. Once programmed, that information would inevitably influence 95 percent of that individual's behavior for the rest of his or her life."

[4] *Britannica.com* › science › information-theory › Physiology
[5a] *The Backwards Brain Bicycle* – Smarter Every Day-133; youtube.com/watch?v=MFzDaBzBlL0&feature=youtu.be
[5b] smartereveryday.com
[6] *En.Wikipedia.org/wiki/*Neuroplasticity, Research and Discovery
[7] *The Oxford Book of Exploration,* Page 415 Robin Hanbury-Tenison - 2005- History;

[8] *How Our Eyes See Everything Upside Down*; By Mental Floss, UK; February 10, 2017

[9a] *JAMA Ophthalmology, December 8, 2008;* The Study of the Wonderful; The First Topographical Mapping of Vision in the Brain; Arch Ophthalmol. *2008;126(12):1767-1773. doi:10.1001/archopht.126.12.1767*

[9b] *Hubel, David H., and Torsten N. Wiesel.* "Receptive fields of single neurons in the cat's striate cortex." *The Journal of physiology 148.3 (1959): 574-591;* "The period of susceptibility to the physiological effects of unilateral eye closure in kittens." *The Journal of physiology 206.2 (1970): 419.*

Blakemore, Colin, and Grahame F. Cooper. "Development of the brain depends on the visual environment." (1970): 477-478.

Journal of Neurophysiology Vol. 41. No 4, July 1978

"Yanny-Laurel" vocabulary.com - Laurel

"The Dress"

[10] Slate.com/technology/2017/04/heres-why-people-saw-the-dress-differently.html

Goliath- The Enormous Underdog

[11] Malcolm Gladwell TEDTalk "The unheard story of David & Goliath"

[12] Jets 50/3 (September 2007) 489–508

[13] Saul's exact height is not given, but he was "a head taller" than anyone else in all Israel (1 Samuel 9:2), which implies he was over 6 feet tall, approximately 1 foot taller than David

Chapter 3, The Lucky Chosen to be Chosen

[1] According to data released by the Pew Forum on Religion and Public Life (2009 survey), 24% of American Christians expressed a belief in reincarnation, a belief common in Jesus' day [Matt 11:14, 17:11, Mark 9:11-13] and did not easily disappear after Nicaea's council (325AD) banned the belief. It persisted for centuries. In the early 13th century, the Pope launched a crusade against the Cathars, a reincarnationist Christian sect in Italy and Southern France, and wiped them out completely. [2] Clements, Ronald (1968). *God's Chosen People: a Theological Interpretation of the Book of Deuteronomy.* In series, *Religious Book Club*, 182. London: SCM Press.

[3] Isaiah 13:16, 1Peter 2:9

Chapter 4, The Fundamentals of Fundamentalism

[1] Source Pew Research, August 9th, 2012
pewforum.org/2012/08/09/the-worlds-muslims-unity-and-diversity-3-articles-of-faith/

[2] Heresy: a belief or opinion contrary to orthodox religious (especially Christian) doctrine.

[3] Selah is a Hebrew word found at the ending of verses in Psalms and has been interpreted as an instruction calling **for a break;** or it may mean "forever." An example of Selah is seeing the term used seventy-one times in the Psalms in the Hebrew Bible. In either interpretation, it calls for **a moment of reflection**.

[4] puckermob.com/kids-doing-funny-things/teacher-asks-3rd-grade-class-to-write-letters-to-god-and-the-result-is-hilarious/ By: Lex Gabrielle

[5] en.wikipedia.org/wiki/Bible translations into English manuscripts

[6] Ehrman; *Misquoting Jesus,* Introduction, Ehrman uses a range 200,000 – 400,000 differences or errors among surviving manuscripts are in a general agreement among numerous other textural critics and Biblical scholars, some of which assert there are more than 600,000 differences.

[7] Ehrman, *Misquoting Jesus;* Chapter 2 "The Copyist of Early Christian Writings" pages 45-99

[8] "Organized Christianity: global membership ranked by 6 major ecclesiastico-cultural megablocs and 300 major traditions AD 1970-2025." This chart is found on pages 16-18 of the World Christian Encyclopedia; Oxford University Press.

Chapter 5, A Conundrum of Biblical Proportions

[1] *Grace, Predestination and Original Sin.* Summer 2003, Religion and Spirituality, *The Original View of Original Sin,* Peter Nathan: vision.org/the-original-view-of-original-sin-1140

[2] Tornau, Christian, "Saint Augustine", *The Stanford Encyclopedia of Philosophy,* (Winter 2019 Edition), Edward N. Zalta Manicheans, Platonists

[3] Excerpt from: The Original View of Original Sin- Peter Nathan Summer 2003, Religion & Spirituality, Vision.org

Augustine didn't devise the concept of original sin. It was his use of specific New Testament scriptures to justify the new doctrine. The idea itself was shaped from the late second century onward by certain church fathers, including Irenaeus, Origen, and Tertullian. *Irenaeus did not use the Scriptures at all for his definition; Origen reinterpreted the Genesis* account of Adam and Eve in terms of a Platonic allegory and saw sin deriving solely from free will; Tertullian's version borrowed from Stoic philosophy. Though his earlier patristic peers' arguments convinced Augustine, he made use of the apostle Paul's letters, especially the one to the Romans, to develop his own ideas on original sin and guilt. Today, however, it is accepted that Augustine, who had never mastered the Greek language, misread Paul in at least one instance by using an inadequate Latin translation of the Greek original. Augustine's Neoplatonic, dualistic concept of physical being evil and spiritual being good does not coincide with Paul's view. This leads us to a second influential idea of Augustine's relating to sin. He proposed the concept of the "fall of man" as a result of sin. In Augustine's view, humanity lost its spiritual relationship with its Creator and fell to a lower state. Tragically, Augustine's misreading and misinterpretation of sin based on looking at Scripture through the prism of dualism is accepted as dogma by most contemporary Christian theologians. The doctrine of original sin owes more to Augustine's desire to emulate the philosophers than the Scriptures.

Pentateuch Origins

[4a.] "The composition of the Torah (or Pentateuch, the first five books of the bible: Genesis, Exodus, Leviticus, Numbers, and Deuteronomy) was a process that involved multiple authors over an extended period of time. While Jewish tradition holds that all five books were originally written by Moses sometime in the 2nd millennium BCE, this view began to be seriously questioned in the 17th century, and today scholars are virtually unanimous in rejecting Mosaic authorship." *ehrmanblog.org/modern-views-of-the-authorship-of-the-pentateuch.*

[4b.] Mosaic authorship of the Torah was unquestioned by both Jews and Christians until the European Enlightenment, when the systematic study of the five books led the majority of scholars to conclude that they are the product of many hands and many centuries. McDermott, John J. (2002). *Reading the Pentateuch: a historical introduction.* Pauline Press. ISBN 978-0-8091-4082-4.

[4c.] "It has long been recognized that the traditional view—- not stated in the Pentateuch itself, but already assumed elsewhere in the Old Testament— that Moses was the author of the Pentateuch cannot be correct." *Introduction to The Pentateuch;* R. Norman Whybray; Page 12

[5] *The Making of the Pentateuch* ("A Methodological Study", JSOT Press, Sheffield, 1987) by R. N. Whybray, Professor of Hebrew and Old Testament Studies at the University of Hull (UK), was a major contribution to the field of Old Testament studies, and specifically to theories on the origins and composition of the Pentateuch. Its originality lays in its detailed critique of the D.H. (documentary hypothesis,) and it remains a standard text for Old Testament studies. *The Making of the Pentateuch* has been described as "the most compelling critique of the hypothesis" ever made, and its arguments are frequently cited by evangelical Christians who wish to state the case for Mosaic authorship (Whybray explicitly rejects this notion and regards the Pentateuch as fiction)

[6] pg. 4 *"Making Waves Gently"*: Norman Whybray's Contribution to British Old Testament Study', David J.A. Clines University of Sheffield; also in *"I have taught you the way of wisdom"* (Prov 4.11): Articles on Wisdom by R. Norman Whybray (ed. Katharine Dell and Margaret Barker; Society for Old Testament Study Monograph Series; Aldershot, Hants.: Ashgate Publishing).

[7] *The World and the Word*: An Introduction to the Old Testament;
Eugene H. Merrill, Mark Rooker, Michael A. Grisanti – 2011; page 164 "In this
view the Pentateuch is a thoroughly late composition with respect to both the time
of its writing and the traditions it [...]Van Seters rejects most of the traditional
criteria for source analysis (except for alleged "doublets") and proposes that the
books of the Pentateuch should be understood as ideological fiction rather than
history.
[8] In 1650, the Anglican archbishop James Ussher calculated that the world was
created around 4004 BC based on the genealogies said to go back to book of
Genesis.
[9] Dalrymple, G. Brent (1994-02-01). The Age of the Earth. Stanford University
Press. ISBN 978-0-8047-2331-2.
[10] *Tim Sledge,* Four Disturbing Questions: One Simple Answer, pg.58
[11] pg.35 ibid
[12] *Ehrman,* Misquoting Jesus, pg. 33,34
[12] Macrione; Lily C. Vuong Gender and Purity in the Protevangelium of James
[Note] If you wish to suffer unnecessarily, 'google' anything on this subject and
prepare to be dumbstruck at how thick, deep, and competitive the numerous
arguments in the doctrinal weeds are.
[13] John Shelby Spong, *A New Christianity for a New World*, page 150
David Bentley Hart, *That All Shall Be Saved: Heaven, Hell, and Universal
Salvation*
A Larger Hope? Volume 1: Universal Salvation from Christian Beginnings to
Julian of Norwich Ilaria L. E. Ramelli, Richard Bauckam

Chapter 6, Quoting Misquotes
Quotes early in this chapter are taken from the Introduction portion of *Misquoting
Jesus; Jesus Interrupted*; *Forged.* Author, Bart Ehrman, Ph.D., M.Div., Moody
Bible Institute; Wheaton College; Princeton Theological Seminary. Examples
of conflicts, errors and contradictions presented in this chapter are taken from the
debates: Bart Ehrman vs Mike Licona, Ph.D. 2018, Kennesaw State University;
Bart Ehrman vs Mike Licona, Ph.D. 2009 Southern Evangelical Seminary in
Charlotte, NC; Bart Ehrman & Daniel Wallace. February 1st, 2012, University of
North Carolina at Chapel Hill, Memorial Hall Performing Arts Theater.

Chapter 7, A Hell of an Idea
[1] Chapter 3 Pg. 59-61

[2] Moloch—Leviticus 18:21, Leviticus 20:2 - 20:5, 2 Kings 23:10, Jeremiah 32:35 Deuteronomy 18:10–13, 2 Kings 16:3 and 21:6 and Ezekiel 20:26,31 and 23:37
[3] news.harvard.edu › gazette › story › 2009/12 › revelations-on-revelation
[4] Ehrman, "Heaven and Hell: A History of the Afterlife
[5] Norse mythology of Pagan origin. Hel, the location, shares a name with Hel, a being who rules over the place. Late Icelandic sources give inconsistent descriptions of Hel and describe various figures as buried with items that facilitate their journey to Hel after death. The Poetic Edda describes Brynhildr's trip to Hel after her death. Odin, while alive, visits Hel upon his horse Sleipnir. In Snorri Sturluson's Prose Edda, Baldr goes to Hel on his death, and subsequently, Hermóðr uses Sleipnir to attempt to retrieve him. Old Norse feminine proper noun Hel is identical to the name of the entity that presides over the realm, Old Norse Hel. The word has cognates in all branches of the Germanic languages, including Old English hell and thus Modern English hell. Old Frisian helle, Old Saxon hellia, Old High German hella, and Gothic halja. All forms ultimately derive from the reconstructed Proto-Germanic feminine noun *xaljō ('concealed place, the underworld). In turn, the Proto-Germanic form derives from the o-grade form of the Proto-Indo-European root *kel-, *kol-: 'to cover, conceal, save.' The term hell is etymologically related to Modern English Hall and, therefore, Valhalla, an afterlife 'hall of the slain' in Norse Mythology. Hall and its numerous Germanic cognates derive from Proto-Germanic *hallō 'covered place, hall', from Proto-Indo-European *kol-. *Wikipedia*
Orel (2003:156 and Watkins (2000:38)
Orel, Vladimir (2003) A Handbook of Germanic Etymology.
Watkins, Calvert (2000) The American Heritage Dictionary of Indo-European Roots. Houghton Mifflin Company. IBSN 0-395-98610-9
[6] The late Gary Amirault's Tentmaker.org has the most extensive available collection of texts on Universal Reconciliation and Christian Universalism available.
[7] Some examples include the Concordant Literal N.T. Young's Literal, 20th Century N.T., Rotherham's Emphasized, Weymouth's N.T. in Modern Speech, and there are many others
[8] Moloch's anthropomorphized bull figure was typically pictured in Rabbinic Judaic texts as a bronze statue internally heated by a fire. Inside this construct, priests or parents placed their children to be consumed by fire as a sacrificial offering.
[9] Research sourced in part from an article written by Bryan T. Huie [10]
("Purple," p. 863). The Eerdmans Bible Dictionary
[11] New Bible Dictionary ("Linen," p. 702)
[12] The New International Dictionary of New Testament; (vol. 2, p. 206)

[13] Kittel's Theological Dictionary of the New Testament

Chapter 8, A Universal Loss

[1] *"Encyclopedia of Wars,"* authors Charles Phillips and Alan Axelrod document the history of recorded warfare, listing 1763 wars of which 123 are classified to involve a religious cause, accounting for less than 7 percent of all wars and less than 2 percent of all people killed in warfare. Estimates of one to three million people were tragically killed in the Crusades, and perhaps 3,000 in the Inquisition.
[2] Calvin's letter to Farel on 24 July; Selected Works of John Calvin
[3] "On only two counts, significantly, was Servetus condemned —- namely, anti-Trinitarianism and anti-paedobaptism." Roland H. Bainton, *Hunted Heretic (The Beacon Press*, 1953), p. 207. Regarding his rejection of infant baptism, Servetus said, "It is an invention of the devil, an infernal falsity for the destruction of all Christianity" (Ibid., p. 186.)
[4a.b.] Schaff-Herzog *Encyclopedia of Religious Knowledge* (Baker Book House, 1950), p. 371
[5] *The Wycliffe Biographical Dictionary of The Church* (Moody Press, 1982), p. 73.
[6] Stephen Hole Fritchman, *Men of Liberty* (Reissued, Kennikat Press, Inc., 1968), p. 8
[7] Walter Nigg, *The Heretics* (Alfred A. Knopf, Inc., 1962), p. 328
[8] VHS recording Hour of Power – Billy Graham-Robert Schuller
[9] Gen. 12:3; 1 Tim. 2:4-6; 4:9-11; John 4:42; 12:32; 12:47; 1 Jn 4:14; Col. 1:16-20; 1 Cor. 15:22; Phil. 2:9-11; Acts 3:20, 21; Rev. 5:13. For an excellent, extended summart:Tentmaker.org/books/ScripturalProofs
[10] Origen and universalism, Origenist controversy-churchhistory101.com/feedback/origen-universalism.php
[10] Church Fathers & Universalism since Early Church times ....
christianforums.com/threads/church-fathers-universalism-since-early-church-times.8042013/
[11] Justice, Ginny, "The Role of Indulgences in the Building of New Saint Peter's Basilica" (2011). *Master of Liberal Studies Theses.*
7. https://scholarship.rollins.edu/mls/7
[12] *Disputation on the Power and Efficacy of Indulgences* (a.k.a. Luther's Ninety-five Theses) and the subsequent Reformation.
[13] *Note:* Regardless of doctrinal affiliation or agnosticism, when in Rome, make time for an immersive experience in St. Peters Basilica's magnificent structure. The scale. The beauty. The art. Allow time to ascend into the cupola (the dome). Many people are unaware that it's possible to climb up the dome and access the rooftop terrace to a spectacular panoramic view of the Vatican gardens &

museums, St. Peter' square, and a large part of Rome up to the Mediterranean Sea. A most memorable and educational trip. Rome, Italy (the Eternal City) - Best Catholic. bestcatholic.com/rome.shtml

[14a] tentmaker.org/articles/Carlton_Pearson-Doctrine_of_Inclusion
[14b] tentmaker.org/ScholarsCorner.html

Chapter 9, The End of the World— Again

[1] Eschatology is a highly controversial part of theology that packages various versions of the return of Christ, death, judgment, the final destiny of the soul, of humankind. The science of last things.
[a.] en.wikipedia.org/wiki/Dispensationalism
[b.] Exhibit Comparison of Futurist, Preterist and Historicist beliefs.
[2] **Eisegesis**: the interpretation of a text by reading into it one's own ideas (Webster)
[3] **Exegetics**: the science of interpretation especially of the Scriptures (Webster)
[4] Ezekiel 38
[5] Rev.14:20 (NLT)
[6] Revelation 6:2–8.
[7] en.wikipedia.org/ wiki/Dispensationalism media/File: History of Dispensationalism
[8] *The Wars of the Judahites, Flavius Josephus*
[9] Josephus: The Complete Works *ccel.org/ccel/josephus/complete.iii.viii.i.html.* Ernest L. Martin, Ph. D, 2000 New Evidence for the Site of the Temple in Jerusalem: "Significantly, Jesus said the same thing as Josephus. Jesus said that Jerusalem was to be *"laid even with the ground."* Josephus explained the reason why every stone was overturned in the city (including those that made up the very foundations). The Jews were accustomed to hide their gold and other valuables in the walls of their homes. The Temple itself was also the treasury of the Jewish nation. When the fires consumed the whole of the Temple and City, the gold melted and descended into the cracks and crevices of the stone foundations. In order to recover the melted gold, the Tenth Legion had the Jewish captives uproot every stone of the Temple and the whole of the city. So much gold was recovered that the price of the metal in the Roman Empire went down *half of its pre-war value*. Looking for gold by overturning the stones (including all foundation stones) left Jerusalem as a vast quarry of dislodged and uprooted stones in a state of unrecognized shambles."
[10] *neh.gov/humanities/2017/winter/feature/the-late-great-planet-earth-made-the-apocalypse-popular-concern* HUMANITIES, Winter 2017, Volume 38, Number 1, Erin A. Smith
[11]*"The Prophet Hen of Leads, Modern Prophecies, pg. 256, Random House*

[12] *A Christian Student's Survival Guide Pg. 154*

[13] *Millennial fever and the end of the world: a study of Millerite Adventism*

[14] *Imagining the End: The Apocalypse in American Popular Culture; pg. 155*

[15] *Manifest Insanity: Or How I Learned to Stop Worrying and Think for Myself*

[16] *88 reasons Why the Rapture Will Be in 1988: The Feast of Trumpets (Rosh Hash-Ana) September,*

[17] *Final Shout Rapture Report 1989 1990 1991 1992 1993*

Sidebar: Regularly consuming "the news" will program you with fear. The vast majority of us spend our day in a waking trance, making our minds more susceptible to the increasingly negative news cycle. <u>Ration</u> the time you spend in front of the now countless sources *spewing endless negativity.* When I was a child, there were three television networks, and I was Dad's remote control. What we saw on the evening news often happened days before it aired. Today's 24 hours news networks, satellite communications, and social media platforms make the world seem very small. We get news seconds later, not days later, and by and large, it is the worst of what is happening in our world. They do not report the tens of millions of good things happening every minute all around the world. That which is good doesn't sell ad space. I stopped watching the local News more than a decade ago. I am increasingly careful about how I consume world news today. There is a rule in the news: "If it bleeds, it leads." Create fear, and all will draw near. Would you allow someone to back a truck up to your door and shovel load after a load of garbage into your home? Be as protective of what you allow into your mind. It is much harder to clean.

[18] *Heaven's Gate: Postmodernity and Popular Culture in a Suicide Group edited by George D. Chryssides*

[19] *nasa.gov/topics/earth/features/2012.html*

[20] *The Prophecies of Nostradamus (In English and French Languages); By Nostradamus*

[21] *"5/5/2000: Pg. vi; Richard William Noone*

[22] *2008: God's Final Witness - Page 244; Ronald Weinland - 2007*

[23] *Moffitt, Mike (May 17, 2011). "The end-of-the-world FAQ sheet". San Francisco Chronicle.*

[24] *"A Conversation with Harold Camping, Prophesier of Judgment Day". New York Magazine. May 11, 2011. Retrieved October 13, 2011*

[25] *"Judgment Day". Family Radio. Archived from the original on June 8, 2011. Retrieved May 16, 2011.*

[26] Pastor, John Hagee

[27] Prophet, Hank Kunneman

[28] Rabbits are at home in briars, the resourceful Br'er Rabbit escapes. Using the phrase "please don't **throw me in the briar patch**" refers to the idea that it gets

Quantum
Brook

worse the more one struggles against it" became part of the wider culture of the United States in the mid-20th century.

Chapter 10, Gob Smacked

[1] The Physics of God, pg. 24 -Pew "Religion & Science"
[2] I had saved and retrieved the actual experiment and results notes to ensure that I accurately restated the results.
[3] *Power vs Force*, The Hidden Determinants of Human Behavior, David R. Hawkins, M.D., Ph.D. Chapter 2, History and Methodology, pgs. 53,54
[4] Kendal, Kendal and Wadsworth 1971
[5] *Power vs. Force*, Hawkins, Pg. 68 Map of the Scale of Consciousness
[6] Goodheart coordinated his work with German-born acupuncturist Felix Mann, who stressed the medical significance of the acupuncture meridians. *Mann 1974.* Meanwhile, Goodheart's book on applied kinesiology quickly reached its 12th edition and started a revolution. David Walther followed with an extensive work on applied kinesiology in 1976.
[7] Diamond, 1979
[8] *Power vs. Force,* Hawkins, Pg. 57,58
[9] ibid Pg. 59
[10] ibid pg. 60

[11] Dr. Albury Gardner (December 28, 1953 - September 10, 2015) was a Lt. Commander in the Navy, later getting a degree in structural engineering before discovering his passion and greater calling in the field of alternative medicine. He would get his DC in Clinical Nutrition, and Chiropractic Neurology, degrees which were little more than the doorway to all he would soon learn.
[12] *scientificamerican.com*/article/how-einstein-revealed-the-universe-s-strange-nonlocality/
[13] *The way of Qigong* Kenneth Cohen; Sources of qi. Pg. 32

Chapter 11, Conclusion & A Glimpse Beyond the Spin

[1] *The Enigma of Reason;* Hugo Mercier and Dan Sperber (cognitive scientists, Harvard)
[2] From the Bohr model or Schrodinger equation for hydrogen, the electron energy levels' solution shows that they depend only upon the principal quantum number. For hydrogen and other nuclei stripped to one electron, the energy depends solely upon the primary quantum number (n). hyperphysics.phy-astr.gsu.edu › quantum › qnenergy
[3] heartmath.org/about-us/

[4] **conductor**: (physics) material capable of transmitting another form of energy (such as heat or sound.) Webster

[5] **resistor:** (physics) the opposition offered by a body or substance to the passage through it of a steady electric current. Webster

[6] John 14:12 NIV

[7] In a paper published in 2013, Eva Bianconi of the University of Bologna in Italy and her colleagues outlined a method for estimating the number of cells in a "standard human being," Dr. Bianconi and her colleagues concluded that there were an average of 37.2 trillion cells in each of us. New York Times. June 19, 201

[8a] *London Real*. Bruce Lipton, Ph.D., [8b] *The Biology of Belief: Unleashing the Power of Consciousness, Matter & Miracles*. Lipton, Bruce H, Ph.D., Anniversary Ed. Carlsbad, CA: Hay House, Inc., 2005

[9]. *Zero Limits, The Truth Behind the Story*, Joe Vitale; Ihaleakalá Hew Len, Ph.D.

Note: Web addresses referenced here are current as of publication date. If an address fails due to a change in address, Google the *entire* old address for the new link.

Quantum
Brook

Permissions

Photos used in whole or in part in the cover design and those used in Chapters 1-11 arc licensed through Shutterstock.

QuantumBrook Publishing provides charts or diagrams which are not otherwise attributed.

"Love Story", and "Dear Joe" fonts licensed through MyFonts.

Scripture taken from The Holy Bible, NEW INTERNATIONAL VERSION®, NIV® Copyright © 1973, 1978, 1984, 2011 by Biblica, Inc.® Used by permission. All rights reserved worldwide.

Quotations by David Hawkins, MD, Ph.D., taken from Power Vs. Force used by permission from Veritas Publishing. Specific uses cited in the Bibliography

All Quotes by Dr. Barth Ehrman are used by permission.

Quotes from John Shelby Spong used by permission.

Brief quotes from numerous sources used under "fair use" law.

Material excerpted from The Way of the Explorer, © 2008 Edgar Mitchell used with permission from Red Wheel/Weiser, LLC Newburyport, MA www.redwheelweiser.com

"The Dress" photo has been in ubiquitous use on the internet for over four years. We've made "good faith" efforts to contact Buzzfeed, who *may* own the copyright.

MEME "This is True this is Truth" pg. 37. is in ubiquitous use on the internet. Good faith efforts to identify the unknown source.

Image Screenshot "the backward brain bicycle" YouTube, used by permission from, Smarter Every Day.

About the Author

Jerry spent virtually his entire career in the technology sector, mostly in the Healthcare Information, Electronic Medical Record, Laboratory, and Payor Analytics space. Throughout his career, he produced hundreds of millions in accumulated contract value for startups and Industry Leaders like Siemens, McKesson, and Sunquest Information Systems. His experience included a variety of sales and marketing, sales management, and business development roles, including business plan development, capital raise, and Mergers & Acquisition.

His experience involved extensive systems vendor selection processes working closely with the "C Suite" partnering with firms such as Ernst &Young, Deloitte Touche, Accenture, First Consulting Group, and Price Waterhouse in complex system evaluations. Jerry worked broadly with both the provider and payor sides of the healthcare continuum in the hospital's inpatient, ambulatory, and post-acute care settings and the physician practice space.

In his most recent role as Vice President of Population Health, he consulted solutions that leverage technology to streamline—*proactive care.* Proactive care aims to keeps patients healthy, lower cost, produce superior outcomes, and extend life expectancy. The goal is to reduce costs while improving outcomes through early detection and intervention. The challenge underlies increasingly complex revenue cycles and shrinking reimbursements. The efficient use of technology is the only way to achieve the goal.

As this book highlights, for more than 50 years, Jerry was extensively involved in the church as a musician, board of directors, youth counselor, and various leadership roles. He was ordained in the 90s and briefly considered ministry as a full-time vocation. Instead, his passion became righting the wrong of Christian Fundamentalism's *overt declaration* of an exclusive relationship with God and the discovery of an astonishing, Conscious Universe, a reality increasingly evident through explorations in quantum physics.

Jerry is semi-retired, to entrepreneurial pursuits, and writing. He lives in a suburb north of Atlanta with his childhood sweetheart Ronda, and wife of 45 years. They have a son, daughter and four granddaughters.

Quantum Brook

www.ingramcontent.com/pod-product-compliance
Lightning Source LLC
LaVergne TN
LVHW051502080426
835509LV00017B/1875